HISTORIC PRESERVATION

HISTORIC PRESERVATION

AN INTRODUCTION TO ITS HISTORY, PRINCIPLES, AND PRACTICE

SECOND EDITION

Norman Tyler

Ted J. Ligibel · *Ilene R. Tyler*

W. W. NORTON & COMPANY

NEW YORK · LONDON

For information about permission to reproduce selections from this book,
write to Permissions,
W. W. Norton & Company, Inc.,
500 Fifth Avenue, New York, NY 10110

For information about special discounts for bulk purchases, please contact
W. W. Norton Special Sales at specialsales@wwnorton.com or 800-233-4830

Manufacturing by Edwards Brothers
Book design by Jonathan Lippincott
Production manager: Leeann Graham

Library of Congress Cataloging-in-Publication Data

Tyler, Norman.
   Historic preservation : an introduction to its history, principles,
and practice / Norman Tyler, Ted J. Ligibel, Ilene R. Tyler. — 2nd ed.
     p.   cm.
   "1994 edition published as Issues of historic preservation"—T.p. verso.
   Includes bibliographical references and index.
   ISBN 978-0-393-73273-3 (pbk.)
   1. Historic preservation—United States. 2. Historic
sites—Conservation and restoration—United States. 3. Historic
buildings—Conservation and restoration—United States.
4. Architecture—Conservation and restoration—United States.
I. Ligibel,Ted. II. Tyler, Ilene R. III. Title.

E159.T   95 2009
363.6'9—dc22   2008027409

ISBN 13: 978-0-393-73273-3 (pbk.)

W. W. Norton & Company, Inc.
500 Fifth Avenue, New York, N.Y. 10110
www.wwnorton.com

W. W. Norton & Company Ltd.
Castle House, 75/76 Wells Street, London W1T 3QT

0 9 8 7 6 5 4 3

CONTENTS

1. Introduction 11
2. The Preservation Movement in the United States 27
3. Architectural Styles, Contextualism, and Design Guidelines 63
4. The Legal Basis for Preservation 121
5. Designation of Historic Properties 135
6. Historic Districts and Ordinances 155
7. Intervention Approaches, Documentation, and Technology 189
8. Preservation Economics 237
9. Preservation Planning 269
10. Sustainability and Partnering with the Environmental Community 299
11. Heritage Tourism, Cultural Landscapes, and Heritage Areas 321

Notes 337
Further Reading 345
Preservation Resources 349
Degree and Certificate Programs in Historic Preservation 356
Architectural Terms 360
Index 365

Therefore, when we build, let us think that we build for ever. Let it not be for present delight, nor for present use alone; let it be such work as our descendants will thank us for, and let us think, as we lay stone on stone, that a time is to come when those stones will be held sacred because our hands have touched them, and that men will say as they look upon the labor and wrought substance of them, "See! this our fathers did for us." For, indeed, the greatest glory of a building is not in its stones, or in its gold. Its glory is in its Age.

— John Ruskin

ACKNOWLEDGMENTS

——◆——

The fortieth anniversary of the National Historic Preservation Act of 1966 provided a unique opportunity to reflect on the successes and shortcomings of the historic preservation movement in the United States. The interest of the American public in historic preservation has grown tremendously in recent decades, aided by such events as the nation's bicentennial, the turn of both a century and a millennium, rampant development, and unexpected events such as Hurricanes Katrina and Rita. There has been an explosion of preservation activity throughout the country. Web sites, blogs, listservs, and publications concerned with these issues are profuse.

Although information on historic preservation is readily available, this book fills a void in the preservation literature. It presents the full range of preservation topics, from a look at basic preservation philosophies to techniques of rehabilitation and economic analysis. Although other authors—many listed in the Notes and Further Reading—explore such topics in greater detail, this book is a primer on historic preservation issues. In layperson's language, it serves as a reference for students, historic district commissioners, local officials and community leaders, homeowners, and others.

Originally written to serve as a text for an introductory course in historic preservation, this much-revised book has benefited greatly from the review and comments of others. Thanks go to a number of individuals, representing member schools of the National Council for Preservation Education, who responded to a call for revision suggestions, including Bonnie Stepenoff (Southeast Missouri State University), James Garman (Salve Regina University), Lauren Bricker (California State Polytechnic University), and Jeff Tilman (University of Cincinnati). Others who responded were Peter Brink and Daniel Carey of the National Trust for Historic Preservation, Rachel Bankowitz of the Commonwealth Cultural Resources Group, and Barry Stiefel. Special thanks goes to Tom Visser of the University of Vermont for his review of the text. Ioana Campean contributed many of the sketches in the Architectural Terms section. The authors gratefully acknowledge Michael Quinn and the architectural firm of Quinn Evans Architects of Ann Arbor, Michigan, and Washington, D.C., for contributing information and graphics for many of the case studies, and Carl Elefante and Ruth Mills for contributing to sections on sustainability and cultural landscapes. We are grateful for the time and thoughtfulness these individuals devoted to making this a better and more accurate text.

Chapter One

INTRODUCTION

Historic preservation has played an increasingly important role in American society in recent decades. It has grown from an activity of a few dedicated individuals and organizations to become an activity engaged in, at some level, by millions of citizens. Virtually every one of our communities now recognizes the significance of the historic heritage represented in its built environment. A significant number have taken steps to ensure the protection of historic structures and other properties through their designation and regulation. Such involvement is now an accepted practice of local government, acting in the public interest.

This book introduces readers to the many facets of historic preservation. As a society, we have always had some appreciation of our cultural and architectural heritage, but in the last few decades Americans have become increasingly aware of the significance of our historic structures and sites and have recognized how fast we have been losing many of them. They are irreplaceable. It is our duty as a society and as members of our own local communities to protect and preserve our heritage, which is deep and rich. Preservationists in every state of the union have campaigned to preserve the best of it, with the help of organizations ranging from the National Trust for Historic Preservation to statewide preservation networks to local historical associations and historic district and landmark commissions. The preservation movement has established itself as both powerful and integral to thousands of communities across the country.

One aspect of historic preservation has remained consistent throughout its relatively brief history: it is an intensely "grass-roots" movement. More often than not, efforts to save a particular place are rooted at the local level and grow from there. Especially since the bicentennial year of 1976, the American public has developed deeper interest in the preservation of the country's architectural heritage. Individuals and organizations have supported historic preservation activities for over a century, but in the last three decades interest on the part of the general public has increased markedly.

What role is historic preservation meant to play in American society? This question is debated continually by organizations, agencies, and individuals across the country. Among property owners and developers, in city council chambers, even during historic district commission meetings, persistent questions arise: Does preservation stand in the way of progress? Is it appropriate to establish new restrictions on property owners? Who should determine what is historically significant?

The role of historic preservation is constantly being defined and redefined. Many perspectives continue to be explored. The typical perspective of Americans has focused on new opportunities, not on our heritage. Even the founding fathers could be seen as opportunistic, for they strove to leave their old-world traditions behind and strike forth on an adventure in the uncharted wilderness of the new frontier. Such expansionism was long ago recognized as this country's "manifest destiny." That the entire country already was inhabited by myriad Native American groups was an afterthought to many of these early settlers, as was the idea that the new nation's seemingly boundless resources were, in fact, exhaustible. "Go west!" was the ubiquitous call that attracted hundreds of thousands of explorers and the settlers who followed.

Reflecting on this American spirit of opportunism, writer Clem Labine considered the role of preservationists in a seminal article from 1979 titled "Preservationists Are Un-American":

> And then it hit me. The more I inquired into the forces that make preservationists do the things we do, the more I realized that preservation is really un-American. . . .
> The fact is that preservation goes against the basic historical thrust that built America into a world power. America was built on the concept of the frontier. Land was limitless. Resources were never-ending. The pioneer way was to use it up, throw it away and move west. . . .

American Progress, *Representing the Spirit of Manifest Destiny, painting by John Gast,*
1872. Courtesy of the Library of Congress.

So where do preservationists fit into this scheme of things? Are we merely folks
who think that the apex of civilization was reached in the 19th century and are
vainly trying to recreate that vanished world? No, we are not making futile, reac-
tionary gestures. Rather, we represent the cutting edge of a true cultural revolution, a revolution generating new perceptions that will have a dramatic impact on
America's way of thinking in the next 50 years.

Preservationists oppose the conventional American idea of consuming ever
more. We are actually the new wave of pioneers. We are struggling to reverse the
"use it up and move on" mentality. We are moving in and picking up the pieces. We
are taking individual buildings and whole neighborhoods that have been discarded
and trying to make them live again. We are cleaning up after society's litterbugs.[1]

Why do preservationists feel so strongly committed to preserving the past,
when America's greatest challenge has traditionally been thought of as its future?

To answer that question, it is important to recognize that preservationists are not against growth and development. Rather, they see growth as built on the past. "The past is prologue," a Shakespearean phrase commonly used to represent this perspective, challenges us as a society to base our plans for future growth on our past, to look at how our society has evolved historically, and to have that past serve as a guide for the future. The word *preserve*, when broken into its root forms "pre-serve," includes the concept of contributing to the future. As stated by John Lawrence, former dean of Tulane's School of Architecture, "The basic purpose of preservation is not to arrest time, but to mediate sensitively with the forces of change. It is to understand the present as a product of the past and a modifier of the future."[2]

The twentieth century was an era of unprecedented change. As a people, we realized we could accomplish virtually anything—and in shorter and shorter periods of time. In the twenty-first century, the process of change was so rapid it was almost impossible to observe. That is why historic preservation has taken on such significance in recent decades. Adele Chatfield-Taylor, founder and former executive director of the New York Landmarks Preservation Foundation, discussed this perspective in a presentation celebrating Columbia University's program in historic preservation:

> So it is no wonder that an interest in historic preservation (a puny term to describe a gigantically important moment in this progression) surfaces in earnest in the early part of the twentieth century, in the swirling midst of these other developments. . . .
>
> It is our increasing lack of access to a familiar world that has generated a hunger for the sight and touch of a gritty reality that old buildings provide—and not impenetrably preserved, bionic old buildings—but buildings that have registered the imprint of the passage of time. Old buildings that are a time line, old buildings that are real. . . .
>
> [T]he technological ability to build 100-story buildings on every square inch of the face of the earth—whether it be Madison Avenue, Times Square, or the plains of Kansas—is not necessarily a mandate to do so. . . . In a sense, then, historic preservation represents a desire to reduce this power to a possibility rather than an inevitability.[3]

In the past, many felt a need to "tame" the vast landscape of the United States. Powerful eighteenth- and nineteenth-century Americans saw themselves, by necessity, as conquerors of nature and as builders of cities. But now nature is conquered and most of the habitable American landscape is either cultivated or built upon. In fact, some communities are at, or rapidly approaching, a "closed to development" status, with any available land already farmed, built upon, conserved, or secured for development. This reality should reorient us to address issues not of growth but of quality of life, recognizing elements worthy of preservation. Our society will have matured when its primary focus shifts from the quantitative to the qualitative—when we recognize the need to preserve our built heritage because it represents who we are as a people.

NOUNS AND VERBS

One can develop an understanding of historic preservation in many ways. A useful analogy is to think of the preservation of buildings in terms of nouns and verbs. When buildings are viewed as objects, they are nouns. They make up a part of the physical presence of a space and are the "subject" of that space. Thinking of historic buildings in terms of their physical structure is the most common approach to understanding their significance, but it is not the only one. They also can be seen as places of involvement—where historic events took place. From this perspective, they can be seen as verbs, based on the action that took place there, similar to the use of a verb in a sentence. In other words, buildings can be seen not only as static structures but also as essential carriers of our community's history.

Just as nouns and verbs are both needed to make a complete sentence, both the noun and verb aspects of historic buildings are needed to describe their full significance. Preservationists need to recognize that the preservation of historic buildings should include not only the physical structure but also the history of the place. Only in this way does a historic building maintain its full meaning. To consider the spaces within and around buildings, and even the events that took place there as part of their living history, allows historic structures a more active and significant role within the community. Historic preservation is more than old buildings, and it is more than historical account; it can be described as "applied history," for it puts history to good purpose through use of historic structures as sources of community revitalization.

Historic preservation should be seen as more than the protection of older buildings. Preserving buildings only as inanimate structures makes them period set pieces—objects of curiosity, but not much more. This attitude can lead to the kind of preservation represented by the term "façadism," wherein only the front façade of a structure is preserved and the rest of the structure is demolished, as absurdly represented by the text on a sign found in a South Carolina gas station:[4]

> **In order to preserve the architectural traditions of Charleston, the brickwork and woodwork of the demolished Gabriel Manigault house 1800 AD were used in this station.**

Sign from South Carolina gas station.

A similar analogy often can be applied to exhibits found in historical museums. Conventionally, such museums are places where historical items are collected, archived, and displayed. The basic function is to display artifacts in a gallery for the public to view. Curators have become aware, however, that visitor interest increases significantly if objects are displayed in their actual environment, which gives the artifacts a richer context, rather than in museum display cases. The impression on a visitor can be enhanced even more through live recreations of historical events by reenactors in period costumes. Sometimes this format is carried even further and visitors are drawn into the enactment, becoming active participants.

The venerable "Hall of Presidents" at Disney World, for example, uses life-sized animated figures to bring to life important figures. More recent technological innovations have allowed more advanced levels of recreation and interpretation of historic figures, events, and sites. Some exhibits have blurred the line between education and entertainment, leading to a new term, "edutainment," which combines the two into one presentation. Many historic sites have taken advantage of the modern technology fostered by movies such as *Star Wars*, with its use of holographic images and computer-generated "spectral imagery." At the Herbert H. Dow Historical Museum in Midland, Michigan, the founder of Dow Chemical Company springs to life as a three-dimensional holograph and walks and talks as if alive while describing the founding of the company. In Philadelphia, a pint-sized Benjamin Franklin can be seen discussing the benefits of electricity. The Cave of Altamira, a World Heritage site in Spain, cannot host its many visitors, so figures representing prehistoric artists responsible for the dramatic cave drawings are realistically projected full-size within an exact replica of the main cave. Such technologies are becoming more common in an attempt to bring history to life.

A good example of a "living history museum" is Plimoth Plantation in Massachusetts. In 1969, this village began to replace its conventional static exhibits with a daily reenactment of seventeenth-century life in the original Plimoth colony, and a personalized approach was adopted. Plimoth Plantation now is inhabited, at least during museum hours, by "residents." Everyday village activities are performed by staff dressed in period costumes. The public is invited to walk

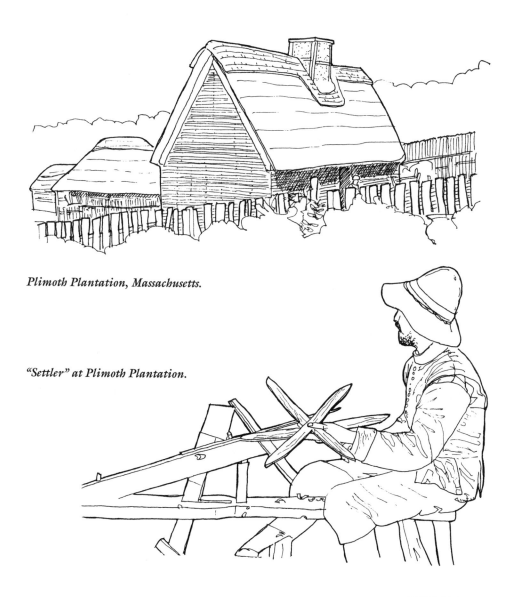

Plimoth Plantation, Massachusetts.

"Settler" at Plimoth Plantation.

through the recreated 1620s settlement and strike up neighborly conversations with whomever they wish. The actors, who have thoroughly studied the lives of the individuals they portray, pretend to know only seventeenth-century life, so visitors must adapt to that historical perspective in order to talk with them. The plantation's residents often question visitors on their strange dialect and look askance at their "heathen" manner of dress. However, they are a friendly group and willing to share information about their activities. The ability to go beyond static representation of artifacts (history as nouns) and to present history as a complete environment (history as verbs) is the source of the success of Plimoth Plantation and other such museums.

PRESERVATION PHILOSOPHIES

The underlying philosophy of the historic preservation movement in the United States is defined more through activities than theory. One could rationalize that "preservation is as preservation does," for preservationists bring many perspectives to the field. Some see their role primarily as saving old buildings, some as preserving a cultural heritage, some as fostering urban revitalization, and some as contributing to sustainability and an alternative approach to current development practices.

Preservationists bring a diversity of approaches even to so basic an activity as saving old buildings. For instance, some feel that historic structures should be kept in their original state or, if they have been altered, that they should be returned to their original condition. Others feel they should protect what remains of a structure's significant historic character but that change also can and should be accommodated. The pendulum swings with the times and the circumstances as well as with the flow of available monies to a project. What is considered an appropriate response in one instance may be seen quite differently in another.

As a society, Americans have changed considerably in their views toward their architectural heritage. In the 1950s and 1960s, in an age of space travel, new technologies, and unheard of changes in transportation and communication technologies, the new was considered far superior to the old. Attitudes have shifted considerably since then. Some now see new development as the cause of a significant deterioration of our communities and the environment. This debate will continue without resolution, of course, as it has for generations.

This issue of old versus new was also part of the debate among nineteenth-century "preservationists." The contrast in opinions was nowhere greater than that found in the writings of the French architect Eugène Emmanuel Viollet-le-Duc (1814–1879) and the English art historian and essayist John Ruskin (1819–1900).

Viollet-le-Duc

Eugène Emmanuel Viollet-le-Duc was one of the first master builders concerned with the restoration of landmark structures. Previously, buildings either followed a natural course of deterioration or were informally maintained by local craftsmen. Viollet-le-Duc changed this attitude. He not only devoted his career to

Church of La Madeleine, Vezelay, France.

restoration work (and is considered the world's first restoration architect), but also presented his methods, technology, and philosophy in a series of books, including a ten-volume dictionary of architecture. Although much of his philosophy of restoration is now discounted by historic preservation professionals, the historical and technical information that he cataloged has proven to be invaluable. His work had no precedent and was highly influential in early restoration efforts throughout Europe.

Viollet-le-Duc's restoration philosophy was based on the principle that important monuments should be rebuilt not necessarily as they originally were, but as they "should have been." As he stated, "To restore a building is not only to preserve it, to repair it, or to rebuild, but to bring it back to a state of completion such as may never have existed at any given moment."[5] For example, his first major project, the church La Madeleine de Vézelay in Vézelay, France, used new stone elements sculpted to duplicate the old, but also used new statuary, not based on the original design but based on what Viollet-le-Duc deemed compatible.

After Viollet-le-Duc's death, one critic, Paul Léon, disagreed with his approach, saying, "A monument to be a testimony to the past must stay as the past has bequeathed it. To pretend to restore it to its original state is dangerous and deceitful; we must preserve buildings as they are, respecting the contribution of successive generations."[6] Because he added new elements and embellished without appropriate historical basis, Viollet-le-Duc's restoration methods are now largely discredited, but his contributions are significant nonetheless because of the recognition he gave to the need for restoration of significant historic structures.

A limited number of contemporary examples of restoration based on his philosophy exist. The city of Santa Barbara, California, for example, was largely destroyed by an earthquake in 1925, and the downtown had to be rebuilt almost from scratch. City authorities saw this as an opportunity to establish rigorous new design controls. They determined that newly constructed buildings should be built in a single architectural style; they wanted to improve on the beauty of their city by limiting new designs to the older Spanish Mission pattern, and they established a board of architectural review to ensure a consistent approach. Indeed, much of the new construction since then has been done in this style, giving an almost unparalleled uniformity to the streetscape. The guiding philosophy adopted by Santa Barbara during this period was that the historical image of the city should be better than before, just as Viollet-le-Duc had advocated a century earlier.

Santa Barbara County Courthouse.

It also could be argued that the restoration of Colonial Williamsburg subscribed loosely to Viollet-le-Duc's philosophy in the sense that all post-1775 changes and additions to the original town were planned to be removed. In several cases, the restorations and reconstructions were based on scant evidence. Whether Williamsburg is an example of a site being brought back to a state of completion such as may never have existed at any given moment has been the subject of debate for many preservationists.

John Ruskin

In contrast to Viollet-le-Duc, nineteenth-century writer and critic John Ruskin posited that older buildings should not be restored; they should remain untouched. He argued that a society has no right to improve, or even restore, the craftsmanship of another era. As he explained in *The Seven Lamps of Architecture*, "It is impossible, as impossible as to raise the dead, to restore anything that has ever been great or beautiful in architecture." Old buildings should be left to look old, he argued. They gain their beauty only after four or five centuries, and the richness of their beauty is enhanced when seen as ruins. As noted in the epigraph to this book, "The greatest glory of a building is not in its stones, or in its gold. Its glory is in its Age." Ruskin felt that buildings should be built to last. "When we build, let us think that we build for ever."[7]

Who are we to try to restore a former glory? Ruskin asked. In his mind, restoration was comparable to erasing the character evident in the face of an older person through plastic surgery, trying to make that person look young again. The beauty in age lines should be respected rather than artificially changed. We often want to make older buildings look too perfect, to restore them to a state where they look more like museum pieces than buildings in daily use. "We have a tendency to clean old buildings too much, to strip them of their age and character, to make them look too new, and to turn them into spectacles, rather than allow them to look old and merely befriended." Ruskin saw restoration as that same type of artificiality, which he termed an "indiscreet zeal for restoration."[8]

> Restoration may possibly . . . produce good imitation of an ancient work of art; but the original is then falsified, and in its restored state it is no longer an example of the art of the period to which it belonged. [In fact,] the more exact the imitation the more it is adapted to mislead posterity.
>
> No restoration should ever be attempted, otherwise than . . . in the sense of preservation from further injuries. . . . Anything beyond this is untrue in art, unjustifiable in taste, destructive in practice, and wholly opposed to the judgment of the best Archaeologists.
>
> Do not let us talk then of restoration. The thing is a Lie from beginning to end.[9]

Viollet-le-Duc and Ruskin present two opposing perspectives on the restoration of historic perspectives. Both can be viewed as extreme, so it can be instructive to consider more pragmatic current practices.

Restoration of a ruin presents a unique challenge, exemplified in the treatment of the Bay Furnace project on the shores of Lake Superior. After seven short years of producing pig iron for shipment, a fire destroyed the entire site, includ-

Bay Furnace, Alger County, Michigan.

ing much of its tapered masonry tower. The location was largely abandoned for a hundred years; the original tower disintegrated into a heap of rubble overgrown with plants. The National Forest Service, which manages the property as a picnic site and campground, decided to clean up the furnace and make it an interpretive history site for visitors. It considered several options for treatment of the tower itself, ranging from erection of a protective covering structure to reconstruction of the full height tower to stabilization of the extant form. Selecting the latter option resulted in a partial reconstruction of the tower's original form. Stabilization of the site as a ruin illustrated the tower's original purpose but stopped short of a full restoration. Native plants were reintroduced, and wild plants were even allowed to reestablish themselves on the reconstructed furnace. The site is preserved as a ruin—a relic of a long-lost industry.

Ruskin's philosophy has a ring of truth when looking at historic structures that have been sanitized rather than merely restored. The Isaac Ludwig Mill is another example of the potential conflicts inherent in developing an appropriate approach to restoration. This mill is the oldest remaining mill on the Maumee

River, which drains northeast Indiana and northwest Ohio into Lake Erie. It was saved by the local park system. But in the process, the workers cleaned the mill of its saw and grain dust and cobwebs and put aluminum siding on its head-house. The overall feel of the old, authentic mill faded. That initial sanitization process has since ended, and the mill has been returned to a more realistic "working" state.

OTHER PERSPECTIVES: CHINESE, NATIVE AMERICAN, AND JAPANESE VIEWS OF PRESERVATION

Not all cultures see preservation as saving older structures. Three cultures (Chinese, Native American, and Japanese) represent interesting alternative perspectives. For example, the Chinese put more value on the saving of images through art or writings. Perhaps because theirs is an ancient culture in a crowded country, whose thousands of historic sites all bear many layers of history, the Chinese do not consider the preservation of physical structures as critical. As described by David Lowenthal, professor emeritus of geography at University College, London:

> The Chinese endorse tradition in language and ideas but discard material remains or let them decay. Mao's orders to demolish ancient monuments were easy to carry out; few old structures had survived recurrent iconoclasm. Revering ancestral memory, the Chinese disdain the past's purely physical traces. Old works must perish for new ones to take their place. And Confucian precepts judge material possession a burdensome vice. In the traditional Chinese view, preserving objects and buildings reduces creation to commodity; it demeans both object and owner.[10]

Some Native American cultures hold views similar to the Chinese regarding the physical remains of the past. To many, the geographical place itself holds the overriding significance, and many such places are considered sacred. In contrast, ancient adobe buildings in the Southwest can be found in a ruinous state, and their restoration is not likely a primary concern of these indigenous tribes. Holding onto the physical presence of these structures is unimportant. Indeed, their deterioration is viewed as a natural act—as Mother Earth reclaiming temporal objects.

The Japanese lend a different perspective, perhaps best represented by the cyclical reconstruction of the Ise Shrine in Ise City. The earliest construction of

Ise Shrine, Ise, Japan.

this shrine is said to date from the third century. It was originally built as a simple structure dedicated to the Sun Goddess, and its design was derived from the granaries and treasure storehouses of prehistoric Japan. Built of sacred cryptomeria wood, it was situated on a cleared site and surrounded by carefully manicured large white pebbles.

To ensure the structure's continuing preservation, every twenty years the shrine is torn down and a new one built on an immediately adjacent site, matching the previous site and structure in every way. At each time cycle, the shrine shifts back and forth between sites. The present structure, dating from 1993, is the sixty-first iteration, with the next rebuilding scheduled for 2013. The Japanese consider each structure not a replication of the original but a *recreation* of it. This philosophy reflects the natural order of things, for nature allows things to live and die, and from that cycle comes perpetual renewal.

Chapter Two

THE PRESERVATION MOVEMENT
IN THE UNITED STATES

Preservation in the United States has followed two distinct paths from the earliest activities in the eighteenth century until its full flowering in the last half of the twentieth century. Private-sector activities tended to revolve around important historical figures and associated landmark structures, whereas government involvement was limited to preserving natural features and establishing national parks. This chapter describes these parallel paths and how they finally merged with the establishment of the National Trust for Historic Preservation in 1949 and passage of the National Historic Preservation Act in 1966.

EARLY ACTIVITIES

Many early preservation activities took place throughout the nation in the eighteenth, and more prominently in the nineteenth, centuries, but often under the banner of "antiquarianism." Genealogists, historians, conservationists, collectors, associations and societies, and individuals often carried out preservation work before it was known as such.

One of the nation's first acts of preservation was the successful effort in 1816 to save Independence Hall (then known as the Old State House) from demolition. This Philadelphia building has tremendous historical significance, as every student of American history recognizes. Nevertheless, the site had been offered for subdivision into smaller parcels. Fortunately, a number of historical associations launched strong appeals, and the city of Philadelphia purchased it for preservation.

Independence Hall, Philadelphia.

Awareness of the American past and historic preservation are not new ideas. Indeed, they enjoy a long heritage of interest and support in this country. Countless Pioneer and Historical Societies/Associations were founded shortly after Euro-American settlements had taken hold in the early to mid-1800s. As early as the mid-1840s, efforts were underway to protect sites associated with the late-eighteenth- and early-nineteenth-century American frontier, as seen in northern Ohio and Indiana, where individuals acting on their own saved two major sites associated with that era: Gen. Anthony Wayne's fortification, Fort Wayne (1794), at present-day Fort Wayne, Indiana, and the site of the Battle of Fort Meigs (1813) at Perrysburg, Ohio.

The Mount Vernon Ladies' Association of the Union is generally considered the first nationwide preservation group organized in the United States. It was founded in 1853 to save deteriorating Mount Vernon, George and Martha Washington's homestead. The association presented a petition to Congress for "The Proposed Purchase of Mount Vernon by the Citizens of the United States, in Order that They May at All Times Have a Legal and Indisputable Right to Visit the Grounds, Mansion, and Tomb of Washington." The petition failed, and the federal government showed no interest in taking care of the property. As a result,

Mount Vernon, Fairfax County, Virginia.

Ann Pamela Cunningham chartered the Mount Vernon Ladies' Association. Motivated primarily by patriotism, she offered the challenge, "Those who go to the Home in which he lived and died, wish to see in what he lived and died! Let one spot in this grand country of ours be saved from change!"[1]

Cunningham found other women of means who had both the time and the inclination to help, and through this private organization, they raised the money to acquire Mount Vernon. The association's members, who were located in each of the states of the Union at that time, spearheaded a bold and successful campaign that saved and allowed for restoration of the structure.

The association served as an early model for organizations involved in saving landmark structures threatened by the encroachment of development or by time. Their significant effort also helped form some of the early trends of the preservation movement in the United States: for example, the early tradition that preservation activities were largely supported by private individuals, and that women had a prominent role in these activities. Out of these founding traditions also came the commonly adopted goal of saving individual landmark buildings.

With the emphasis by early preservationists on saving landmarks, there was little interest in preservation for the sake of architectural history. Nineteenth- and early-twentieth-century organizations, including historical or patriotic societies, family organizations, and government agencies, saved landmark buildings more for patriotic reasons than for their architectural ones. During that period, the historical connections of structures to great men and important events, the earlier the better, were the only criteria worth considering for preservation of a structure. It was not until the mid-twentieth century, when our society began to realize what was being lost to demolition and neglect, that buildings began to be considered for preservation based on their architectural significance as well.

ACTIVITIES OF THE FEDERAL GOVERNMENT

Throughout the nineteenth century, the federal government took virtually no active role in preservation and showed no inclination to recognize or protect buildings of potential historical significance. Instead, the government's interest was oriented toward the protection of the expanding nation's natural features, especially in the West. In 1872, the federal government established Yellowstone National Park as a protected area and the world's first national park comprising

Casa Grande, Arizona.

land in three states. In the Southwest, the federal government showed interest in preserving adobe dwellings, some of which dated to the fourteenth century, since settlers exploring this new territory often looted and destroyed these dwellings to get artifacts to sell back east. In 1889, Congress designated the Casa Grande ruin in Arizona, abandoned in the mid 1400s, as the nation's first National Monument and appropriated $2,000 to protect it—the first federal funding ever allocated for preservation.

At that same time, two cowboys looking for cattle in Arizona came across a spectacular site, the Cliff Palace dwellings of Mesa Verde. For the next eighteen years, word of the site spread back to the East Coast. Scavengers came to take well-preserved artifacts, selling them on the international market for good profits. Recognizing the loss at this significant site, Congress established Mesa Verde National Park with the intention of preserving the dwellings and remaining artifacts.

The Antiquities Act of 1906 established stiff penalties for destroying federally owned sites. Giving the president authority to designate "historic landmarks, historic and prehistoric structures, and other objects of historic or scientific interest"

Mesa Verde, Mesa Verde, Colorado. Courtesy of Barry D. Kass, Images of Anthropology.

situated on federal lands, the act was the nation's first historic preservation legislation. It prompted the surveying and identification of historic sites throughout the country and transferred authority for administering preservation activities at the federal level from Congress to the executive branch of government, allowing for more efficient management. The Antiquities Act further established the administration of preservation efforts through the office of the Secretary of the Interior, where it remains today.

The National Park Service

The National Park Service was established in 1916 within the U.S. Department of the Interior as the administrative agency responsible for national parks. The goal was to establish an apparatus to handle sites too large for private protection or preservation, such as the Jamestown and Yorktown sites in Virginia, which were combined to form the Colonial National Historical Park. It also began a program of acquiring Civil War battlefield sites to protect them from development.

nation of properties for the National Register. This process is one of the most important aspects of preservation work.

Perhaps the best way to describe the National Register is to identify what it does and does not do, for there are common misconceptions about designation.

The National Register *does:*

- Identify historically significant buildings, structures, sites, objects, and districts according to the National Register Criteria for Evaluation.
- Encourage the preservation of historic properties by documenting their significance and by lending support to local preservation activities.
- Enable federal, state, and local agencies to consider historic properties in the early stages of planning projects.
- Provide a list identifying historic sites that might be affected by new development for review by the Advisory Council on Historic Preservation (discussed later in this chapter).
- Provide for review of federally funded, licensed, or sponsored projects that may affect historic properties.
- Make owners of historic properties eligible to apply for federal grants-in-aid for preservation activities.
- Encourage the rehabilitation of income-producing historic properties that meet preservation standards through tax incentives; discourage the demolition of income-producing properties through federal income tax disincentives.

Listing a property on the National Register *does not:*

- Restrict the rights of private property owners in the use, development, or sale of privately owned historic property.
- Lead automatically to local historic district or landmark designation (although some communities and states have tied such federal designations to state or local designations).
- Stop federal, state, local, or private projects on the site.
- Provide for review of state, local, or privately funded projects that may affect historic properties (although some states and communities have tied such designation to environmental reviews).
- Guarantee that grant funds will be available for all significant historic properties.
- Provide tax benefits to owners of residential historic properties, unless those properties are rented and treated as income-producing by the Internal Revenue Service.

Some preservationists argue that the federal government should change its policy of not providing protection for National Register properties and legislate some form of protection for all listed properties. Although it was politically necessary to leave such control out of the original act, historic preservation has since proved its worth, and many would argue that the ability of private developers to destroy national landmarks with impunity is no longer justifiable.

The Concept of Historic Districts

The National Register defined the concept of historic districts. Before 1966, only individual structures or objects were designated at the federal level. The National Historic Preservation Act recognized the need for the designation of individual properties, but also recognized that in many instances it is necessary not only to preserve a building but also the context in which it and adjacent buildings are placed. Therefore, the idea of designating groups or assemblages of buildings as historic districts represented a significant conceptual shift. There are now over 2,300 local historic districts listed with the National Park Service. For many, the residents and local elected officials decided they would like to protect the area's historic character by also adopting a local historic district *ordinance*. Such local legislation is one of the best ways to protect the historic character of buildings and places while allowing appropriate change to happen.

Advisory Council on Historic Preservation

The 1966 act, as amended, also established the Advisory Council on Historic Preservation. The Advisory Council is an independent federal agency, appointed by the president and under the executive branch, that advises the president and Congress on historic preservation policy. The council also reviews and comments on federal and federally-assisted activities that affect properties listed in, or eligible for listing in, the National Register of Historic Places.[10] In essence, the council was established to provide a check against unwarranted demolition and destruction of historic resources as a result of federal activities and programs. It is the only federal entity created solely to address historic preservation issues. It currently has twenty members, including the Secretaries of the Interior, Transportation, Housing and Urban Development, and Agriculture.

Section 106 Review

Most of the Advisory Council's budget and personnel resources are used each year to fulfill its primary mandate, a process known as Section 106 review (referring to its section in the National Historic Preservation Act of 1966). This process involves reviewing and commenting on federal and federally supported projects that affect historic properties—properties either on or eligible for listing on the National Register of Historic Places. Such review recognizes that federal policy and expenditures can cause great harm to historic properties. For example, the widening of an existing two-lane highway may impact a designated historic farmstead along its route. The Section 106 process ensures that such properties are considered during federal project planning and implementation. In any given year, thousands of such projects are reviewed. The National Historic Preservation Act also requires that special consideration and planning be undertaken for properties designated as National Historic Landmarks.

The review procedures are described in the Advisory Council's regulations, "Protection of Historic Properties." The regulations define an "area of potential effects" as the "geographical area within which an undertaking may directly or indirectly cause alterations in the character or use of historic properties, if any such properties exist." Federal agencies must assume that there is the potential for historic properties to exist until the identification step of the review process has been completed. Simply stated, the process works in this way:

1. The federal agency involved with the project identifies historic properties that may be affected and consults with the State Historic Preservation Office (SHPO) or the Tribal Historic Preservation Office (THPO) to determine which properties are listed on, or are eligible for listing on, the National Register.

2. For each historic property the agency determines whether the proposed project will have (a) no effect, (b) no adverse effect, or (c) an adverse effect.

3. If an adverse outcome is anticipated, the agency consults with the SHPO or THPO and others to determine how to minimize the negative impact. This step results in a memorandum of agreement (MOA) which outlines the mitigating measures to be taken.

4. If an MOA is executed, the agency can proceed with the project under its terms.

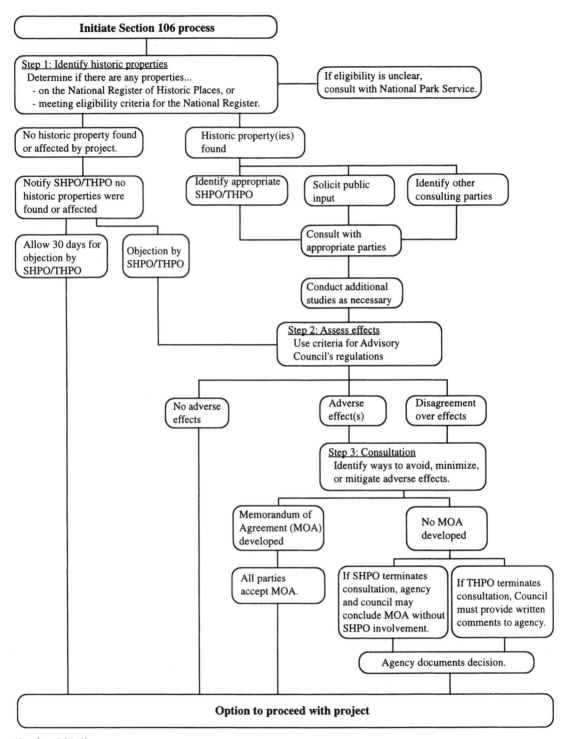

Initiate Section 106 process

Step 1: Identify historic properties
Determine if there are any properties...
- on the National Register of Historic Places, or
- meeting eligibility criteria for the National Register.

If eligibility is unclear, consult with National Park Service.

No historic property found or affected by project.

Historic property(ies) found

Notify SHPO/THPO no historic properties were found or affected

Identify appropriate SHPO/THPO

Solicit public input

Identify other consulting parties

Allow 30 days for objection by SHPO/THPO

Objection by SHPO/THPO

Consult with appropriate parties

Conduct additional studies as necessary

Step 2: Assess effects
Use criteria for Advisory Council's regulations

No adverse effects

Adverse effect(s)

Disagreement over effects

Step 3: Consultation
Identify ways to avoid, minimize, or mitigate adverse effects.

Memorandum of Agreement (MOA) developed

No MOA developed

All parties accept MOA.

If SHPO terminates consultation, agency and council may conclude MOA without SHPO involvement.

If THPO terminates consultation, Council must provide written comments to agency.

Agency documents decision.

Option to proceed with project

Section 106 diagram.

When no agreement can be reached among the parties interested in the project, the Advisory Council may try to develop an alternative agreement. As shown in the diagram, the Section 106 review process does not have the power to stop work even if it will have significant negative impact on a historic property. Likewise, it does not insist that certain procedures are followed in order to proceed with proposed work. The process mandates only that there must be an impact review and an opportunity for interested bodies to make comment. If the review shows that serious harm would be done to a designated property, federal funding may or may not be withdrawn, but in any case a project could proceed without the use of federal funding if an owner so chose.

An example of the use of the Section 106 process was a proposal for a new residential development in the Lower Coastal Plain area of Georgia. Because the project required review under the federal Clean Water Act, the Section 106 process was initiated. The review resulted in an archeological excavation showing clear evidence of slave settlements containing patterns based on African traditions, including housing layouts, pottery shards, and religious artifacts. In addition to the unique and unusual nature of the archeological findings, the site also was the location of a mansion and laboratory built by Henry Ford, already listed on the National Register. The Section 106 process indicated that the adverse effects to these sites caused by the proposed development should be mitigated. As a result, the project's boundaries were redrawn and landscaping included giving visual separation between the new project and the historic sites. Also, the new housing was designed to complement the existing architectural style of the Ford properties. A monitoring process was established to ensure long-term compliance with the agreement.

CHANGES IN THE PRESERVATION MOVEMENT

Since the passage of the National Historic Preservation Act in 1966, the preservation movement has undergone significant changes. The act not only instituted structural changes in preservation programs, as described above, but also changed the way preservation is conceived and who is involved.

First, the notion of historical significance underwent revision. Preservationists no longer focused on saving aged national landmarks as museum pieces. Instead, entire areas were designated as historic districts. Also, more recent buildings were recognized for their historic importance. A distinctive gas station or motel could be seen as an important representation of society's cultural heritage and therefore worthy of recognition. Buildings with local or statewide significance were seen as contributing to the larger historic context and worthy of National Register status alongside nationally recognized landmarks. But these buildings were not considered frozen in time as museum pieces. Through the concept of adaptive use, alterations were allowed that would enable buildings to continue to contribute to the economic vitality of a community.

Thanks to the National Historic Preservation Act, many new preservation initiatives were undertaken. In 1968, the National Trust produced the first film on preservation for national distribution, "How Will We Know It's Us?" attracting more people to the movement. Also in 1968, American and Canadian preservationists joined together to form an international organization, the Association for Preservation Technology (APT) International, focusing on conservation and restoration techniques. Additional focus was brought to historic preservation during the 1976 bicentennial celebrations taking place across the country. Local celebrations stimulated increased interest in "heritage tourism," and Americans recognized, many for the first time, that their culture had a significant heritage of its own.

A tax incentive program for the rehabilitation of historic structures, created under the Tax Reform Act of 1976, represented a significant shift from public-sector involvement to private-sector initiative. For the first time, investors who were not supporters of preservation became integral players because of new economic incentives. Older structures could be viewed as financial opportunities rather than as obstructions to development. As Michael Tomlan, professor of historic preservation at Cornell University, wrote in *Past Meets Future*: "It was in the 1980s that preservationists launched feverishly into the 'business' of preservation. The move was not without its irony: on one hand we preservationists continued to try to control development, while on the other we promoted business interests."[11]

Preservation also became an important tool of urban revitalization during this period. Through the Main Street Program established by the National Trust in 1980 (see Chapter 9), the preservation and adaptive use of older commercial buildings became an important tool of downtown renewal. This successful program changed perceptions of older and blighted downtowns and provided the framework for a complete revitalization program that transcended typical rehabilitation efforts to include recognition of the importance of organization, promotion, design, and economic restructuring.

As a result of these new perspectives, preservation advocates took a more activist role, sometimes with missionary zeal. Lobbying efforts by groups such as the National Trust for Historic Preservation and Preservation Action pushed through other beneficial legislation. The ranks of preservation advocates swelled. This expansion was tied closely with the environmental movement, which grew after the passage of the National Environmental Policy Act (NEPA) of 1969. NEPA established a national policy on the protection and preservation of the nation's natural environment, authorizing a listing of environmental amenities and a process of review when such sites were impacted by federal actions or funding of development. The environmental movement had many parallels with the preservation movement in terms of activities, policies, legislation, and timing.

THE STATE ROLE

Many states had preservation programs prior to the National Historic Preservation Act of 1966, but they tended to be limited in scope. Typically, they included the operation of state-administered museums, historic sites, and highway or structure marker programs. As a result of the 1966 act, states took on a larger and more uniform role.

State Historic Preservation Offices (SHPOs)

The National Historic Preservation Act authorized grants to help establish state-level offices. In a federal–state partnership, these offices became the chief administrative agencies for most preservation programs. To be eligible for federal funding for preservation administration and projects, states were required to establish an official State Historic Preservation Office (SHPO, pronounced variously as "shpoe" or "ship-poe").

SHPOs are assigned a number of responsibilities. Each:

1. Is responsible for conducting systematic surveys of historic properties and sites throughout its state. These surveys are intended to establish a list of individual structures, objects, or districts that have historic significance. The surveys should indicate properties needing designation because they are threatened.

Originally, the surveys were comprehensive in scope, and SHPOs tried to recognize and document virtually every historic resource in a state. Lowered funding in subsequent years caused downscaling, and state surveys now have two primary thrusts. The first is an effort to prioritize the survey work to provide documentation for the most significant properties. Second, local citizens are encouraged to do the survey work themselves in a manner consistent with the state's established procedures.

2. Processes nominations to the National Register of Historic Places. The SHPO sends approved nominations, with comments, to the National Park Service, where it is again reviewed and certification either granted or denied. Although the National Park Service may override decisions made at the state level, this seldom occurs, and most of the processing and review work is carried out directly between the property nominator and the state office. The process may take as little as sixty days or as long as a year or more.

3. Administers grants to individual projects throughout the state, serving as the funding conduit from the national to the local level.

4. Advises and assists in the efforts of local agencies (but it cannot regulate). Under the United States system of government, states authorize powers to local governments, but local governments need not accept them. Thus, the power states can give to local governments to regulate historic properties does not necessarily mean that local governments must take on this power. They may choose not to be involved in preservation regulation at all. Although the power to regulate resides with the state, typically the initiative for preservation lies at the local level.

5. Provides consultation on Section 106 review.

6. Reviews applications for federal investment tax credits and makes recommendation to the National Park Service. An increasing number of states are now supplementing the federal tax credits with historic tax credits applicable to state income taxes.

7. Administers the Certified Local Government (CLG) process.

SHPOs are represented nationally by the National Conference of State Historic Preservation Officers, a nonprofit professional association. The NCSHPO acts as a communication vehicle among the various SHPOs and their staffs. It also represents SHPOs to federal agencies and national preservation organizations.

The president of the NCSHPO acts as an ex-officio member of the Federal Advisory Council on Historic Preservation.

In 1992, Congress adopted amendments to the 1966 act to allow Native American tribes to assume any or all of the functions of SHPOs. Tribal Historic Preservation Offices (THPOs) may maintain inventories and registers of places historically significant to the tribes. They can also nominate properties to the National Register, conduct Section 106 reviews of federally supported projects on tribal land, and conduct education programs on the importance of preserving historic properties. Native Americans tend to preserve their heritage more

Alaska's SHPO brochure.

through language, oral tradition, arts, crafts, and dance than through buildings, so the federal- and state-level programs may have a different emphasis, giving less importance to the preservation of historic structures. Congress recognized the distinctive link between tribal cultures and tribal religions with the American Indian Religious Freedom Act of 1978. Indeed, the term *historic preservation* may not be inclusive enough to represent the appropriate meaning to Native Americans.

State Historic Preservation Review Boards

Historic preservation review boards have been established in some states. Composed of professionals in the fields of American and architectural history, architecture, cultural geography, prehistoric and historic archeology, historic preservation, and related disciplines, such boards can serve several functions. Most commonly, they review nominations submitted to the state for properties to be listed on the National Register and recommend that the SHPO accept or reject those nominations. In some instances, the state review board also serves as the final board of appeal for property owners who do not agree with a determination made by a local historic district commission. Although each case must be decided on its own merits, generally it is inappropriate for a state review board to rethink the judgment of a local commission. The board's review determines only whether the local commission's action was within the rights provided by the local ordinance or whether rights of the property owner were not properly protected.

THE LOCAL ROLE

In many ways, historic preservation is most meaningful at the local level, where the process of designating historic structures is initiated. Preservation ordinances, regulations, and incentives are drafted at the local level, where authority is given to review and approve or disapprove changes to historic structures. Property owners deal directly with local officials.

The roles of the various levels of government—federal, state, and local—are quite distinct. The federal role is to fund activities, set out an overall superstructure of preservation activities, and ensure consistency of approach from state to state. The federal government also monitors its own properties and activities and provides incentives to encourage appropriate work at historic buildings. But it has virtually no regulatory power and thus no ultimate power over owners of historic properties. At the state level, SHPOs encourage surveys of significant historic resources and facilitate federal activities, providing a link between the federal and local levels of government and state laws authorized for local programs. But state preservation officials also have limited regulatory power over historic properties.

The real protective power of historic preservation is found at the local level. This point cannot be overemphasized. Only at the local level can historic properties be regulated and protected through legal ordinances. The process of administering local historic ordinances is in the hands of historic district commissions, which are made up of either appointed or elected local residents. The National Historic Preservation Act of 1966 enabled local governments to establish such review agencies. These powers are reserved for local governments because of the underlying philosophy that each community should determine for itself what is historically significant, what is of value to the community, and what steps should be taken to provide protection. As historian Antoinette Lee with the National Park Service put it, "Architectural historians give you information; the neighborhoods give you passion."[12]

The Range of Local Government Programs: The Charleston Principles

A document referred to as the *Charleston Principles*, written in 1990, represents a national consensus on the activities of local governments and agencies in historic preservation. Its general principles can guide preservation activities in any community:

A Call to Action for Community Conservation

Members of the national historic preservation community, assembled on October 20, 1990, in Charleston, South Carolina, for the 44th National Preservation Conference, sponsored by the National Trust for Historic Preservation, adopted unanimously the following principles for comprehensive local government programs to conserve community heritage and made a pledge to have these principles become part of the policy of their communities.

We call on local leaders to adopt and act on these principles in order to improve their citizens' quality of life, increase their economic well-being, and enhance their community's heritage and beauty.

Principle I: Identify historic places, both architectural and natural, that give the community its special character and that aid its future well-being.

Principle II: Adopt the preservation of historic places as a goal of planning for land use, economic development, housing for all income levels, and transportation.

Principle III: Create organizational, regulatory, and incentive mechanisms to facilitate preservation, and provide the leadership to make them work.

Principle IV: Develop revitalization strategies that capitalize on the existing value of historic residential and commercial neighborhoods and properties, and provide well designed affordable housing without displacing existing residents.

Principle V: Ensure that policies and decisions on community growth and development respect a community's heritage and enhance overall livability.

Principle VI: Demand excellence in design for new construction and in the stewardship of historic properties and places.

Principle VII: Use a community's heritage to educate citizens of all ages and to build civic pride.

Principle VIII: Recognize the cultural diversity of communities and empower a diverse constituency to acknowledge, identify, and preserve America's cultural and physical resources.[13]

SUMMARY OF THE HISTORY OF PRESERVATION

The preservation movement has changed dramatically from its early years to today's organized and systematic activities. Local, state, and federal government agencies work to complement one another and support the actions of nongovernmental groups found across the country. The history of historic preservation in the United States can be briefly recounted through dates important to the movement:

1816 Philadelphia State House (Independence Hall) saved from demolition.

1853 Mount Vernon Ladies' Association formed to save President George Washington's home, regarded as the first private group to mount a national preservation effort; property opened to the public in 1859.

1872 Yellowstone National Park made a federally protected area, leading to interest in protecting Southwestern adobe dwellings.

1889 First national funding for historic preservation, as Congress appropriated $2,000 to preserve Casa Grande ruin in Arizona.

1890 Creation of Yosemite and Sequoia National Parks in California; also first national military park established at Chickamauga Battlefield in Georgia, followed shortly by Gettysburg and Shiloh.

1895 Adirondack Forest preserve (now Adirondack Great Park) instituted by the State of New York; over six million acres to remain "forever wild" in a public–private partnership.

1906 Antiquities Act passed, the country's first national preservation legislation, designating monuments on federal land and establishing penalties for destroying federally owned sites.

1916 National Park Service established to administer areas too large to be preserved privately (e.g., Colonial National Historical Park in Virginia, including Jamestown and Yorktown, Virginia).

1920s Geographer Carl Sauer first describes the concept of "cultural landscape."

1926 John D. Rockefeller Jr. begins funding the restoration of Williamsburg, Virginia.

1929 Henry Ford establishes Greenfield Village.

1931 Charleston, South Carolina, establishes an "Old and Historic District," the country's first designated historic district.

1933 Historic American Buildings Survey (HABS) authorized by President Roosevelt.

1935 Historic Sites Act passed by Congress, setting historic preservation policy; it "established policy . . . to preserve for public use historic sites, buildings and objects of national significance for the inspiration and benefit of the people of the United States."

1949 National Trust for Historic Preservation established.

1964 First graduate-level course in Historic Preservation offered at Columbia University's Graduate School of Architecture, Planning, and Preservation.

1966 National Historic Preservation Act passed; major provisions established preservation roles for federal, state, and local levels of government, which led to the creation of the National Register of Historic Places, local historic districts, State Historic Preservation Offices, and the Advisory Council on Historic Preservation.

1969 National Environmental Policy Act (NEPA) enacted, setting in motion legal and policy-based actions to encourage environmental awareness and protection.

1975–76 National celebration of United States bicentennial brought preservation and conservation ethic to forefront of communities across the country.

1976 Tax Reform Act removed incentive for demolition of older buildings.

1978 Revenue Act established investment tax credits for rehabilitation of historic buildings.

1978 U.S. Supreme Court upholds New York City's local preservation law in *Penn Central Transportation Co. v. City of New York.*

1980 Main Street Program established by the National Trust for Historic Preservation.

1980 Amendment of National Historic Preservation Act of 1966 and inclusion of provision for Certified Local Government status.

1984 First National Heritage Corridor established for the Illinois and Michigan Canal.

1991 Congress passed Intermodal Surface Transportation Efficiency Act (ISTEA) with provision under the Enhancements section to provide funding from U.S. Department of Transportation for transportation-related historic preservation projects.

1998 National Trust for Historic Preservation becomes independent of federal funding.

2006 One-hundredth anniversary of the Antiquities Act; Fortieth Anniversary of the National Historic Preservation Act.

Chapter Three

ARCHITECTURAL STYLES, CONTEXTUALISM, AND DESIGN GUIDELINES

Historic buildings are commonly described in terms of their architectural style. This enables us to place buildings in their historic context by describing styles that came before and after and the cultural impact of each style during its time period. It also allows us to evaluate whether a building is a good or poor example of a particular period and style.

A discussion of architectural styles found in the United States also is a discussion of a continuing search that has taken place over more than two centuries for an "American" style. For many generations, we have been searching for our cultural identity, partially through our architecture. Americans have long wanted to define themselves as a culture separate from their primarily European roots. However, with no strong sense of our own history, the older architectural heritages of the mother countries inevitably were used as a starting point in defining our own.

To trace the evolution of American architectural styles is to follow a process beginning in the seventeenth century and coming to a form of resolution only in the twentieth century. It begins with European precedents and the ways in which early settlers imitated familiar styles from their homelands (primarily England). The search continues with experiments in the nineteenth century with both classical and romantic trends and culminates, at least for a while, in the twentieth century with a truly original American style. This chapter presents a summary of the major architectural styles that were prominent throughout American history, starting in the early colonial period. Each succeeding style represents a shift in America's self-image.

It should be noted that many of the major, more formal styles described in the following sections, particularly after the mid-seventeenth century, were designed by architects or master builders/carpenters/masons and reflected an architectural fashion of the times. However, there are many sub-styles and types of architectural expression that were not architect- or builder-designed. Often referred to as *vernacular* (or ordinary) structures, such places reflected the availability of local materials, local idioms, prevailing environmental conditions, or ethnic preferences. For example, the unique "shotgun houses" of the Gulf Coast region reflected locally available materials, environmental conditions, and the African and Caribbean heritage of many of the early inhabitants. Log cabins, Native American wigwams, cobblestone homes, I-houses, and the American "four-square" residence are other examples. Works such as folklorist Henry Glassie's *Pattern in the Material Folk Culture of the Eastern United States,* geographer Fred Kniffen's seminal article "Building in Wood in the Eastern United States," and *A Field Guide to American Houses* by Virginia and Lee McAlester are excellent primers on American vernacular architectural forms. For other references on architectural styles and vernacular types, see the Further Reading list at the end of this book.

ENGLISH STYLES

Colonial

Buildings constructed during the colonial period (generally considered to be up to 1776) were basic in plan and typically only one room deep. Common characteristics of early colonial houses in the North included steep roofs, which were needed to shed snow, and chimneys placed centrally within the structure to keep the heat radiating within the building. As typified by the Parson Capen House, Colonial houses often had two stories for more centralized heating, with the upper floor projecting a foot or two over the lower wall at the front and giving some weather protection to the entry.

Structures were built with locally available natural materials. Pegged post-and-beam construction was common in the North because of the availability of hardwood. Early structures sometimes had thatch roofs, but these were soon replaced with more durable wood shingles. Rooms were added to the first floor by extending the roof at the rear to form the familiar saltbox shape. Wattle and daub or brick infilled the walls, which were usually covered on the exterior with clapboard siding to provide protection from the elements. Small casement windows were common until the end of the seventeenth century, when sliding-sash double-hung windows became popular.

Other features were specific to certain locations or circumstances. For example, the Boxford House in West Boxford, Massachusetts, built during the colonial period, has a black band painted around the top of the chimney, reportedly to signify a safe house on the Underground Railroad during the Civil War period. This suggestion is supported by a hideaway chute with false floor located behind an attic chimney.

In the Southern coastal colonies, houses varied from those in the North. They were typically constructed of brick instead of wood, often had one story, and chimneys were located on the ends of the house, rather than in the middle, to minimize heat buildup.

Parson Capen House, Topsfield, Massachusetts.

Georgian

Colonial builders were not necessarily concerned with questions of architectural style; they dealt with construction details that related to basic existence. Late in the colonial period, however, settlers began the search for a more refined style to present an identity through their buildings and to express a more civilized nature through architecture. British colonists initially established this identity by using the Georgian style, named after King George III, with which they were very familiar, and which was the most prominent style of the eighteenth century in England. Pattern books illustrating the style began arriving in the colonies soon after 1700 and were influential in establishing its significance during a period of increasing wealth, urbanization, and building in New England. Cliveden Mansion, the site of an important battle of the Revolutionary War, is an excellent example of the Georgian style.

Georgian houses were both formal and symmetrical. The style included a symmetrical arrangement of rooms, typically two rooms deep and two stories high ("four over four"), allowing more privacy for families by separating cooking, dining, sitting, and sleeping into separate rooms. The Georgian style was influenced largely by the architecture of Palladio, a prominent sixteenth-century Italian architect who derived much of his detailing from classical Greek and Roman

Cliveden Mansion, Historic Germantown, Philadelphia.

Palladian window.

elements, including pediments, pilasters, dentils in the cornice, and the familiar rounded Palladian window. Side gable roofs had little overhang, and casement windows gave way to sliding single-hung or double-hung windows, with each sash divided into as many as twenty individual panes. This style became one of the most durable in America, and still is used as a basic pattern in the reproductions found in many traditional, but newly built, residential neighborhoods.

Federal

As indicated by the name, the Federal style was popular during the period just after the American Revolution, from about 1780 to 1820. First developed by the Adam brothers in Scotland (and also called the Adam style), it soon was adopted by Americans, especially in seaport towns around Boston and eastern Massachusetts. The exterior and interior elevations of Federal-style buildings share classical detailing and symmetry with the Georgian and are considered derivative of the earlier style. However, the detailing differs noticeably. Federal-style roofs had a shallower pitch; window and door detailing was lighter and simpler and in some instances even delicate. The Federal-style entrance usually placed an elliptical

Abraham Jones House, Libertytown, Maryland.

fanlight over the doorway, with sidelights under the arch. In the more prominent examples, interiors may have oval- or circular-shaped rooms circumscribed by their rectangular floor plans. The Abraham Jones House represents one of the best examples of the decorative treatment found in a Federal-style house, as shown in its main entrance door, 12-over-12 windows, and parapet side walls.

CLASSICAL STYLES

Greek Revival (Classical Revival)

Although Georgian and Federal buildings featured some classical elements, the intentional replication of classical Greek and Roman buildings began in the late eighteenth century, largely through the influence of Thomas Jefferson. While serving as minister to France, he became enamored of the Maison Carrée at Nîmes in southern France. This Greek-temple-style structure was a prototype for Jefferson's design of the Virginia State Capitol in Richmond, completed in 1792. As the first public building in the United States in neoclassical temple form, the capitol building significantly influenced the design of other public structures. Soon the classical style, associated with Greek city-states and republicanism, was accepted as the style most fitting to represent the new American republic, and the nation's search for an appropriate architectural style seemed to have been satisfied. Jefferson's design for the University of Virginia in 1817, one of this country's most admired pieces of architecture, was a tour-de-force in this classical style. After the War of 1812, it was less politically correct to use British styles such as Georgian and Federal. The Greek Revival style (sometimes referred to as Classical Revival), representing Greek independence and democracy, became much more favored.

Greek Revival structures are most readily distinguishable by a temple-style pediment on a gable-front roof supported by freestanding Greek- or Roman-style

Judge Robert S. Wilson House, Ann Arbor, Michigan.

columns. Although the main structure could be stucco, board siding, or brick, the front elevation is typically enhanced with a white portico (porch) with a full-width pediment and columns. Greek Revival structures are rectilinear, and their interior spatial arrangement has height and width proportions and window arrangements that originate in the design needs of the temple form on which it is based. The front of the Judge Robert S. Wilson House in Ann Arbor, Michigan, built in the 1840s, was based on the proportions of the Temple of Athena Nike at the Greek Acropolis. Its finely proportioned columns, regular window placement, and overall plan have led to it being called "one of the finest Greek Revival houses in America."[1]

Although the style remained popular for certain building types, especially formal buildings used by governments or banks, the eventual decline of the Greek Revival style in the North was due partially to its association with the mansions found on southern plantations. It also was less favored because of the inherent restrictiveness and inflexibility of its plan. As society grew increasingly urban, buildings closely placed along busy streets became more appropriate and workable than buildings situated temple-like on selected hilltops. This change in thinking was described by John Maass in his book *The Gingerbread Age*.

> The Victorians, of course, moralized on every possible occasion and they attacked the Greek style upon moral grounds. Actually, the Greek Revival had run its course in the [1840s] because it was no longer adequate. This beautiful, serene style is essentially an architecture of façades. Fenestration was always a problem in a porticoed building; even such a lover of the antique as Goethe had recognized that "columns and windows are a contradiction." The Greek temples had of course been windowless and the dwellings of the ancient Greeks and Romans were without columns. The ground plan of a Greek Revival building had to conform to the symmetrical elevation. This could be made to work in formal designs like royal palaces, state capitols and even town halls but it was a straitjacket for builders who were called upon to solve the everyday problems of an increasingly complex industrial civilization.[2]

Italianate (Renaissance Revival)

Italianate, another formal, symmetrical style, first came to prominence in the 1850s and remained popular through later revivals well into the twentieth century. Although the style first became popular in England, its stylistic elements were

Boston Public Library. Courtesy of the Historic American Building Survey.

derived from Italian Renaissance architecture and distinguished by an almost severe, blockish form similar to the Italian palazzo (hence the style's alternate name, Renaissance Revival). The Boston Public Library, the largest municipal library in the country, opened its Renaissance Revival style McKim Building in 1895. With its grand Italian palace design and layout, it was referred to as a "palace for the people."

Italianate house.

An important feature of the style is a wide, projecting cornice supported with elaborate double brackets. Windows with rounded or segmented arch tops typically have an eyebrow hood. Low-sloped or flat roofs make the roof form recede and give primary importance to the wall elevations.

The lack of projecting elements, like the portico of Greek Revival structures, makes Italianate buildings fit better on city streets, so this style became popular for downtown commercial buildings. In fact, it was the style of choice for common commercial buildings from the 1850s until the turn of the century. Because the timing of its ascendancy matched the period when most American cities beyond the East Coast experienced their most rapid growth, in many parts of the country downtowns, large and small, have a preponderance of Italianate storefronts.

Italianate storefront.

Italian Villa residence.

Italian Villa

The Italian Villa style became popular in the 1840s, when A. J. Downing included examples in his books, such as *The Architecture of Country Houses* (1850), and recommended it as both picturesque and practical. The style is basically a less formal, asymmetrical Italianate structure with a prominently featured tower rising above the roofline, typically offset within a two-story *L*- or *T*-shaped floor plan. Because of its less symmetrical plan, additions can be incorporated freely without losing the essence of the style. The Italian Villa style was used by the wealthy, typically as a country home in a garden setting, with multiple roofs, porches, and four prominent elevations, rather than one.

Balconies with balustrades are common to the style, as are classically detailed verandas. Roofs with gentle slopes may have wide projecting eaves supported by Italianate-style bracketing. Windows can be rounded at the top and set in groupings of two or three. Bay windows are used to increase the interface between interior spaces and the outdoors. Walls are typically stone, stucco, or brick; only in less distinguished residences are they wood clapboard.

Beaux-Arts Classicism

The French term *beaux-arts* means "fine arts" and refers to the approach to architectural design taught at the École des Beaux-Arts (School of Fine Arts) in Paris from the seventeenth century to the twentieth century. Beaux-Arts (or Academic) Classicism is characterized by grand, formal compositions with elaborate stone detailing. Multistory Greek columns or pediments typically are grouped in pairs to define projecting façades or pavilions. Symmetry is important on all of the façades, and detailing is much more exuberant than in other classical styles. Cornice lines have elaborate moldings and dentils, and both rooflines and windows

Library of Congress, Washington, D.C.

Columbian Exposition Administration Building.

include carefully detailed stone balustrades. Although Beaux-Arts structures commonly used rusticated stone bases, smooth stone exteriors capped by elaborate carved stone cornices, and grand masonry and marble interiors, steel framing was often used in construction in the United States after the turn of the twentieth century.

The influence of the Beaux-Arts school was particularly strong at the World's Columbian Exposition held in Chicago in 1893. The planners of the fair wanted to make it one of the most significant events of the age. Still recovering from the Great Fire of 1871, Chicago was to rise, phoenix-like, from the ashes. After the Civil War, many Americans toured Europe and returned aware that the United States had no city that could vie with the beauty of Paris or the prominent cities of Italy. One of the primary purposes of the fair was to demonstrate that America was a culture of destiny and that its architecture could showcase that culture, even if only as a temporary façade that would last but one summer. The fair was a huge success. Great numbers of Midwesterners who had never visited a big city before came and saw what they considered the ideal world created by the architects. So great was the exposition's architectural impact that the Beaux-Arts influence remained a force in architecture for another forty years.

Many notable American architects were trained at the École, among them Richard Morris Hunt (in 1846, the first American to attend), Louis Sullivan, H. H. Richardson, and Bernard Maybeck. Their rigorous classical training greatly influenced the grand public architecture in the United States between the 1890s and 1920s. Prominent American buildings in the Beaux-Arts style include Union Station (1907) and the Library of Congress (1897) in Washington, D.C., the Metropolitan Museum of Art (1895) in New York City, and the San Francisco Opera House (1932).

THE ROMANTIC STYLES

Gothic Revival

In the mid to late nineteenth century, when many of the formal styles, with their controlled elegance and symmetry, were evolving toward grander structures and grandiose detailing, a new movement arose that incorporated more romantic notions of architectural design. Influenced greatly by English landscape design, with a free-flowing interpretation of nature and natural forms, the romantic period of architecture in the United States was ushered in by architect A. J. Downing. The son of a nurseryman, Downing was the author of an influential book, *Treatise on the Theory and Practice of Landscape Gardening* (1841). In his later books, *Cottage Residences* and *The Architecture of Country Houses*, he laid out design principles that provided a significant counterpoint to the more formal styles still prevalent at the time. The Delamater House, in Rhinebeck, New York, is an excellent example of Downing's Carpenter Gothic Cottage. (It is now operated as one of the country's oldest inns.)

The romantic style of choice was Gothic, the only "rational" style considered flexible enough to adapt to all of a building's functional requirements. As opposed to the symmetrical perfection sought in classical design, Gothic was a freely interpreted style subject to the whims of its designer. The Gothic Revival style was expressed through pronounced features—most distinctively, the pointed

Delamater House, Rhinebeck, New York.

arch form. This element is so integral to the style that any building with pointed arches can almost instantly be recognized as Gothic Revival. Other elements common to the style include freely laid out asymmetrical floor plans; tall, narrow windows; and steeply pitched roof forms. Window tracery and pinnacles may also be used.

Although at its roots a masonry style, many smaller wood frame buildings were built in the Gothic mode and considered to be in the derivative "Carpenter" Gothic style. Typically they featured vertical board siding, elaborately cut decorative vergeboard trim under the eaves, and a veranda.

Richardsonian Romanesque (Romanesque Revival)

The Romanesque style is somewhat similar to Gothic in massing, if not in detailing. Based on the ancient Roman basilica prototype, it is differentiated by its use of rounded instead of pointed arch forms for windows and entrances.

Oliver Ames Memorial Library, North Easton, Massachusetts.

The Romanesque style was popularized in the 1880s by Henry Hobson Richardson, an influential and dynamic architect of the period. Richardson was a large man with a commanding presence who exuded confidence. He represented the spirit of the age, a spirit that wanted to present itself boldly to the world. Because of his personal influence, the new style became popularly known as Richardsonian Romanesque. During the relatively short span of twenty years, Richardsonian Romanesque architecture became an almost universal prototype for public buildings and was often used for churches, libraries, train stations, and other large institutional structures. Many of Richardson's buildings include prominent masonry towers with multiple-arched openings at the top. Among Richardson's most representative and important buildings are Trinity Church (1877) in Boston, the Allegheny County Courthouse and Jail (1888) in Pittsburgh, the Marshall Field Wholesale Store (1887) in Chicago, and the State Hospital (1880) in Buffalo, New York. A concentration of five Richardson buildings were built in North Easton, Massachusetts, supported by the Ames family. They include the Oliver Ames Memorial Library.

Richardsonian Romanesque residence, Chicago.

Most buildings in the Richardsonian Romanesque style have exteriors of heavy masonry punctuated with groupings of windows with transoms. A large arched opening forming a deeply recessed entrance is a signature. The proportions in Romanesque architecture are heavier than Gothic and do not stress verticality nearly as much. Monochromatic masonry emphasizes the prominent exterior forms of openings and recesses more than the details. Chimneys are low, in keeping with the horizontal massing, and eyebrow windows often provide openings through roofs.

Second Empire

The Second Empire style is modeled on French architecture from the period of the Second Empire of Napoleon III. The Louvre Museum in Paris is the building that best represents its French roots. In the United States, Second Empire style was elaborate and exotic enough to satisfy the need for extravagance felt by many of those who had become rich during the Civil War. At the time, it was considered a modern style, one of the first based not on a historical style but on the contemporary environment of Paris of the 1870s. Prominent American examples of the style are the State, War and Navy Building in Washington, D.C. (now the Old Executive Office Building), built between 1871 and 1875, and the Philadelphia City Hall (1874–81). Second Empire style was commonly used for large resi-

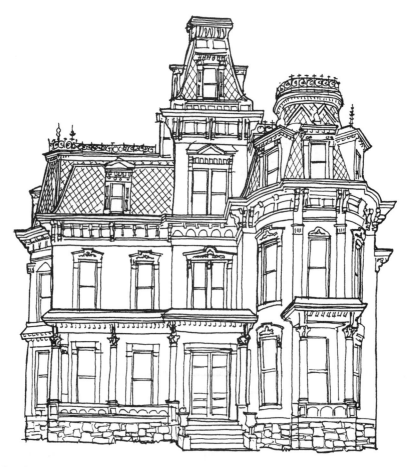

Charles Ficke Mansion, Davenport, Iowa.

dences during the period from the 1860s to the 1880s. During the late nineteenth century it became a widespread, if not pervasive, style. As an example, Charles Ficke moved his family into a larger house in Davenport, Iowa, to give space for his extensive art collection. The Ficke Mansion represents one of the best examples of a Second Empire residence.

The primary distinguishing feature of Second Empire buildings is the distinctive upper-story mansard roof. The defining Parisian mansard roof (named after the seventeenth-century architect François Mansart) allowed a three-story structure to be kept more in scale with two-story structures while capturing usable floor area in the attic. However, lower stories were often classical in character and included Italianate detailing. Without the mansard roof, a Second Empire building could be considered Italianate in form and detailing.

Queen Anne

The Queen Anne style, most popular from the 1870s to the 1920s, is a residential style that represents the culmination of the picturesque, romantic styles of the nineteenth century. Historically, it has no real link to Britain's Queen Anne but is closely associated with the Victorian era. (Although "Victorian" is often discussed as an architectural style, the term is correctly used only to represent the period of Queen Victoria's reign, not a style.)

Queen Anne designs thrived on decorative excess and best represented the wealth of the "Gilded Age." Variety was encouraged, as was freedom of expression. The use of historical detailing was not predetermined in this style; instead, details casually intermingle. The overall effect is one of studied busyness—partial- or full-width porches with ornamented spindles, decorated brick chimneys corbeled prominently, and multiple turrets and roof gables facing in every direction. Wall surfaces are of masonry, wood shingles (either plain or fish-scale) or clapboard, and freely project and recess. Windows come in various sizes and shapes, often with small sections of leaded or colored glass. Brick chimneys are prominent and sculptural in form.

Although the Queen Anne style was primarily used for residences, it found its way into some commercial structures. The style was more subdued in this building type, but it can be recognized in freely expressed wall surfaces and roof combinations. A commercial structure with a gable roof form typically indicates Queen Anne elements.

Queen Anne house.

A derivative of Queen Anne, often listed separately, is the shingle style. Its overall forms and detailing follow the Queen Anne pattern, with its primary distinction being the extensive use of wood shingles on the exterior walls. In some cases, shingles are found only on upper stories, but in the best examples shingles are used on virtually all exterior surfaces, upper and lower, large and small. It is almost always used for residences, and was most popular in New England coastal towns, where the salty air weathered the shingles to a natural gray.

Colonial Revival

From the 1890s to the 1920s, elements of the earlier colonial and Georgian styles were reinvented with modifications. Called Colonial Revival, it remained popular as one of the most common residential styles through the 1950s. Colonial Revival houses represented a rebirth of interest in the historic architecture found along the East Coast. A formal, distinguished style, it was favored by wealthy clients who desired the character of the old while enjoying the convenience of a modern facility.

Colonial Revival houses have one or two stories with a symmetrical front façade, double-hung windows, a classic Greek cornice, and a formal entrance door with a prominent pediment, sidelights, a transom, and classic columns or pilasters (attached columns). In more elaborate examples, the plans may include large porches and porticos. Also common were significant side porches or sun-rooms. White is the color of choice for wood-sided homes, although brick houses are also common.

The Colonial Revival style has remained popular for residential architecture because it combines historicism with modern conveniences. A more recent resurgence followed the American bicentennial year of 1976.

Colonial Revival residence.

Spanish Colonial Revival (Mission)

The Spanish Colonial style remained a dominant architectural influence for centuries in the southwestern United States. Based on the heritage of the Spanish colonists, the style fit well with planning dictates put forward in King Philip's 1573 Law of the Indies, which required that buildings in the colonies be uniform in design for the sake of the beauty of the town. Because the Spanish Colonial style was most often found in Spanish mission outposts, it is also called, in its more inclusive nomenclature, Mission style. It lasted from 1600 to the mid-nineteenth century. A revival from the 1890s to World War II incorporated more architectural diversity and included residences, institutional buildings, and railroad stations. The style became the popular contemporary Spanish Colonial Revival starting in 1915, based on the success of the opening of the Panama Canal and new interest in Central America. That surge of popularity extended through the 1930s, and it is still found today throughout the Southwest, although typically constructed with more modern materials. It remains localized,

Country Club Plaza, Kansas City, Missouri.

extending from Texas to California, but also including Florida. Many excellent examples of the style are found in historic Santa Fe, New Mexico.

The style used building materials indigenous to the regions, most often incorporating Indian adobe in thick, windowless walls for coolness in the desert climates, with timber-supported low-slope roofs using clay tile or flat roofs. Spanish Colonial is known for its exuberant baroque curves applied to plain stucco walls and surfaces. Iron trim is often used for decorative features.

Tudor

Primarily used for homes and residential club buildings, Tudor style comes from sixteenth-century England. Its proportions and detailing are medieval in character, with steeply sloped roofs, massive chimneys, and tall, narrow windows with small panes and sometimes intricate muntin patterns. Its most prominent feature is half-timbering with stucco infill, a detail that essentially defines the revival style. The steep gabled roof typical of the style usually has a cross-gable that accentuates

Tudor house.

the front façade and helps define the front entrance, often a heavy wooden door recessed in an arched opening.

The Tudor style was especially popular from the turn of the nineteenth century through the 1930s. Even today it remains a common style for larger houses built as manors, and is used regularly in upscale residential developments and college fraternity and sorority houses.

Late Gothic Revival and the Chicago Tribune Competition

After the 1893 Chicago Exposition closed, with its abundance of classical white architecture, architects in this country became even more interested in finding an American idiom. The styles reinforced by the exposition had served the nineteenth century but did not meet the needs of the twentieth century. High-rise, steel-framed structures had no historical precedent, and it was unclear what form or style they should adopt. Many architects of the period were uncomfortable with the new construction mode, which minimized the need for decorative exterior walls, and they searched for a form appropriate to this design challenge.

Tribune Tower, Chicago.

Attempts to adapt earlier styles to the new skyscraper form led to incongruous solutions and culminated in the most publicized solution of all: the Chicago Tribune Tower of the early 1920s. The Tribune Tower design competition was significant because it was an open call to architects to present their best ideas for a prestigious new high-rise building. With entries submitted by the world's most prominent architects, the competition brought to the fore all the current thinking on high-rise design. Some submissions were whimsical; others were precursors of the modern style. However, the winning design was solidly in the historical revival style, a Gothic Revival scheme that clearly represented the traditional corporate tastes of the day. To many, the selection was a major disappointment and represented American unreadiness to take off the cloak of architectural historicism. The nation was unsure of the future and compensated by clinging too firmly to the past.

TWENTIETH-CENTURY STYLES

As America entered the twentieth century, a division remained between advocates of the romantic styles and the classical styles. Each felt that their favored architecture represented the true spirit of the nation. In a way, American architects were frustrated because many styles had been embraced and were still in evidence, but it was unclear which style was most representative of American culture. This problem was pondered by traditionalist architect Bertram Goodhue in 1916 as he considered whether there should be a new approach to architectural design for the new century. In an article he wrote for *The Craftsman*, Goodhue observed:

> I think you may expect me to say "Throw away traditions," but that I cannot do. I feel that we must hold tradition closely, it is our great background; as a matter of fact, good technique is born of tradition. We cannot start each generation at the beginning in our mastery of workmanship. The big universal progress in art moves on the wings of tradition. The nervousness about tradition in America springs from the fact that we have used it too much in place of imagination, in place of solid practical thought. Tradition has made us a little lazy about our own needs and our own inspirations. I feel that we should use tradition, and not be used by it.[3]

Even with this embrace of traditionalism, architects of the period realized that the search was still on, for there was no one style America called its own. Every other great civilization had a style to represent it—why not this country?

The Chicago School of Architecture

By the early 1900s, the need for an architecture to satisfy the new functional needs of twentieth-century building types was more and more apparent. Traditional styles were still found acceptable for churches and residences, but businessmen, with their new skyscrapers, factories, and offices, sought a way to represent the entrepreneurial spirit of the times. This led to a new style based not on historical

Reliance Building, Chicago.

precedents but on the utilitarian needs of tall, urban commercial buildings. The style was fully developed in the Loop area of downtown Chicago and eventually became known as the Chicago School of Architecture. Many of the best examples are still found there. In 1890, the Reliance Building, considered to be the world's first high-rise structure, was built in downtown Chicago. It provided an innovative and beautiful solution to this early functional design problem. Other prominent examples include the Carson, Pirie, Scott and Company building, the Marshall Field Wholesale building, and the Gage Building.

Chicago School buildings exploited new technologies and were possible because of two important developments: the advent of steel framing for tall structures and the invention of the first safe elevator by Elisha Otis. Other technologies also made high-rise construction possible, including improvements in foundation construction, wind bracing, fireproofing, and plumbing.

Primary ornamentation of these new Chicago-style buildings was based on the repetition of windows across multistoried, rectangular façades. The most distinctive window unit, known as the Chicago window, completely filled the void between steel columns with glass and was typically made up of a large fixed-glass picture window in the center with double-hung windows for ventilation on either side.

Louis Sullivan, Frank Lloyd Wright, and the Prairie Style

Throughout his career, Chicago architect Louis Sullivan considered the question of functionalist design for a new age. He was an early architectural innovator, and his Transportation Building was the only nonclassical building built on the main concourse of the 1893 Chicago Columbian Exposition. Sullivan's credo was "form follows function." This notion of having a building's design spring from its function, rather than applying a decorative style to its surface, was an entirely new way of looking at design. Architects of this school no longer perceived the function of a building and the style applied to it as separate decisions, but acted on the assumption that the form of a building should be a direct expression of its function.

Sullivan gave first expression to the new skyscraper form by offering an innovative design approach for the high-rise building type. He looked at high-rise buildings as having three parts: base, middle, and cap. Both the base and the cap of a building were similar to those in traditional building styles, but the number of middle floors was seen as flexible. These floors could be arranged to express the typology's verticality, and any number of floors could be added to the middle without destroying the overall form. But Sullivan did not eschew decorative treatment. He simply redefined it in his own distinctive design vocabulary and created unique ornament to accent functional aspects. An early example of this approach is seen in Sullivan's Wainwright Building in St. Louis.

Many architectural historians consider Sullivan the first Modern architect. He was also the leading architect in a group that became known as the Prairie style, representing the architecture of the Midwest. Sullivan's greatest pupil was Frank Lloyd Wright, who was to become America's most influential architect. Wright's genius was his ability to make the new principles of architectural design distinctly

Wainwright Building, St. Louis, Missouri.

his own. He developed a design vocabulary with horizontal open floor plans representing the prairie, uniquely American in derivation and Midwestern in its influence. His style was not derived from any historical precedent but was formulated according to his own criteria, which represented perfectly the new freedom found in the American lifestyle.

Features of the Prairie style, as developed by Wright and others, typically include long bands of horizontal windows, recessed protected entrances, integral planters, and long, low chimneys at the intersection of the roof planes and usually defining the location of the family hearth. Stucco or red brick was used for exteriors; often Norman brick was chosen because its natural tones and longer, horizontal form better represented the essence of the style.

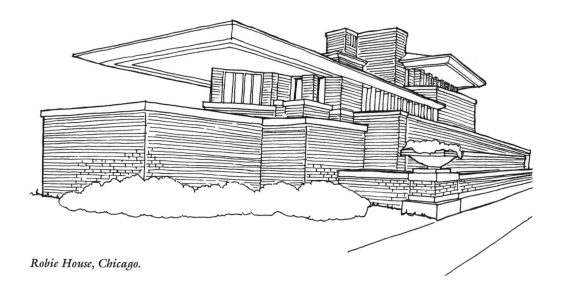

Robie House, Chicago.

The Robie House of 1906 in Chicago is one of the best examples of Wright's early work. Wide overhanging eaves and a strongly horizontal emphasis accentuated by low-sloped hip roofs are meant to represent protective yet expansive forms. The rooms are not constructed as traditional box forms; instead, walls are broken into planes, allowing rooms to become continuous spaces, flowing one into another naturally, with indoor spaces flowing as well into the outdoors.

Craftsman

The Arts and Crafts movement originated in England under William Morris, a designer of great note and innovation. The Craftsman approach to design was a reaction against both the excesses of the Victorian period and the plainness inherent in the designs of the Industrial Revolution. Its proponents tried to reestablish the importance of the individual workman by emphasizing the value of the hand-made over the mass produced.

Craftsman-style houses drew inspiration from historical precedents, but their detailing incorporated a distinctive contemporary flair. Although the informal exterior arrangement was similar to earlier styles, such as the Queen Anne, the interiors were noted for the craftsmanship of their wood detailing, including stairs, window and door trim, and room dividers, as well as the use of decorative leaded-glass windows. Other earthy materials, such as warm-tone tiles and stone,

Interior of Greene and Greene's Gamble House, Pasadena, California.

were used for a natural effect. American architects Charles and Henry Greene were the most prominent of the style's proponents; they combined their Craftsman-style houses with Arts and Crafts décor including the sturdy wood furniture of Gustav Stickley. The style remained popular from the turn of the century through the 1930s, and its original houses remain popular among contemporary families who appreciate their craftsmanship.

Bungalow

The word *bungalow* derives from the Hindi *bangla*, which denotes a style from India favored by the colonial British for its broad overhangs and open porches, desirable in a warm climate. The style was adapted to U.S. needs and was popular throughout the country from the turn of the century to the 1930s. Many older

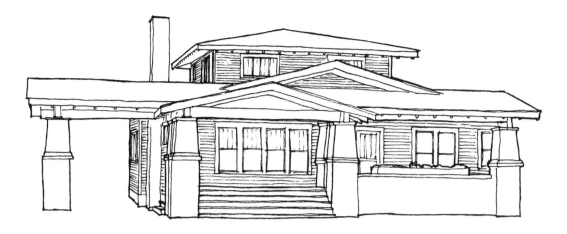

Bungalow house.

urban neighborhoods can easily be dated by the preponderance of this residential style.

The bungalow style is meant to give the appearance of a small, one-story cottage even when used for larger houses. A definitive feature is a broad front porch, usually supported by substantial square or tapered columns resting on the porch rail. Typically, a front-sloping roof continues from the main house and sweeps over the porch in a continuous line. The bungalow-style house often has dormer windows in the center of the roof, facing front, with the result that a two-story house often looks like a low, one-story structure. Much of its detailing uses design ideas from the Arts and Crafts movement.

Catalog Houses

Although not a style, catalog, or precut, houses were an important and popular product from about 1900 to 1940. Houses were manufactured and shipped in their entirety from the factory or mill to a buyer's lot. All lumber pieces were sized, numbered, and cut accurately to length at the factory, and doors, windows, hardware, decorative treatments, paint, and other building components were delivered as a package on a train or truck, ready to be assembled on site. Many of these catalog homes could be classified within the realm of vernacular types in that they were so ubiquitous that they became the most common residential architectural expression of many cities, towns, rural areas, and neighborhoods.

Catalog houses also included hundreds of designs in various popular architectural styles. They were indistinguishable from custom-built houses except for the manufacturer's trademark (Sears, Aladdin, Montgomery Ward, and numerous others) stamped on rafters and joists. Precut homes conferred the advantages of quick construction and low cost. Detailed instructions came with each kit, making it possible for owners to do much of the assembly themselves.

Until World War II, catalog houses were an important and large segment of the U.S. housing heritage. Enormous numbers of precut houses still stand. According to Robert Schweitzer, who has researched catalog houses, the seven major national kit house companies operating from 1900 to 1940 shipped about half a million kit homes, and there are several hundred thousand still standing. (Chevy Chase, Maryland, and Dearborn, Michigan, boast large numbers, and each year owners host historic-home tours featuring their catalog houses.) Aside from an ever-increasing nostalgic interest and a growing respect for their historic value in the development of early twentieth-century communities, they offer a level of quality in construction methods and materials that would be hard to duplicate. Many now are listed on the National Register of Historic Places and sometimes command prices that would stun their early owners.[4]

Art Deco/Moderne

Art Deco is sometimes seen as the representative style of the 1930s. It was popular in such varied contexts as Hollywood fantasy sets, theaters, and fair and exposition buildings, but was rarely used for residential architecture. The name is taken from an exposition held in Paris in 1925, Exposition des Arts Décoratifs et Industriels Modernes, to showcase innovative industrial design.

The chief characteristic of Art Deco is its stylized decoration, which represents a conscious rejection of historical precedents found in most earlier styles and instead is based on geometric and naturalistic forms. Its use of new and different materials, including aluminum, stainless steel, lacquered surfaces, and inlaid wood, made for a unique architectural palette. In its attempt to be of the "modern" age, the forms and detailing of its decoration express a machine-age aesthetic. Its forms include sweeping curves, stepped (zigzag) patterns, and a popular sunburst pattern. The Berkeley Shore Hotel in Miami Beach, Florida, includes many of these interpreted decorative elements, and is a popular icon of South Beach for photographers.

Berkeley Shore Hotel, Miami Beach.

Moderne (often considered a derivative of Art Deco) was an architectural expression of the streamlined design aesthetic that became popular in the 1930s and 1940s and remained so well into the 1950s. Based on the principle of airflow

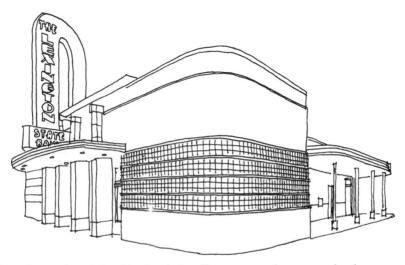

Moderne bus station, Columbia, South Carolina, converted to use as a bank.

design used in aeronautic technology (during this period, tail fins were added to automobiles), the Moderne style was horizontal, as opposed to Art Deco's more vertical treatments, and used streamlining to look up-to-date. Instead of decorative treatment, it relied on horizontal banding of windows, canopies, and other features to represent motion. The Moderne style incorporated high-technology materials, especially aluminum, glass and other smooth, hard-surface finishes.

International (Modern)

In the 1920s a revolution was born in architecture. Louis Sullivan first expressed the principle that function should be the basis for design, not historical precedents. What became known as the International style, and later the Modern style, took this principle as a philosophical base and posited that superfluous decoration should be completely eliminated. Whereas architects of the previous two decades had experimented with many new and eclectic approaches—including Art Deco and Prairie style—the International movement established severe restraints that grew into an almost dogmatic approach to design. The style was based on three fundamental concepts:

1. Function, the prime motivation of design, is the only valid element to express.
2. New construction technologies should be utilized.
3. Completely free of historical references, modern architecture should express no period other than its own.

To Modernists, the new style was both a product of its times and an immutable expression of truth. It was first identified in *The International Style*, a book written by Henry-Russell Hitchcock and Philip Johnson about the Interna-

Barcelona Pavilion, Barcelona, Spain.

tional Exhibition of Modern Architecture, held in New York City in 1932.[5] The authors were inspired by the work of many contemporary European architects, including Le Corbusier, Walter Gropius, and Ludwig Mies van der Rohe. More a crusade than a preference, the International/Modern style so completely dominated American architecture for thirty years that it seemed an important milestone had finally been reached. The centuries-long search for a truly American style was over!

Ironically, the project that perhaps had more influence than any other in establishing the language of the Modern style was the German Pavilion at the 1929 World's Fair in Barcelona, Spain (commonly known as the Barcelona Pavilion), designed by German architect Mies van der Rohe. With vertical marble slabs defining wall planes, light steel columns, and glass walls, it completely broke the mold of building as box. Using Frank Lloyd Wright's more organic schemes as a starting point, Mies's design used severe, crisp forms and new materials in a completely original way.

The style became prominent after World War II and was used extensively for institutional and corporate "image" buildings. Mies later practiced in Chicago,

Lake Shore Drive Apartments, Chicago.

where at the Armour (later Illinois) Institute of Technology he was an influential professor of architecture for many years. Among his most notable and influential projects was the Lake Shore Drive Apartments (1948–51), designed as a pair of towers that conveyed a simplicity and straightforwardness expressive of the Modern style in its purest form.

Typical elements of the Modern style are flat roofs with little or no overhang and flat, smooth cornices. Smooth wall surfaces appear engineered with one material and little relief, and windows are typically flush so that they appear to be a continuation of the exterior walls, rather than an opening in them. Large expanses of wall are broken only by projecting and penetrating planes, such as balconies and entrances. The absence of decoration is inherent in the style; the Modern style used materials in their purest form. Architects chose glass not only for windows but also for entire façades; the glass curtain wall became a common high-rise form. Steel, no longer covered and ignored, was displayed freely and openly as a major design element. The goal was not only to express a universal style but to invent a universal building type that could be adapted for virtually all uses. This architectural tradition arose out of industrial design and structural engineering.

Some in the architectural profession feared the trend, feeling it would eliminate the need for architects as purveyors of design. In any case, the American

Architectural Office, Seattle (1956).

search for a national architectural style seemed to be over. Modern architecture represented the newness, innovation, strength, and universality from which both Americans and Europeans drew inspiration. Residential design remained very traditional in comparison, but Modern expressed America's best and broadest goals.

Postmodern

The International/Modern style is still used prominently for many large buildings, but it is no longer sufficient to satisfy every architectural design urge. In response to the need for a change from the limitations of the Modernist aesthetic, and lack

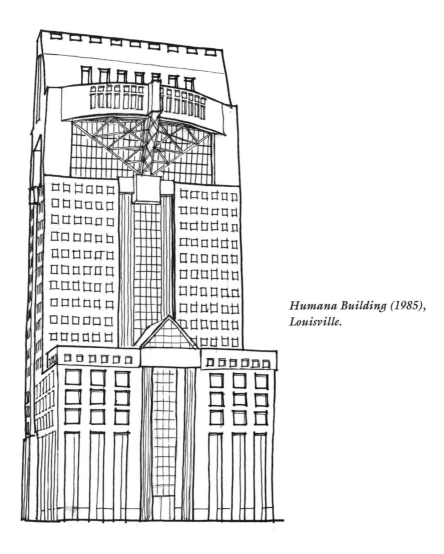

Humana Building (1985), Louisville.

of design flexibility, Postmodernism took form. First more a movement than a style, its philosophy was more important than its design palette. With faint beginnings in the 1960s—expressed more often in architectural treatises than in actual buildings—its popularity, which peaked in the 1970s and early 1980s, continues to this day. One of its most recognizable examples is the Humana Building in Louisville, Kentucky.

Postmodern design returned to the use of historical references, and many architects looked once again at traditional design elements for inspiration. The Postmodern period can be seen as a necessary catharsis that liberated designers from the severe strictures of Modernist dogma. Architects were relieved to again have the freedom to explore alternatives. Robert Venturi expressed the Postmodern manifesto in his book, *Complexity and Contradiction in Architecture*.

> Architects can no longer afford to be intimidated by the puritanical moral language of orthodox Modern architecture. I like elements which are hybrid rather than "pure," compromising rather than "clean," distorted rather than "straightforward." . . .
>
> I am for richness of meaning rather than clarity of meaning; for the implicit function as well as the explicit function.[6]

Postmodern architects do not advocate wholesale duplication of earlier historical styles, but rather a selection of elements from earlier periods, reinterpreted in a decorative, sometimes whimsical, fashion. Various styles may collide as they

House at Half Creek, Water Mill, New York.

meet each other on a single building. Elements such as column capitals and broken pediments were enlarged to such a degree as to provide a completely different relationship of scale. Architect Philip Johnson's AT&T (now Sony) Building in New York,[7] for example, features a Chippendale broken pediment as the enormous cap on a high-rise building. Architect Robert A. M. Stern took a Postmodern design approach with a residence in Water Mill, New York, with its Dutch gambrel roof form, heavily columned loggia, and retro-style tower.

The CAD Revolution (or "New Techtonic")

A revolutionary type of architectural design has grown from expanded and experimental use of computer software and computer-aided-design (CAD).[8] Exemplified by the work of architect Frank Gehry, a leading proponent of this design approach, CAD allows designers to develop construction drawings for buildings that were unbuildable previously because their sculptural free-form design could not be drawn using traditional drafting methods. However, computer software now allows structural engineers to design and specify components with no regular order or dimensions to their form. As evidenced in Gehry's renowned

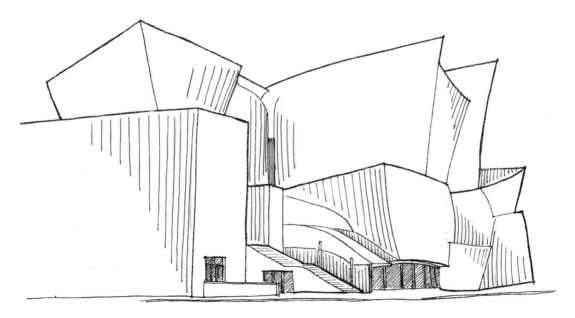

Walt Disney Concert Hall, Los Angeles.

Guggenheim Museum in Bilbao, Spain, and Walt Disney Concert Hall in Los Angeles, architectural design has reached a level to which it could only aspire previously. However, complications and delays have been an inherent part of the design and construction of these sculptural forms. For example, design for the Disney Concert Hall began in 1987 and it took sixteen years for the project to reach completion, opening in 2003 at a total cost of $274 million.

This free-form type of expression may not yet have a name as an architectural style, but because of its dependence on CAD technology, as well as its enormous price tag, it could be referred to as CADillac style. Perhaps a more appropriate name would be "New Techtonic," based on its reliance on new architectonic technologies. Whether or not it has a generally recognized name, such architecture represents a significant and exciting new direction in building design.

The history of American architecture is the tale of a search for an architectural style to truly represent our evolving American culture. Beginning with the most basic colonial structures and extending through the Georgian and Federal periods, builders first borrowed from familiar English styles. The search for a style then took architects and builders to other countries and other periods for their inspiration: Greek, Gothic, Romanesque, Italianate, and French, and even back to England for the popular Queen Anne style.

Only in the twentieth century did architects develop forms unique to U.S. culture. Louis Sullivan and Frank Lloyd Wright originated a new aesthetic of the American prairie. Contemporary art forms inspired the Art Deco and Moderne styles in the 1920s and 1930s.

But the search ended, at least temporarily, with the evolution of a style derived from the machine age—the Modern (or International) style, whose roots lie in the turn-of-the-century Chicago School. Although many important examples of Modern architecture came from European architects in the 1920s and 1930s, it was the dominant style in the United States for most of the twentieth century. Only recently has Modern architecture been joined by other styles, still being defined.

Presented in this chapter are only some of the architectural styles documented and categorized by American architectural historians. Many of the early revival styles had later revival periods as well, when the styles metamorphosed into newer forms. Likewise, the Modern period is represented as a single style; this brief discussion does not reflect its many variations, including Brutalism, Expressionist Modern, Deconstructionism, and others. The serious student may refer to more complete style texts, such as those listed in Further Reading, to better appreciate how the search for an American style followed many paths paralleling those represented here.

Contextualism

From the 1930s through the 1960s, Modernist-trained architects generally ignored older buildings and their styles and tried to design in the new mode. Respect for historical elements was not looked upon favorably, which led to the covering or defacement of many elegant nineteenth-century façades. Architectural critic Brent Brolin noted:

> The modernist architectural code of ethics maintained that history was irrelevant, that our age was unique and therefore our architecture must be cut off from the past. Just a few short decades ago modernists argued that everyone in the world, their tastes freed by the Movement, would soon want to live in the same kind of houses, in the same kind of modern cities, all of which would reflect the spirit of our times. (While the "times" were always "ours," the decision as to which forms characterized them was always "theirs," the architectural elite.) Because of this overwhelming belief, several generations of architects have felt little need to accommodate their work to the older, theoretically obsolete architecture around it.[9]

More recently, the stylistic straitjacket of Modernism has loosened. As architects gained increased awareness of, and appreciation for, historic preservation, they also saw the need to design new buildings that were compatible with historic buildings. This design approach, called *Contextualism*, yields contemporary architecture that is sensitive to, and compatible with, its surroundings.

The Context of *Time*

The element of *time* is important to historic preservation. More and more, we recognize that our past is integral to our future. Peter Eisenman, architect and theorist, gives a graphic example to consider. Imagine, he suggests, a picture of an arrow:

Eisenman's arrow.

An object (the arrow) is represented in this picture. Whether the arrow is static or in flight cannot be perceived. And yet the object is entirely different depending on its context. An arrow at rest is simply an object, but an arrow in motion is part of a much richer story, for it has both a shooter and a target. How can we understand the arrow without understanding where it began and where it is going? Its current position, as portrayed in the drawing, is but a small part of that story, and much of the meaning is lost without knowing the larger context.

Similarly, a building does not represent just its current state; it is part of a longer time continuum. Buildings as they exist today, whether new or old, are links between what came before and what will come in the future. Contextual design represents this approach of bringing historic and contemporary buildings together compatibly.

Architects should recognize that a design they create today will continue to resonate over time. Planning theorist Kevin Lynch once asked the question, "What time is this place?," suggesting that time is as important as place. Contemporary architects have often lost sight of this fact, designing buildings that make no reference to what has come before and ignoring what should come in the future as part of a community's overall context. They choose the latest style from a current professional journal and make their design statement. Unfortunately, often that statement is, "Forget the rest; my building is unique." The preservation perspective makes us realize that "the rest" *does* matter, and it encourages architects to see their "statement" as fitting in, over time, with its architectural neighbors.

An older district in an American city is often seen only in terms of its current condition. It may be viewed as a collection of neglected structures and businesses with little to offer. However, this perspective overlooks much that has value. To fully appreciate an older historic district, we must consider its current status within the context of time and look both at its past and its future. As we recognize its richness by looking back in time, we are able to better understand its potential as we look forward. Perhaps William Faulkner stated it most succinctly when he said, "The past isn't dead. It isn't even past."[10]

The Context of *Place*

As the preservation movement has made architects and designers more conscious of the element of time, it has encouraged them to consider the context of *place* as well. Virtually all buildings have neighbors and are part of a collection of structures and spaces that form, in some way, a community or cultural landscape. Preservationists should view old and new structures as part of the same ensemble. All play a role within the spatial context. Whether or not they work well together depends on how well they relate.

Architects and historic preservationists should ensure that such critical perspectives as *time* and *place* are not ignored. It is critical to carefully consider, as a society, both where we have been and where we are going.

Contextual design emphasizes compatibility. This approach asks architects to respect the scale, height, setback, materials, and detailing of surrounding older buildings. This does not mean that new designs need to look old; in most cases, this would be inappropriate. Rather, it means that contemporary design should blend with the old so that new and old are distinguishable but compatible. This sense of continuity and basic sensitivity to the old has been referred to as an "architectural genetic code,"[11] a code of craftsmanship worked out over generations of trial and error. Though often controversial, a new, compatible design can offer a contemporary look and vibrancy to a vintage historic structure without compromising the architectural character of either.

The contextual design approach reminds architects, planners, and developers to look at what surrounds the site of a new building. A design device to aid in this approach can be something as simple as drawing a site plan that includes all surrounding buildings. For example, to get a better feel for contextualism, an architect could try placing a new structure *not* in the center of the site plan drawing, but in one corner of the sheet, giving more prominence to adjacent existing, and perhaps more significant, structures. This simple exercise can reveal new design possibilities.

Clements Library, The University of Michigan, Ann Arbor.

MATCHING, COMPATIBLE, OR CONTRASTING?

When designing an addition to a historic building or a new building in a historic district, an architect or designer should carefully consider the question of contextualism. How closely should the new design "fit in" with the old? Generally, one of three design approaches can be taken: matching, compatible, or contrasting.

The historic Renaissance Revival style William L. Clements Library at the University of Michigan in Ann Arbor presents an interesting case study. Studies completed by architecture students in their classroom design studio compared these three design approaches, illustrating various possibilities for contextual design.

Matching

In the matching approach, new architecture imitates the old. The new addition, shown on the right of the sketch opposite, top, is meant to fit in as a coherent piece of the original historic fabric. Additions are designed in the same style as original buildings, using similar materials and detailing, at least on the public exterior. Some critics question this approach, saying the new is not clearly differentiated

Sketch of matching approach from student design project, side view.

from the old, and may fool an observer into thinking a recent construction is older, part of the original historic structure. Although this criticism is valid, and is counter to design standards established by the Secretary of the Interior, there are instances where such an approach may be considered both acceptable and appropriate.

Compatible

Compatible design, the most common of the three approaches, suggests that new design be sensitive to historic structures and compatible with them in terms of "size, scale, color, material, and character of the property, neighborhood or environment." [12] For example, the elaborately detailed windows of a historic building can be suggested in simpler form in a new addition, or a new cornice can be similar in height and proportion, but designed with a simple horizontal line, rather than the more elaborate dentils found on the original.

The compatible approach sketch below defers to the original building through a simplification of its design details. Windows are much simpler, lacking the limestone surrounds and smaller glass panes. The cornice does not rise as high as the original building, and the original arched windows are represented with contemporary windows.

Sketch of compatible approach from student design project, side view.

Contrasting

Contrasting design follows the logic that the new and old should be distinct because each is a product of its own era. Often, the contrasting approach uses simple, modernist surfaces and materials to serve as a counterfoil to the elaborate detailing of historic structures. The buildings may be designed either as background structures, with little identity of their own, or may aggressively compete with their historic context. In the latter case, the architect may be unconcerned about context because he or she feels the new building will one day be a historic structures itself, seen as a product of its own time.

In the sketch below, the student decided to expose all four elevations of the original building, including the upper floors of the rear, as shown. By stepping the entrance down to the basement level, the maximum amount of original wall is exposed. The contrasting triangular additions on either side of the rear entrance reflect the pattern of diagonal walkways found throughout the campus leading to the rear of the building.

Designers who use the contrasting approach may perceive that most historic districts consist of a variety of architectural styles from many periods. As a result, they see no need to stay closely tied with the existing design context and instead feel they enrich the district through architectural diversity.

Achieving good new design in a historic district cannot be obtained simply by establishing an ordinance addressing design in historic areas. Good design must come from architects, designers, and preservationists who understand the dynamics of contextualism and are sensitive to the relationship of new to old.

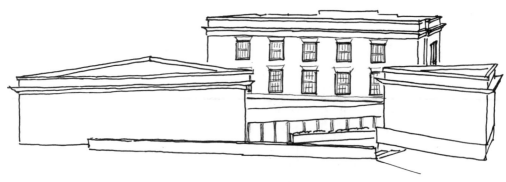

Sketch of contrasting approach from student design project, rear view.

Church Court condominiums, Boston.

CASE STUDY: CHURCH COURT CONDOMINIUMS

An interesting and complex architectural project using a contextual design approach is the Church Court condominiums in Boston. Architect Graham Gund purchased the shell of a burned-out church building, of which only the corner tower and two exterior walls remained. Rather than demolish the structure, he incorporated it into the design of a new condominium complex. The stone walls of the old church serve as entrances to an interior court. The new building, where the condominium units are located, picks up design suggestions from the old church, but old and new elements are distinguishable. The project thus makes reference to the 1892 church and recognizes its former significance to the community, but adapts the site and the remaining structure to a new use.

CASE STUDY: A TOWNHOUSE IN GREENWICH VILLAGE

A good way to understand contextual design is by example. The first sketch shows townhouses that are part of a block of similar townhouses located in the Greenwich Village neighborhood of New York City. The gap in the middle of the

Greenwich Village townhouses.

sketch represents a space created when, in 1971, a revolutionary group, the Weathermen, built bombs in a rowhouse and accidentally detonated dynamite stored in the basement.

The empty site was purchased by new owners, who asked the architectural firm of Hardy Holzman Pfeiffer to design a new townhouse as infill. The architects faced a critical decision with how to approach this project. Their site was the only gap in a block-long progression of historic townhouses, all similar in design. Should they take a matching approach and restore the original character of the historic block? Should they represent the new contemporary owners by designing a contrasting façade? Or should they try to blend the two and develop a compatible but contemporary façade with the scale and detail of the original? There is no truly right or wrong approach, but the issues can be better understood by considering the problem as one of contextual design.

The architects' solution was to design an infill structure that satisfied diverse criteria. The upper (third) floor was designed to match the adjacent townhouses, with a similar brick front and identical windows. However, the windows on the lower two floors were more contemporary, with the façade turned at an angle to

Greenwich Village townhouses with infill design.

the street. This angle, the architects explained, expressed the historic significance of the place by symbolizing the explosion of the previous structure. This attempt to use both compatible and contrasting elements of architectural design to express a significant historical event was criticized by some as inappropriate and others as truly innovative. However, it illustrates the latitude that can be brought to the question of contextual design.

THE NEED FOR DESIGN GUIDELINES

Any discussion of contextual design must acknowledge the subjectivity of the issue. What one person deems appropriate may be frowned upon by another. This variability can lead to problems when proposals for new construction in historic districts are reviewed. It is unfair for property owners to be governed too subjectively, so procedures must be instituted to rationalize this process as much as possible, both through the adoption of design guidelines and with the establishment of design review boards and commissions.

To address the public's need for design guidance, the National Park Service, acting on behalf of the Secretary of the Interior, publishes standards and guidelines dealing with several forms of building renovations intended for historic places. Known as "The Secretary of the Interior's Standards for the Treatment of Historic Properties," this useful document addresses the preservation, restoration, rehabilitation, and reconstruction of historic structures.[13] The most frequently utilized section of these guidelines, "The Secretary of the Interior's Standards for Rehabilitation," covers in detail both the rehabilitation of historic buildings and new design in historic districts.

This document presents ten clear standards that now are commonly accepted practice for preservation design. Supplemental to these standards is an extensive set of principles that provides more specific guidance on exterior surfaces, roofs, windows, interiors—even sites and districts. These standards and guidelines, revised a number of times since their first publication in 1979, are adopted by historic district commissions to assist in determining whether or not to approve petitions for proposed changes to historic structures. The standards and guidelines are nationally accepted and represent the best thinking on appropriate methods of intervention.

The ten standards for rehabilitation, as stated in the original document and clarified in the 1995 revisions, are as follows, with commentary (italics added):

1. "A property shall be used for its *historic purpose* or be placed in a new use that requires minimal change to the defining characteristics of the building and its site and environment."

   Commentary. As an example, consider a historic church, no longer needed by its congregation, that has been sold. What is compatible with its historic use? Appropriate uses might include a community center or religious bookstore. Less appropriate uses include conversion to a boutique clothing store, bar, or gym.

2. "The *historic character* of a property shall be retained and preserved. The removal of historic materials or alteration of features and spaces that characterize a property shall be avoided."

   Commentary. As part of a building's historic designation, the significant historic characteristics should be clearly identified. These historic features, whether arched windows, steeply sloped roofs, or terra-cotta details, should be kept even if the structure is modified for a new use.

3. "Each property shall be recognized as a *physical record of its time, place, and use.* Changes that create a false sense of historical development, such as adding conjectural features or architectural elements from other buildings, shall not be undertaken."

   Commentary. Additions and alterations should not try to look original. To maintain the integrity of the original elements, the new should be clearly differentiated from the historic. (Refer to the previous discussion of Contextualism.)

4. "Most properties *change over time*; those changes that have acquired historic significance in their own right shall be retained and preserved."

   Commentary. As an example, a black Carrara glass front that was put on an 1880s Italianate commercial building when it was converted to a jewelry store in the 1930s has been in place long enough to have developed historic significance of its own; hence, the building façade may be most appropriately restored to its 1930s period, leaving the glass in place.

Carrara glass front on Italianate commercial building.

5. "Distinctive features, finishes, and construction techniques or examples of craftsmanship that *characterize a property* shall be preserved."

   Commentary. Perhaps a designated building has a magnificently crafted staircase in its foyer. Although the stair opening may not satisfy current fire safety codes for egress, and other stairs will need to be built, plans should retain the staircase as an elegant example of the building's original craftsmanship.

6. "Deteriorated historic features shall be *repaired rather than replaced.* Where the severity of deterioration requires replacement of a distinctive feature, the new feature shall match the old in design, color, texture, and other visual qualities and, where possible, materials. Replacement of missing features shall be substantiated by documentary, physical, or pictorial evidence."

   Commentary. This standard often applies to wood windows. It is commonly assumed that old windows should be replaced with new, thermally efficient insulated units made of modern materials, such as vinyl. However, this standard urges owners to repair their original windows if possible and, if the windows are beyond repair, to replace them with similar painted wood sash to retain as much as possible the original appearance and proportion of muntins, whether using single or insulated panes.

7. "Chemical or physical treatments, such as sandblasting, that cause damage to historic materials shall not be used. The surface cleaning of structures, if appropriate, shall be undertaken using the *gentlest means possible.*"

   Commentary. This guideline directly responds to early attempts to restore painted brick buildings by sandblasting their exteriors. The integrity of soft bricks can be destroyed when sandblasting removes the bricks' outer crust, resulting in exposure of the soft core.

8. "Significant *archeological resources* affected by a project shall be protected and preserved. If such resources must be disturbed, mitigation measures shall be undertaken."

   Commentary. Preservationists tend to limit their involvement to existing structures, but it is essential to recognize the importance of preserving archeological artifacts as well, and to engage archeologists when necessary.

9. "New additions, exterior alterations, or related new construction shall not destroy historic materials that characterize the property. The *new work shall be differentiated from the old and shall be compatible* with the massing, size, scale, and architectural features to protect the historic integrity of the property and its environment."

Commentary. Contemporary design in a historic district can be perfectly appropriate as long as the new is designed based on a recognition of the old and is compatible with it. There is a danger in insisting on nostalgic design. As humorist Garrison Keillor observed, "The past was copied, quoted, and constantly looked at until one day, the country looked more like it used to than it ever had before."[14]

10. "New additions and adjacent or related new construction shall be undertaken in such a manner that if removed in the future, the essential form and integrity of the historic property and its environment would be unimpaired."

Commentary. New construction, often designed for an economic lifespan of thirty to forty years, rarely lasts as long as original historic architecture. Therefore, new construction adjacent to historic carries with it the assumption that if it is eventually removed, the integrity of the historic would still be preserved. This is often evaluated as the potential "reversibility" of the new construction.

DESIGN REVIEW

One of the most controversial aspects of administering historic districts is design review. There are as many as 3,000 communities in the United States that have historic districts, and at least 75 percent of those have some level of design review based on a local ordinance and administered by a design review board, historic district commission (HDC), zoning board of appeals, or similarly empowered entity. As described in Chapter 6, a good ordinance includes sections describing the basis on which approval or disapproval for proposed changes is given. Supplemental guidelines may include provisions regarding the change of a roof slope, the location or type of window, or the enclosure of open front porches. When these are clearly and unambiguously described in the ordinance, few questions arise, but when they are not, confusion, suspicion, and resentment can occur, sometimes pitting neighbor against neighbor and, if a continuing problem, even resulting in the de-commissioning of the design review body.

An issue that often arises is whether historic district commissioners, who are commonly political appointees, are the most capable group to conduct design review. Some communities assign the responsibility either to a trained professional who contracts with the city for design services or to a separate design review board whose members have design backgrounds. These boards operate with mixed success.

In Portland, Oregon, for example, design review is conducted by the Portland Design Commission and the Portland Historic Landmarks Commission. Both boards include members with expertise in design and development. These review commissions give designers flexibility in their design approaches, while ensuring the compatibility of new development with the desired character of the area. The foundational set of design guidelines is the Central City Fundamental Design Guidelines. In historic districts this source is supplemented with more local guidelines that take precedence if there is a conflict. Residents generally feel that the review boards in Portland work well. Virtually every downtown project is subject to review, and the review procedure serves as a public forum for discussion of a project's merits. Developers seem to favor this format because they are exposed to public reaction in a controlled, organized environment rather than in the unpredictable arenas of politics and the media.

Boulder, Colorado, is a city that accepts regulation as good for the community. It has a history of growth control ordinances and has passed laws that preserve solar access, control smoke from wood fires, and promote energy conservation. In recent years, Boulder's downtown community has been increasingly concerned about growing competition from suburban shopping malls. In an attempt to ensure a pleasing environment, the city created an ordinance establishing design guidelines for the downtown. A citizens board was set up to review all proposed downtown projects. The Design Review Committee is made up of two members of the Landmarks Preservation Advisory Board and one Historic Preservation staff person. They meet weekly to review requests for alterations. If a project requires new construction or demolition, it automatically goes to the full membership of the Landmarks Preservation Advisory Board. (There is a separate Design Advisory Board for projects in nonhistoric areas.) If a project requires a site plan review, it is forwarded to the Planning Department and, in some instances, City Council for final approval.

Such a review procedure tends to eliminate the worst projects. Unfortunately, it also can discourage innovative solutions. With such tight review, designers may seek a common denominator and submit designs that are mediocre in an attempt to guarantee approval. In Portland, a design guideline may be waived if it is determined that the proposed design better meets the goals of design review than would a project that had complied with the guideline. This leeway reflects the city's concern that the design review guidelines not become a rigid set of requirements that stifle innovation. When the design review board is well respected, and its determinations are shown to be in the public interest, this approach is a useful protection against inappropriate design.

TEARDOWNS

When land values increase well beyond the assessed value of the buildings that occupy a site, the temptation for many developers and owners is simply to tear down existing structures and rebuild to maximize the economic value of the land. This approach ignores the factors of time and place and typically results in a much larger, super-sized structure. In the case of residential architecture, these are sometimes referred to as "McMansions" (in an obvious reference to the famous fast-food restaurant's generic *super-sized* meals). This trend was first recognized in coastal and resort communities that changed from seasonal habitation to year-round residential use.

The popularity of tearing down structures has spread throughout the nation and has had devastating effects on hundreds of communities where land values have soared, far outstripping the inherent value of the vintage, often historic, structures on the property. There are even Web sites dedicated to helping owners and developers identify sites with teardown potential. The issue is so pervasive that the National Trust for Historic Preservation and many statewide preservation organizations are responding by educating their constituents and local leaders about the issue. The Trust published a booklet, "Protecting America's Historic Neighborhoods: Taming the Teardown Trend," to help communities deal with this important issue.

FAÇADISM

Façadism involves preserving the historic façade of a building while demolishing or severely altering the remainder of the structure. This approach has been used in commercial historic districts subject to pressures for development and represents a compromise between retaining a historic streetscape and allowing more density with new construction. Façadism is viewed by some preservationists as a reasonable compromise because at least some of the original historic elements

Façade of Carnegie Library, Ann Arbor, Michigan.

that face the street are retained. Others see it as an abomination that makes a mockery of history and historic architecture, or at least, reduces a historic building to a single-plane work of street art.

Much of the success of the technique depends on the design sensitivity of the architect or designer. Although sometimes done well as a form of preservation, façadism (also humorously referred to as *façadectomy* or *façadomy*) often results in preserving façades that bear little resemblance to their former historic context. As noted by preservation educator Michael Tomlan, "The overheated real estate

Red Lion Row, Washington, D.C.

market and preservationists' willingness to embrace the business community has led to a tendency to 'switch rather than fight.' The most obvious result is façadism—the deliberate demolition of all but one or more elevations of an old building."[15]

In few cities has the façadism controversy been more heated than in Washington, D.C. A longstanding height limitation for buildings led to intense development within those height parameters. To satisfy the city's historic ordinances, developers have been willing to leave intact three- or four-story façades of older buildings if they are permitted to build to the maximum height limit of ten stories directly behind the façade. They argue, often successfully, that the historic streetscape is not significantly altered with this increased density.

Some preservationists feel that preserving the observer's impression of the historic streetscape is sufficient, even if new construction is inserted behind older façades. Other preservationists view façadism as sacrilege and argue that entire buildings should be preserved to teach future generations about the periods, construction methods, and historical contexts in which they were produced.

Chapter Four

THE LEGAL BASIS

FOR PRESERVATION

⬗

The legal framework for historic preservation is largely based on land use law, with the traditional premise that property owners should have the right to do as they wish with their property. Generally, this right could be infringed upon only if the property's use was a nuisance to the community. In addition, the Fifth Amendment to the U.S. Constitution establishes the principle that private property would not be "taken" for public use without just compensation. The Fourteenth Amendment entitles every citizen to "due process" and "equal protection"; a citizen can expect to be notified of action impacting his or her property and has the right to a public hearing prior to any action affecting that property. The Fourteenth Amendment also ensures that government actions affecting private property must be "reasonable" and "fair" and must advance a legitimate public purpose.

Zoning laws established in the early twentieth century had little impact on preservation. In a landmark Supreme Court decision in 1926, *Euclid v. Ambler Realty Company*, the court determined that zoning was appropriate and in the public interest as a means to reduce nuisances, and as such, overrides the interests of individual property owners, thereby setting the stage for later zoning and preservation legislation.

Although government is expected to protect citizens against negative changes, it is not expected to ensure positive outcomes. Thus, in terms of preservation, the government had no authority to guarantee that neighborhoods would be beautiful, or to regulate property for aesthetic purposes (in this case, historic character), and property owners had no legal obligation to contribute to the public good in the use of their property.

BERMAN V. PARKER

Historic structures, if protected at all, were protected only if regulations involved more than aesthetics. This "aesthetics plus" principle meant that regulation had to be justified by a reason beyond aesthetics or historic character—for instance, public health, safety, or welfare.

The important *Berman v. Parker*[1] case, decided by the U.S. Supreme Court in 1954, changed this premise. The court determined that the District of Columbia could remove a building labeled "blighted" in appearance, pursuant to its negative aesthetic impact on an overall redevelopment plan to address blight. This case established the principle that aesthetics alone (the appearance of a structure) is sufficient to justify government regulation. As Justice William Douglas wrote as part of the decision, "It is within the power of the legislature to determine that the community should be beautiful as well as healthy, spacious as well as clean."[2]

Preservationists realized that this precedent also could be used to justify ordinances protecting historic buildings. If a city could regulate *against* "ugly" buildings based on aesthetics, it could also regulate *for* "beautiful" buildings. The *Berman v. Parker* case provided an initial legal basis for historic preservation regulations. However, the validity of such historic designation is based on the fact that, like zoning, such designation must be developed within a broader effort of community planning, based on an inventory of historic resources. Historic inventories take time, perhaps many years, and they are part of a larger historic survey conducted by local communities that is continually underway.

FIGARSKY V. HISTORIC DISTRICT COMMISSION

In 1976, Connecticut's highest court dealt with a historic district's "vague aesthetic legislation." In *Figarsky v. Historic District Commission,*[3] the owner of a vintage structure facing the historic green in Norwich, Connecticut, was cited by the city's building inspector for unsafe conditions. The building was part of the historic district, but because it had little individual significance, was in an altered condition, and the owner had no good use for the vacant structure any longer, he requested a permit to demolish it. The commission denied the request, stating that the structure was important because it blocked a view from the green of an encroaching commercial area and thus was key to preserving the character of the district. The "precedent" for this action had been established earlier in *Maher v. City of New Orleans*,[4] where the court found that a building in a historic district did not need to have individual significance to merit protection, because just as important is the preservation and protection of the setting and scene in which structures of architectural and historical significance are situated.[5]

In the Figarsky case, the building owner felt that the preservation of the general character of a district was not sufficient reason for the commission to deny a demolition permit and so appealed the commission's ruling, saying it had used "vague aesthetic legislation" and acted illegally, arbitrarily, and in abuse of its discretion. He wanted compensation to cover the cost of making sufficient repairs to satisfy the building inspector. However, the Connecticut Supreme Court ruled that the city's disallowing of the demolition of a structure needing substantial repairs was neither confiscatory nor an abuse of the commission's power, and it upheld the commission's denial of a demolition permit.

THE PENN CENTRAL DECISION

Historic preservation's most important legal precedent is the landmark 1978 U.S. Supreme Court decision regarding *Penn Central Transportation Company v. City of New York*,[6] commonly referred to as the Penn Central decision. The importance of this decision to historic preservation cannot be overstated, as it forms the legal justification for most historic preservation ordinances. The Penn Central case addressed the issue of the right of an owner to develop a property versus the right of a city to review and regulate the development of a designated historic property. The case essentially became the first U.S. Supreme Court decision dealing directly with historic preservation law.

Penn Central Transportation Company, the owner of Grand Central Terminal in New York, had applied to the New York City Landmarks Preservation Commission for permission to construct a fifty-five-story addition over the Grand

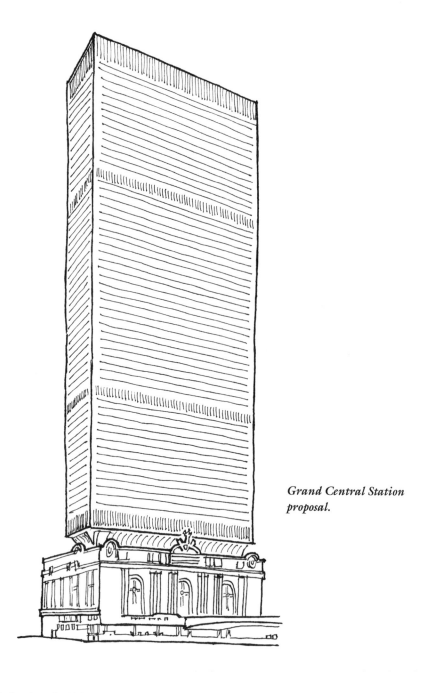

Grand Central Station proposal.

Central Station building, which was designated as a local landmark. The proposed addition was designed by Marcel Breuer, a well-known and influential architect of the time. The design included a new structure cantilevering above the terminal's existing façade.

When the Landmarks Preservation Commission denied approval for the proposed tower, based on the terminal's historic designation, Penn Central claimed a taking, arguing it should get compensation for the loss of rights to use its property as desired (see later in this chapter). The company sought to have the designation overturned, and asked the city for compensation for not being able to develop its property. Many saw the proposal as a desecration of this landmark building, which was important to the life of New York City. The case became a *cause célèbre*, with many notables, including Jacqueline Kennedy Onassis and architect Philip Johnson, marching in the streets to "save Grand Central."

A primary question this case presented was whether the city's new landmark law discriminated against a property owner who owned a historic structure designated as an individual landmark. Whereas zoning ordinances apply generally across all properties, and the burden of such regulation is more or less evenly shared, landmark legislation applies to a minority of property owners who must bear the burden of community good for all others. As made evident in this case, the passing of the Landmarks Preservation Law "imposed a substantial cost on less than one one-tenth of one percent of the buildings in New York for the general benefit of all its people."[7]

The New York Court of Appeals earlier had ruled that there was no taking because the preservation ordinance did not transfer control of the property to the city, but only restricted the appellant's exploitation of it. The appeals court held that the owners had not been denied their rights because:

> (1) the same use of the Terminal was permitted as before; (2) the appellants had not shown that they could not earn a reasonable return on their investment in the Terminal itself; (3) even if the Terminal proper could never operate at a reasonable profit, some of the income from Penn Central's extensive real estate holdings in the area must realistically be imputed to the Terminal; and (4) the development rights above the Terminal, which were made transferable to numerous sites in the vicinity, provided significant compensation for loss of rights above the Terminal itself.[8]

The case went on to the U.S. Supreme Court, where, in a six-to-three decision, the validity of New York's preservation law was upheld as it applied to the Penn Central case. Justice William Brennan described the significance of the case at the beginning of his opinion:

The question presented is whether a city may, as part of a comprehensive pro-gram to preserve historic landmarks and historic districts, place restrictions on the development of individual historic landmarks—in addition to those imposed by applicable zoning ordinances—without effecting a "taking" requiring the payment of "just compensation." Specifically, we must decide whether the application of New York City's Landmarks Preservation Law to the parcel of land occupied by Grand Central Terminal has "taken" its owners' property in violation of the Fifth and Fourteenth Amendments.[9]

In Justice Brennan's notes on the case, he cited the fact that government could not function adequately if it did not have the power to regulate the use of private property or if it had to pay for any reduction in land value or loss of poten-tial value based on changes in the general law. There are numerous examples of this power, including zoning laws restricting the use of property, and even the assessing of property taxes.[10]

This landmark (there is no better word to describe it) decision upheld the legitimacy of historic preservation review ordinances by recognizing that preserv-ing historic resources is a permissible governmental goal and that the city's preservation ordinance was an appropriate means for accomplishing that goal. As such, the Penn Central decision formed the legal basis for legislatures to grant cities the right to establish controls to which the owners of historic properties would be subject. (It is interesting to note that during the 1990s, Grand Central Terminal underwent a successful major restoration, recognized by residents and commuters as a return to its former glory, that has reestablished it as a major commercial and transportation hub and a vital New York City landmark.)

With the Penn Central decision, the Supreme Court did indeed uphold the legitimacy of historic preservation ordinances, but many questions were left unanswered. Primary among these was just how far a public agency could go in limiting the rights of private owners to develop their property. The commission's denial of Penn Central's proposal was upheld because, in the court's opinion, the company had failed to show that it was unable to get a "reasonable return" from its property. What the court did not indicate was how much regulation would be considered too much. If an owner were able to prove that he or she was unable to make a "reasonable return" (left to other courts and other cases to decide), a tak-ing could be claimed, in which case the public agency would need to compensate the owner for the lost use of the property.

*St. Bartholomew's Church,
New York City.*

THE ST. BARTHOLOMEW'S CASE

The constitutional question of whether or not churches and religious buildings should be exempt from historic ordinances is an important one.[11] This issue was addressed most directly and publicly in the case of *St. Bartholomew's v. New York City Landmarks Preservation Commission* (1990).[12]

St. Bartholomew's is a prominent Episcopal church located in the center of one of New York City's prime commercial districts. Built in 1919, the church was designed by Bertram Goodhue, one of the most important architects of the period, and it is an excellent example of late ecclesiastical Gothic architecture.

"St. Bartholomew's Church in New York City is many things to many people. To the passerby, it is a rare breathing space, an interval of gardens and terraces on Park Avenue between Fiftieth and Fifty-first Streets. To the aesthete, it is a beautiful edifice of soft brick and stone. To the religious, it is an oasis of faith in a spiritual wasteland, a monument to God in the land of mammon. And to the homeless, it is a haven where can be found a meal, clean clothes, a night's shelter."[13]

The New York City Landmarks Preservation Commission, recognizing the building's architectural significance as well as the potential threat posed by skyrocketing property values and high-rise development on adjacent sites, designated St. Bartholomew's a historic landmark in 1967. The rector and vestry had opposed the designation.

By the early 1980s, the church had developed plans to replace its adjacent community house with a speculative high-rise office tower. The congregation felt that the substantial income from the investment would both support maintenance costs for the aging structure and finance the church's community outreach and missionary programs. The estimated earnings of the proposed building were as high as $100 million. Following a series of public hearings, the Preservation Commission turned down the plans on the ground that the scale of the fifty-nine-story reflective glass tower was incompatible with the church. According to one commissioner, the project looked like "nothing so much as a noble work of man about to be crushed beneath a gargantuan ice cube tray."[14]

The church fought back. "People think we're vandals," said the church's senior warden. "But preservation of the church is very important to us. If we don't have more money we won't be able to preserve the very building that the preservationists are concerned about: the church sanctuary." To forbid construction would be to take the property out of the church's control and put it "in the hands of a secular agency."[15]

The parishioners were badly split on the issue. Some church members felt that the commission had gone back on its promise to allow changes after designation. As one church member said, "We feel we were lied to at the time of the designation. We relied on a statement made then that would have allowed us to develop our property."[16] A commissioner responded that the 1967 agreement with the church permitted alterations to the property but did not permit the development of a skyscraper. "A one- or two-story addition is one thing, but a forty-seven-story office tower is different. We didn't say nothing could be done, we said this proposal was inappropriate." Other parishioners were opposed to the development and formed the Committee to Oppose the Sale of St. Bartholomew's Church. They charged that "this case is not about religion, but rather it is about a church's efforts, in partnership with a commercial real estate developer, to destroy its landmark property and to develop its site to the highest commercial value."[17]

The battle persisted for more than a decade. The Landmarks Preservation Commission denied the church's plans three times—the original proposal for a fifty-nine-story glass tower, a second for a forty-nine-story tower, and a third application based on economic hardship. The case went to the Federal District Court and then the U.S. Court of Appeals, where two questions were decided:

1. Did the church's historic designation violate the Constitution's free exercise of religions provision?
2. Did the denial represent a taking, and should the church therefore be compensated by the city for not being able to build the office tower?

The church's attorneys first argued the case on a series of general principles. They contended that the designation was against the First Amendment and interfered with the church's ability to raise money for its service programs, thus limiting free exercise of religious beliefs and activities. The court responded that as long as a rational basis for a law of general applicability exists (historic designation and review) and the church was not "impermissibly burden[ed]" in carrying out its religious activities, overruling the designation as illegal or unconstitutional was ungrounded.

Next, the church argued that previous cases had established that historic designation should not take away an owner's ability to make a "reasonable return" on its property. If designation took away the possibility of a reasonable return, then a taking could be claimed. The court, however, said that commercial and charitable entities were not alike. The church was a charitable organization, and the reasonable return provision did not apply because designation did not interfere with carrying out the church's religious purposes.

The church next argued that it had been denied due process in the initial decision on designation. The court responded that the requirements of due process had been met, because (1) prior notice was given of the designation, and (2) there had been a public hearing. The owner's approval was not necessary; the only requirement was that the owner be notified and given a chance to comment. The court thus rejected all three arguments of general principle and, therefore, the church's claims.

The church also argued specific points as applied in this case. The records showed that at the hardship hearing before the commission, the church argued that it would be unable to fulfill its mission of community service and to maintain the main sanctuary without additional income. According to New York law, if it expected to satisfy the hardship provision, the church would have to prove:

- That the landmark designation interfered with its charitable purpose.
- That the cost of renovating the building to suit that purpose would be too great for the church to bear.
- That the church could not afford to maintain the buildings in its present financial condition.[18]

In a hearing before the Landmarks Preservation Commission, the church presented testimony that it did not have the resources to meet its needs. The court noted that the church had a stock portfolio more than sufficient to carry out the proposed renovations, and could increase its income by selling its air rights.

The St. Bartholomew's case is important because of the legal precedent it clarified. It established that religious organizations are subject to historic preservation ordinances of local government, and that such regulations are not a violation of the First Amendment separation of church and state.

FRANK LLOYD WRIGHT'S UNITY TEMPLE, OAK PARK, ILLINOIS

The designation of religious properties is often more controversial than that of any other type of property. Though courts have upheld the right of municipalities to make such designations, churches can be among the most vocal and active opponents of historic designation.

Unity Temple in Oak Park, Illinois, an important early Frank Lloyd Wright project, is another situation entirely. The Unity Temple congregation supported designation and made the landmark structure one of the first religious properties in the country to be voluntarily designated. An agreement guaranteed strict protection for both the exterior façade of the church and the public areas of its interior.

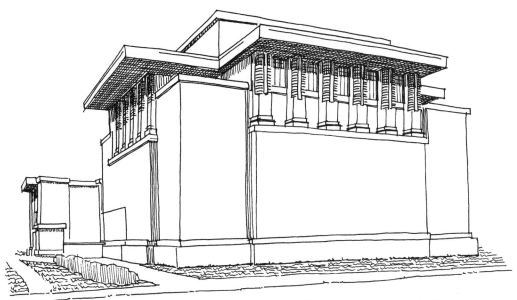

Unity Temple, Oak Park, Illinois.

The designation is significant for a number of reasons. First, the owners voluntarily solicited the designation because they recognized the historic and architectural importance of the structure and wanted to see it protected in perpetuity. Second, the designation included interior spaces; these usually are not designated because it is felt the infringement is too great. Third, protection was secured through an easement (see Chapter 8). As part of this agreement, the Landmarks Preservation Council of Illinois annually inspects the structure to ensure that changes are not made without approval. The building must always be used as a church or similar entity to ensure that the interior spaces will remain as is. In return, the congregation's ability to solicit donations for the church's restoration work is increased, and the easement agreement assures donors that their money goes directly to the building fund rather than the church's general budget.

POWERS INHERENT IN HISTORIC DISTRICTS

The regulatory powers associated with historic districts can be quite considerable. Historic district commissioners are given power of approval over exterior modifications, proposed additions, demolition of designated historic structures, and changes within a historic district. Some commissions also are granted the authority to review and approve proposals for new buildings in historic districts. To a significant degree, these decisions are based on aesthetic judgments by commissioners—something that is unusual in local government. This precedent was based on the U.S. Supreme Court decision in *Berman v. Parker* (1954), described above, which stated that aesthetics alone can be sufficient to justify certain specified government regulation. In contrast, other municipal agencies use more quantifiable criteria to evaluate a proposal. For example, the planning department reviews setbacks, heights, and uses; the building department examines construction specifications and building code compliance; and the transportation department evaluates traffic data. Each of these reviews is based on established objective criteria. Historic district commission reviews, by comparison, use more subjective criteria to evaluate the visual impact of proposed changes on historic character. Although based on subjective criteria at least partially, decisions of historic district commissions should not be seen as capricious. Most are guided by provisions established by the U.S. Secretary of the Interior in its *Standards for Rehabilitation* (see Chapter 3). These ten standards, as interpreted and clarified over the years, give well-considered guidance to commissioners and provide a firm basis for determinations. In many communities these are supplemented by the adoption of locally specific design guidelines.

TAKINGS AND LOCAL HISTORIC DISTRICT COMMISSIONS

In recent years the issue of takings—that is, whether a property owner's financial interest has been "taken" (overridden) through a government decision—has been hotly debated. When courts are more conservative leaning, rulings favoring property owner's rights often are more prevalent, whereas more liberal-leaning courts tend to side in favor of the government's right to regulate the use of private property. This is a debate that has waxed and waned throughout the course of American history.

The takings issue remains a primary concern to many historic district commissioners who are challenged by property owners. What should commissioners do to protect themselves from such legal challenges? To avoid controversy about takings, a historic district commission should carefully describe the components of the property included in the designation. Is only the principal structure designated? Are ancillary buildings included? Is the entire site covered, or is the owner permitted to sell or develop sections of the property?

Sometimes permission for new construction to a historic property is granted if an owner makes the case for economic hardship. However, the hardship must be more drastic than difficulty paying taxes or managing operating costs. The inability of an owner to maximize the property's economic return is also not sufficient justification. The owner must prove that the property's existing use is economically unfeasible and that sale, rental, or rehabilitation of the property is not possible.

In some jurisdictions, when historic buildings are owned by nonprofit organizations, the situation is considered differently. As noted in the St. Bartholomew's discussion, religious organizations have long argued they should not be subject to the same requirements as other property owners. Obviously, their issue is not the economic question of reasonable return. Churches sometimes argue they serve a community and a religious purpose and need to retain the right to change their property and buildings to best address that need.

Governments can also apply the principle of eminent domain to purchase private property for public use, with fair compensation given to the owner. The government can take private land through eminent domain only for uses that benefit the citizenry. When this action occurs, affected landowners are often displeased because relocation is usually necessary. Such relocation is especially difficult on the elderly, people with low income and people who work nearby. Compensation is determined by an objective appraisal of the value of the property. Resentment is often prevalent, but the monetary award should be based on fairness nonetheless.

The most common use of the power of eminent domain is for construction of utilities, government buildings, or public transportation. Few would argue with a need for these projects. However, eminent domain has had more controversial uses. In *Kelo v. City of New London (Connecticut)*,[19] the U.S. Supreme Court decided that it was appropriate for government to extend its authority of eminent domain to take land from private owners and sell it to a private developer. The court determined that it would further the community's economic base by building a hotel and resort as part of the city's comprehensive redevelopment plan. The local government sold the land to private companies with the justification that the new development provided expanded economic opportunities within the community. The court found that, if a project creates new jobs, increases tax base and other city revenues, and revitalizes a depressed urban area, then it qualifies as a public use. This decision has been widely criticized, and in this case and others the government has been accused of abusing its authority to seize property. Later court cases have resulted in mixed messages. The uniqueness of these cases has not yet completely clarified the extent of government's right to take private property.

Approvals Through Litigation

A disturbing, and increasingly common, new trend is for developers to gain approvals from city agencies through preplanned litigation. Recognizing that a local government's approval process can be cumbersome, time consuming, and expensive, some developers are finding increased leverage by threatening lawsuits against commissioners who do not give quick approvals to their project proposals. Both planning commissioners and historic district commissioners are subject to this pressure. They may not be able to defend themselves individually against such suits and may find that their municipal government also cannot provide such protection. This situation can be complicated if city council members are in favor of a project, and historic district commissioners are opposed—a not uncommon scenario. Since the same city attorney likely advises both groups, there may be a conflict of interest in being involved and giving legal advice to either group.

It is important for commissions to have an approval system that is timely, fair, and transparent to both the development community and the public. Decisions that are made between attorneys behind closed doors often lead to very poor decisions for the community. Local leaders must better understand how to avoid this increasingly common problem of "approvals through litigation."

Chapter Five

DESIGNATION OF HISTORIC PROPERTIES

————•————

Perhaps nothing comes closer to the heart of a preservationist than researching an individual historic property and preparing its nomination for designation as a historic structure listed on the National Register of Historic Places. The process of determining a structure's historical and architectural significance forms the trunk of the tree from which all other limbs of preservation grow. There are many levels of designation—local, state, regional, and national—available for historic properties. A designation may result from a local historical society's "plaquing" program, a countywide survey of historic farmsteads, a statewide marker program, or a national-level effort. Documentation is also one of a preservationist's most interesting activities, for the research is like a mystery hunt: bits and pieces of information are put together like clues, leading to the answers needed to document a place's historic significance.

HISTORIC SIGNIFICANCE

The term generally used to describe a property's relative importance is *historic significance*. A structure's significance is based on two primary factors: historical or cultural importance and architectural value. Sometimes both historical and architectural aspects contribute, in which case the overall significance is enhanced.

Many factors may increase a historic property's significance; the more that apply, the greater the significance. An estimate of a property's potential significance should be based on the *National Register's Criteria for Evaluation*.[1] This document explains how the historic significance of a proposed property can be established based on any of four criteria:

1. *The property is associated with events that have made a significant contribution to the broad patterns of American history.* For instance, if a city was established along an important rail line, the original railway station or complex of freight buildings from those early years could be considered significant to that city's local history. As another example, Ford's Theater in Washington, D.C., where President Abraham Lincoln was shot, is a landmark representing a very important single event.

2. *The property is associated with the life of a significant person in the American past.* This is the "George-Washington-slept-here" category. Properties may relate directly to significant events in that person's life. Fort Necessity Battlefield, where George Washington fought his first battle, or Graceland, where Elvis Presley lived and worked for many years, are good examples. However, birthplaces and gravesites of important people often are not designated because they are not uniquely representative of the person's significant years.

3. *The property embodies distinctive features of a type, period, method of construction, or high artistic values, or represents a significant and distinguishable entity whose components may lack individual distinction.* This category deals with architectural significance. Usually, association with a well-known architect or builder is cause for increased significance. Thus, even if a property is not associated with an important event or person, it may represent a good example of an architectural style or type of construction from a certain period.

   Selectivity is important in considering properties in this category, for every building represents a period and an architectural style (even if a vernacular type). Therefore, selections should be based on how well the building represents its style. Does it retain most of its original features? Is the style relatively rare? Is it an excellent local example of a particular style or form? These are all questions that should be addressed. The TWA terminal at John F. Kennedy International airport in New York City is an excellent example of a structure whose primary significance is its architectural design. Designed by

TWA Terminal at John F. Kennedy International Airport, New York City.

Eero Saarinen in 1962, its distinctive wing-like form is one of the purest architectural expressions of flight ever designed.

4. *The property and its site yield, or are likely to yield, important information in history or prehistory.* Important evidence of earlier cultures and events can be uncovered through archeological exploration. If major construction is to occur around a historic structure or in any area where the existence of archeological material is likely, it may be necessary to bring in professional archeologists to ensure that such evidence will be properly handled, analyzed, and documented as associated historic resources before construction is permitted. Such evidence may be useful in tracing the evolution of, or in documenting, artifacts used in association with the property. The African Burial Ground in New York City is a sacred space that had been lost to history until 1991, when the planned construction of a federal office building led to its rediscovery. It is now designated as a National Monument. (There are many ethical issues relating to disturbing human and cultural archeological remains; see Native American Graves Protection and Repatriation Act in Chapter 7.)

INTEGRITY

One of the most essential filters through which a property must pass to determine its historic significance is that of integrity. How well does the property represent the period or theme for which it is being recognized? The importance of any historic property must be evaluated according to its integrity, whether historic or architectural. This is such an important condition that the National Register program has developed a list of seven elements to determine the level of integrity necessary for historic significance:

Location: The place where the historic property was constructed or the place where the historic event occurred.

Design: The combination of elements that create the form, plan, space, structure, and style of a property.

Setting: The physical environment of a historic property.

Materials: The physical elements that were combined or deposited during a particular period of time and in a particular pattern or configuration to form a historic property.

Workmanship: The physical evidence of the crafts of a particular culture or people during any given period in history or prehistory.

Feeling: A property's expression of the aesthetic or historic sense of a particular period of time.

Association: The direct link between an important historic event or person and a historic property.[2]

THE EVALUATION OF SIGNIFICANCE

Based on the criteria described above, a structure's overall level of significance can be illustrated through use of a hypothetical *significance thermometer*. The following example shows how such factors may affect the evaluation of historic significance.

If a vintage home is being considered for inclusion as a designated historic structure, the significance of each aspect of the property is assessed. Age is a positive indicator and raises the "reading" of a home on the significance thermometer. Good architectural style is another positive indicator. If a house has not been altered over time and is still largely in its original form, the house's significance level rises even more. In addition, the significance temperature may rise if the property clearly illustrates a unique settlement pattern of the town. The significance of a house that was once owned by an important family in the town's history is elevated even higher, perhaps over the top.

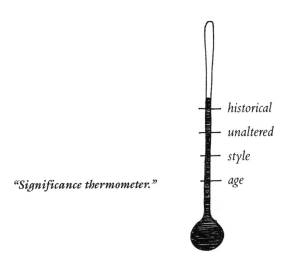

"Significance thermometer."

historical
unaltered
style
age

However, a modern concrete porch built on the front of the house would lower its architectural integrity and thus its level of significance to some degree. Moving a house to a new site would also decrease its integrity, because a property's level of significance is negatively affected by relocation. The degree of significance lost depends on such factors as the appropriateness of the new site, the distance moved, and the number of changes necessary as a result of the move (e.g., building a new foundation).

Thus, up and down goes the property's evaluation on the significance thermometer as each of these factors is considered. The process continues until all relevant information is evaluated. Each detail helps determine the burden of proof and the research needed to substantiate the designation. Each community should determine for itself what minimum level of significance is appropriate for designation. The significance thermometer is only a metaphor for an evaluation process, and numbers should not be assigned, because it is not a quantifiable evaluation. Local historians and preservationists can determine whether a property is significant enough to qualify for designation based on their knowledge and experience. In communities where residents support preservation, the list of designated properties is likely to be more inclusive than in communities where designation and regulation are opposed. If a community's significance threshold is low, many properties may have enough significance to be protected. If the community is more restrictive, only properties high on the significance thermometer are likely to be included.

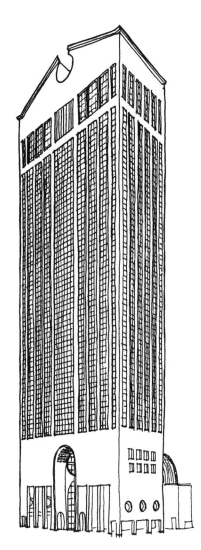

AT&T (Sony) Building,
New York City.

THE FIFTY-YEAR-OLD RULE

A commonly accepted, and government-supported, criterion for historic significance is that a building must be at least fifty years old. This rule is being reconsid-
ered, however, as many newer properties have already taken on historical
importance. The AT&T (now Sony) Building in New York City, designed by
Philip Johnson and his partner John Burgee in 1984, is topped by a prominent
Chippendale-style cap, a novel use of abstracted and amplified ornament.
Although the building was criticized upon its completion, it immediately became

Aerial photo of Getty Center site, Los Angeles. Courtesy of Warren Aerial.

an icon of the Postmodern style of architecture, and its place in architectural history was firmly established. The same could be said for some of Frank Gehry's recent sculptural architecture. Although these expensive labyrinthine structures could only be realized in recent decades using computer-assisted design (CAD) software, and are not yet thought of as "historic," they are architectural landmarks that clearly will increase in historic status over time.

The Getty Center and Museum in Los Angeles is another modern architecture classic that undoubtedly will stand the test of time. A tour de force designed by Modernist architect Richard Meier, these clean white buildings form a large complex that spills over a prominent hill in the Santa Monica Mountains. As Meier himself says of this work, "My wish is to create a kind of spatial lyricism

McDonald's restaurant, Downey, California.

within the canon of pure form. . . . I am expanding and elaborating on what I consider to be the formal base of the Modern Movement."[3] The experience of arrival is enhanced by computer-controlled trams that deliver visitors from street-level parking to the magnificent hillside complex. The $1.2 billion Getty Center opened in 1997. Although it is too recent to be designated as a historic landmark, it will be accepted as such in due time, and should be respected even now as "landmark eligible."

Other relatively new buildings that need to be documented and recognized as important products of their age include fast-disappearing examples of roadside commercial structures, such as diners, motels, and even early McDonald's restaurants such as the one built in 1953 in Downey, California, which now has been added to the National Register. These building types need to be identified and protected as important elements of our mid-twentieth-century lifestyle, with the best representatives deserving status of either national or state register properties.[4]

INTEREST IN THE "RECENT PAST"

Perhaps the growing interest in what the preservation community has dubbed the "recent past" movement comes at a propitious time, when historians will need to accommodate the existence of huge numbers of Modern-era, but aging, structures. Most notably, in the 1990s preservationists began to grapple with the "coming of age" of more recent places, like shopping malls, fast-food restaurants, and suburban developments. Based on largely post–World War II resources found in virtually every community in the nation, interest in the recent past has grown significantly in recent years.

Organizations such as DOCOMOMO (Documentation and Conservation of buildings, sites, and neighborhoods of the Modern Movement), an international effort begun in Europe in the 1990s, or The Recent Past Preservation Network, begun in 2000 in the United States, are examples of groups that are enjoying growing membership. It is interesting to consider the increasing number and variety of activities whose goal is to save resources of the recent past. Richard Neutra's unique Cyclorama Center (1961) at the Gettysburg National Military Park was erected as part of the commemoration of the centennial of the Civil War. The National Park Service has pressed for demolition of the structure, a decision that has led to an active campaign to reverse that decision. Perhaps the architect would be intrigued that his structure is the cause of such a debate, but its impending loss has spurred preservationists, historians, and some local business owners into action, and they are urging the National Park Service to reconsider the decision to demolish the structure.[5]

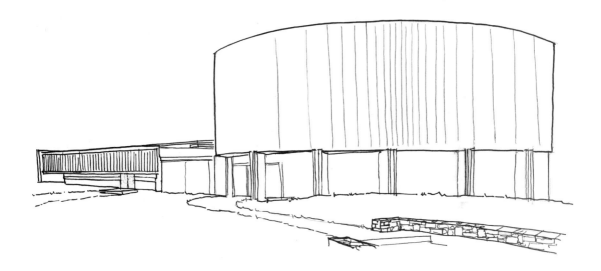

Cyclorama, Gettysburg National Military Park, Pennsylvania.

Interestingly, three of the recipients of the 2007 National Trust's annual National Preservation Awards included recent-past properties. They were architect Louis Kahn's 1953 Art Gallery at Yale University, Oklahoma City's famous Gold Dome Bank (1958), and the space-age-design Hilliard Homes (1966) in Chicago. Organizations such as the National Park Service, the Association for Preservation Technology International, and the National Trust for Historic Preservation have sponsored annual meetings addressing the recent past. In 2008, the World Monuments Fund sponsored its first World Monuments Fund/ Knoll Modernism Prize, to be awarded to a design professional or firm for an innovative design solution that preserved or enhanced a Modern-era landmark.

The national and international awareness of the importance of Modern architecture is strong. Part of this interest comes from the rapid disappearance of post–World War II structures, but it is also based on the recognition that as we enter the twenty-first century, there is a need to both respect and celebrate these more recent design idioms. With interest in sustainable design growing and the need to transform Modern-era buildings into energy efficient structures, this focus will continue.

THEMATIC/HISTORIC CONTEXT AND THE "THEMES AND CONCEPTS" FRAMEWORK

Thematic/historic context is a critical element in assessing historic significance. Determining historic themes associated with a property is necessary when evaluating local, regional, statewide, or national significance. *Historic context* refers to the cultural situation through which a property was created, including its subsequent evolution.

In-depth research is usually necessary to determine historic context. For example, it would be important to know about the evolution of a state and county's educational system when determining the level of significance of a one-room brick schoolhouse remaining in a particular township. This history helps the evaluator gauge the specific level of significance attributable to the building. Identifying the number and type of one-room schoolhouses remaining in a particular county, and ideally the entire state, also would be important. Other aspects of understanding the historic context of a schoolhouse may address the evolution of educational systems or of brick masonry in that region to determine if this one is the only example of its type. Similarly, a historic bridge may be significant because of its age, its integrity, or its structural technology. But it can have additional significance if it represents larger historic themes, such as the development of bridge technology, or a new access link along early settlement routes. All potentially designated historic buildings, structures, landscapes, and archeological sites should be seen in the context of their larger and more sweeping historical patterns.

Archeologists, historians, and geographers have traditionally used the "themes and concepts" process to determine the cultural significance of the subject of their research. The designation process becomes stronger when the specifics of an individual property or district are set within the context of larger trends. Recognizing this, the National Park Service encourages the evaluation of historic properties, districts, and National Historic Landmarks according to such a "thematic framework." First adopted in 1936, the framework was devised for internal use within the History Programs of the National Park Service. These history-based "themes and concepts" guidelines have been revised and expanded in scope numerous times, most recently in 1994, to better reflect the roles of ordinary people and everyday life in our national, state, and local histories. The thematic framework provides a view of cultural resources through three overall historical building blocks: people, time, and place. Within that overall structure, eight thematic categories have been derived, as shown in the diagram and descriptions that follow.

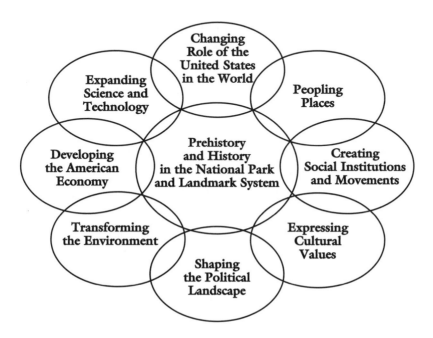

1. Peopling Places: This theme examines human population movement and change. It deals with demographic shifts in American society, including family structure, lifestyle, gender issues, migration, and ethnicity. Topics defining this theme include family and life cycles; health, nutrition, and disease; migration from outside and within; community and neighborhood; and encounters, conflicts, and colonization.

2. Creating Social Institutions and Movements: Social institutions, associations, and organizations, whether temporary or permanent, fill an important role in shaping our society. For example, an African Methodist Episcopal (AME) church may be an important cultural institution for a community's African American population. Topics in this area include clubs and organizations, reform movements, religious institutions, and recreational activities.

3. Expressing Cultural Values: Cultural expressions and their associated institutions comprise this category. The farm in North Carolina where noted American poet Robert Frost lived is an example of a site that has greater cultural value than the property itself. Topics include educational and intellectual currents; visual and performing arts; literature; mass media; architecture, landscape architecture, and urban design; and popular and traditional culture.

4. Shaping the Political Landscape: This theme includes federal, state, local, and tribal institutions that have been politically active and have shaped public policy. Sites associated with influential leaders, movements, campaigns, and grass-roots political activity are included. The Appomattox Court House National Park in Virginia, where General Robert E. Lee surrendered his men to Ulysses S. Grant to end the Civil War, is an example of such a site. Topics that help to define this theme include political parties, protests, and movements; governmental institutions; military institutions and activities; and political ideas, cultures, and theories.

5. Developing the American Economy: Economic development and growth are a major part of the history of the United States, reflected in the way Americans have worked and sustained themselves. Individual sites may represent important points in our economic history, such as mill towns or industrial centers, or workers, owners, and innovators, such as Henry Ford's Highland Park Plant where he established the first automobile assembly line in 1909. Topics considered under this theme include extraction and production, distribution and consumption, transportation and communication, workers and work culture, labor

organizations and protests, exchange and trade, governmental policies and practices, and economic theory.

6. Expanding Science and Technology: This category focuses on science and incorporates physical science, the social sciences, and medicine. The Edison National Historic Site in West Orange, New Jersey, is Edison's ultimate science laboratory and the home of many of this country's most important inventions. Topics under this theme include experimentation and invention, technological applications, scientific thought and theory, and effects on lifestyle and health.

7. Transforming the Environment: Our relationship to our environment is an important thread of our experience as a society, especially in recent decades, when the enormity of our impact has been recognized on a global scale. Our environment today is largely a human artifact, so thoroughly have our settlements affected it in many ways. Yosemite National Park in California, set aside as a protected area in 1890, is one the most dramatically beautiful and, with 4 million visitors a year, one of the most visited areas in the National Park system. Topics under the environment theme include manipulating the environment and its resources, adverse consequences and stresses on the environment, and protecting and preserving the environment.

8. Changing Role of the United States in the World Community: This theme explores diplomacy, trade, cultural exchange, security and defense, expansionism and, at times, imperialism. It looks at our society's relationships with native and indigenous populations, as well as with the international community. It also explores our diplomatic policies throughout history and the individuals involved with creating and administering them. It encompasses the colonial influences of Spanish, French, and British settlers. Topics under this theme category include international relations, commerce, expansionism and imperialism, and immigration and emigration policies.

These eight themes provide a systematic framework for looking at the larger patterns of this country's history, and as such, have true applicability for historic preservation. (A more in-depth explanation of the National Park Service's themes and concepts guidelines can be found at the National Park Service Web site: www.nps.gov/history/history/hisnps/NPSThinking/themes_concepts.htm.)

One role of historic preservation is to ensure that such critical perspectives as time and place are not ignored, and to insist that our society looks carefully both at where it has been and where it is going. In current preservation practice, contextualism also translates into what has become known as the "historic context statement." In preparing for and carrying out site investigations, archeologists have long known the significance of historic context—a concept now pervading most preservation-based research and analysis. Historic Context Statements now are required for many historic designations, including the National Register of Historic Places and National Historic Landmark nominations. They are a summary of the impact of building traditions, development eras, ethnicity, and similar influences on the look of places, both individually and as ensembles.

CRITERIA FOR EXCLUSION

As a counterpoint, it is good to remember that there also are guidelines for identifying properties not considered appropriate for designation. Most such exclusionary clauses are based on those established by the National Park Service for evaluating properties whose nomination to the National Register would fall within certain criteria. As noted, cemeteries and birthplaces are not considered appropriate for designation unless the property is the only remaining evidence from an important person's past. Such properties typically are not acceptable because they have nothing to do with the person's historical importance. A cemetery or birthplace may qualify based on other criteria, however. Similarly, the nomination of statues and commemorative structures is discouraged because they represent an event or person only indirectly.

Religious properties generally are not listed unless they have significant historical or architectural merit that distinguishes them in a special way ("religious status plus"). Many churches are included, however, on the basis of architectural merit or as part of a historic district.

Structures moved from their original sites are considered to have lost much of their integrity, and thus significance, and designations of such properties generally are discouraged. Reconstructed buildings generally are not included, except in rare cases where the work is based on authentic documents and is an integral part of a larger master plan. Buildings less than fifty years old are typically not considered for listing. However, because of the rapid turnover of contemporary buildings, there is increased interest in recognizing buildings representing the "recent past." (See the previous discussion in this chapter.)

NOMINATING PROPERTIES FOR HISTORIC DESIGNATION AND TO THE NATIONAL REGISTER OF HISTORIC PLACES

Many factors influence the research and documentation necessary before a property can be nominated for designation as a historic structure. At the local level, the standards may be different or less rigorous than those required for state or national designation. Most states have their own standards that require a statewide level of significance, and such nominations usually are handled by the State Historic Preservation Office.

Many preservationists aspire to completion of a nomination for listing in the National Register of Historic Places or designation as a National Historic Landmark. The application for National Register designation is submitted to the State Historic Preservation Office (SHPO) for review. Staff review and approval traditionally lead to review by a governor-appointed review board. While a property is being reviewed at this stage, local government officials and property owners are notified and have the opportunity to provide comments. If approved by the review board and signed by the SHPO, the application is then sent to the Secretary of the Interior in Washington, D.C., specifically to the Keeper of the National Register, where a period for review and comment follow. Once approved and signed by the Keeper, a property is considered officially listed in the National Register, and the property's listing is published in the Federal Register. Often the local U.S. Representative and U.S. Senators representing the property location are the first to know when the actual designation occurs. Properties can also be nominated by Tribal Historic Preservation Offices (THPOs) or Federal Preservation Offices (FPOs). Technically, anyone can nominate a property to the National Register, although the research and documentation requirements, as well as the thorough, time-consuming process, have deterred many individuals from pursuing a nomination. Most nominations are prepared by consultants, cultural resource management or architectural firms, or college and university historic preservation, history, architecture, or American Studies students. There are currently over 80,000 National Register listings that include individual buildings, districts, whole towns, cultural landscapes, sites, structures, and objects. The total number of individual properties represented by these listings is over 1.4 million.

The National Register nomination process is formally spelled out in several bulletins issued by the National Park Service, including these basic primers: "How to Apply the National Register Criteria for Evaluation," "How to Complete the

National Register Registration Form," "How to Complete the National Register Multiple Property Documentation Form," and "Researching a Historic Property." These and many other useful publications can be ordered or accessed online through the National Register's publication Web site www.nps.gov/nr/publications/bulletins.htm.

Designation on the National Register of Historic Places gives national recognition to a historic property, though the significance level also can be local or state as well. Because of concern that historic designation would give the federal government new powers over individual property owners, the designation provisions in the National Historic Preservation Act of 1966 did not allow for any direct regulatory power over private properties. National Register listing, although it does provide certain federal incentives (tax credits) and disincentives, does not inherently protect such properties from inappropriate alterations or even demolition. However, once a property has been listed, it generally cannot lose this designation, even if the owner requests it, unless the basis of its significance is proven to have been lost. The same is true of buildings that have been designated as contributing historic structures in a listed historic district. In fact, since the 1980 amendments to the act, such listings can be made only after the owner has been notified and provided the owner does not object. If an owner objects, a historically significant property could be listed as "National Register Eligible."

NATIONAL HISTORIC LANDMARKS

National Historic Landmarks (NHLs) are properties that have national historic significance. They represent a special category of designated historic structures and properties with exceptional value or quality. NHLs are recognized as places that emphasize a common bond between all Americans. For example, Elvis Presley's Graceland Mansion, which had been a designated historic site since 1991, was elevated to NHL status in 2006. Presley's home for twenty years, Graceland represents a twentieth-century cultural icon whose "extraordinary talents produced achievements that remain unparalleled in American and world history"[6] decades after his death. Graceland has been noted as one of the most recognizable residences in the country.

The nominations of NHLs typically are overseen by National Park Service staff, working with preparers across the country. The historic significance of a

Graceland, Memphis, Tennessee.

property is linked to larger theme studies that recently have included such topics as American aviation heritage, American civil rights, architecture (as illustrated by the *Adirondacks Camps* theme study that was completed in 2000), Japanese-Americans in World War II, and thematically related nominations for the War of 1812. This is only a sampling of some of the more current themes that have been studied.

Through this process, outstanding examples of properties meeting the criteria for thematic significance, integrity, historical significance, and national level of significance are identified and designated. The National Park System Advisory Board reviews all nominations, and designated properties are automatically listed in the National Register of Historic Places, if they are not there already. It is important to recognize that listing a private property as an NHL does not prohibit actions that may otherwise be taken by the property owner with respect to the property. As with the National Register, an NHL listing does not necessarily protect these properties from inappropriate alterations or even demolition. The general assumption is that public pressure would deter such adverse actions.

About 2,500 sites (approximately 3 percent of the properties in the National Register) are NHLs.[7] Examples include Mount Vernon, Pearl Harbor, Apollo Mission Control Center, the Martin Luther King, Jr. Birthplace, and the prison on

Alcatraz Island, San Francisco Bay. Courtesy of Philip Greenspun.

Alcatraz Island, just offshore from San Francisco. The National Park Service has published a bulletin, "How to Prepare National Historic Landmark Nominations," that describes in detail the procedures for developing an NHL nomination.

DEDESIGNATION

Sometimes it is necessary to remove historic designation from a listed property. "Dedesignation" may be requested for a variety of reasons. Perhaps a formerly historic structure has been so changed—through conscious alterations, catastrophic damage (weather or fire), or neglect—that designation is no longer appropriate. Though rare, the Secretary of the Interior may find it necessary to remove the designation of NHL or National Register properties and districts if they lose too much of their historic integrity. Four justifications exist for the withdrawal of National Historic Landmark designation: (1) the property has ceased to meet the criteria for designation because the qualities that caused it to be originally designated have been lost or destroyed, or such qualities were lost subsequent to nomination, but before designation; (2) additional information shows conclusively that the property does not possess sufficient significance to meet the NHL criteria; (3) professional error in the designation; or (4) prejudicial procedural error in the designation process.[8]

A properly drafted preservation law should provide a recision procedure. Some communities have established procedures for dedesignation. For example, Detroit's ordinance states that once a historic district is approved, properties can be removed from the district with a majority vote of the property owners within the district. What if an owner of a designated historic property consciously makes inappropriate changes or demolishes a structure without approval? What can be done? Often the penalty for such actions is so low (e.g., a $500 fine) as to be ineffective as a deterrent. However, the owner may be sued in court to have the property reconstructed, with a cloud on the property title until such work is completed. This consequence may not be satisfactory, however, as the damage already has been done. Commonly, a commission and its community react with resignation, saying, "Well, we lost this one, but let's make sure it doesn't happen again." In some cities, inappropriate alterations that were not approved are treated as building violations, and owners can be ticketed by the enforcing agency (e.g., the building department). The best way to avoid these problems is to institute an ongoing program of community surveillance and education. Neighborhood residents who are aware of ordinances should be able to recognize when work does not follow its provisions. It is also important, and in some cases required, to have historic district commissioners serve as monitors for projects under construction.

One of the most prominent examples of the dedesignation of an NHL was a decision made regarding Grant Park Stadium (Soldier Field) in Chicago. Designed by the famous Chicago architectural firm of Holabird and Roche and completed in 1924, Soldier Field remains one of the most significant public spaces in Chicago, with its twin classical Doric colonnades serving as prominent architectural landmarks. It has been the site of many major sporting events, including the famous Jack Dempsey–Gene Tunney boxing championship and many college all-star football games, and for decades it has hosted the Chicago Bears professional football team. In 2003, the field was thoroughly updated with the construction of modern seating that totally envelops the original interior

New Soldier Field stadium, Chicago. *Courtesy of Jonathan Daniel.*

stadium space and dwarfs its classical exterior. The National Historic Preservation Advisory Board made a determination that the scale and scope of these major changes to the stadium caused it to lose its integrity as an NHL. As stated by the Advisory Board in their determination, "During the process of new construction, many historic features and spaces were obliterated. With the exception of the colonnades, exterior walls, and a small seating area on the south end of the bowl, very little of the historic fabric remains."

As of 2007, only twenty-seven NHL properties had been dedesignated. Other examples include the Hotel Breakers at Cedar Point Amusement Park in Ohio, Roosevelt Dam in Arizona, and the *U.S.S. Cabot* in Texas.

The documentation and designation of historic properties are important aspects of historic preservation, for they represent the validation of a structure's historic significance and give it appropriate recognition. Individuals involved in such work find satisfaction in knowing that their contribution continues the process of saving our architectural and cultural heritage.

Chapter Six

HISTORIC DISTRICTS AND ORDINANCES

The first local historic district in the United States was established in Charleston, South Carolina, in 1931, although its establishment was encouraged decades earlier by Frederick Law Olmsted, the nineteenth-century park and landscape planner. To create the district, much work went into documenting a large number of old structures in Charleston. The district was finally approved in 1944 and included 572 historic buildings, although the number of buildings surveyed was much larger.

The second historic district in the United States was established in 1936 in the Vieux Carré section of New Orleans, the old French Quarter. The Vieux Carré district makes up the area included in the original city as laid out by the French in 1721. Over the years this district became a prime tourism destination. After the devastation of Hurricane Katrina, this section of the city, because of its historical significance and tourism draw, was one of the first to reopen and be reoccupied.

These early efforts to establish historic districts helped keep both areas intact. However, the regulatory powers available to agencies administering historic districts in those early years were limited. The value of maintaining the historic appearance of a district was acknowledged, but not legally enforceable. The fate of properties could not be controlled for aesthetic reasons alone but had to rely on the concept of *aesthetics plus*, the idea that there must be a reason beyond historic character (aesthetics) to justify regulatory control (e.g., building codes). It wasn't until the National Historic Preservation Act of 1966 was passed that local governments were given the power to create regulatory historic districts.

Lower Pontalba Building, Vieux Carré district, New Orleans.

Communities establish historic districts for a variety of reasons. Some create them simply as a way to protect significant historic properties. Some establish historic districts to protect against a specific threat of development, whereas others want to encourage development in an older area and look at historic tax incentives as a way to encourage appropriate changes. Some communities use historic districts to maintain property values, and others establish them because they contribute to an improved image of the community at large. These factors are examined in more detail in the following case studies.

REASONS TO ESTABLISH A HISTORIC DISTRICT

There are five reasons to establish a historic district: (1) as protection of historic properties, (2) to control new development, (3) as a redevelopment incentive, (4) to stabilize or increase property values, and (5) to foster public relations and promotion.

Protection of Historic Properties

SAVANNAH, GEORGIA

The primary function of most historic districts is to protect the historic structures within their boundaries. This protection is offered through review of proposed changes by a historic commission, an appointed group that determines whether such changes are appropriate and preserve historic character. The district may be small and include only a few structures, or it may be on a city scale, such as in Savannah, Georgia.

Savannah's original town plan was laid out by Gen. James E. Oglethorpe in 1733. Oglethorpe's very regular grid plan was based on a series of divisions into small neighborhood units, or wards, positioned around squares. This cell plan was quite unusual and remains the defining feature of Savannah's urban plan. Over 1,100 residential and public buildings contribute to the architectural

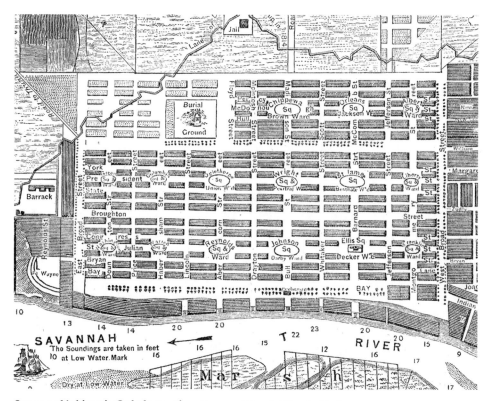

Savannah's historic Oglethorpe plan. Courtesy of Georgia Historical Society.

richness of this historic district, and the fact that the original character is still intact gives this National Historic Landmark district its significance. In 1973, the City of Savannah established the Historic District Board of Review to protect the area's character and architecture as well as its public squares or parks.

ALAMO PLAZA, SAN ANTONIO

Alamo Plaza in San Antonio is a commercial historic district built around the Alamo, the most historic site in Texas. Established as a designated historic district in 1977, the area has a long history. Native American remains confirm a settlement at the site two thousand years ago. Spanish colonists established the Misión San Antonio de Valero in 1724, which later became a military garrison to protect Spanish colonial land from the French. Texan forces used the fort during the famous thirteen-day siege of the Alamo against the Mexican army. Two decades later this area became an important trade terminus, and during and after the Civil War a number of prominent hotels, churches, and commercial buildings were built there. They form the core of the current Alamo Plaza Historic District, which provides protection against inappropriate development in San Antonio's historic downtown.

The Alamo, San Antonio, Texas.

Located just south of Columbus, Ohio, German Village was settled by German immigrants in the mid-nineteenth century. Due to anti-German sentiment during the two World Wars and Prohibition, which led to the closing of the many German breweries, the settlement went into serious decline. Concerned citizens recognized the threat of demolition throughout the community and in the 1960s lobbied to establish a local commission to review and regulate changes to the historic architecture. As a result of this early effort, the 233-acre largely residential district was listed on the National Register of Historic Places. The German Village Society now has more than 1,000 members interested in the preservation of this unique place.

Control of New Development

PIONEER SQUARE, SEATTLE

During its early days as a port for the lumber industry, the Pioneer Square area of Seattle was the city's historic downtown center. It included the original Skid Row, named for the inclined road down which logs were skidded to the waterside for transport to other parts of the United States. By the 1950s and 1960s, Seattle's center city had moved farther north, and the area was a rundown neighborhood full of pawnshops and hotels housing transients.

In 1963, in response to concern over its problems, the city supported a plan to revitalize this depressed area through the construction of new office buildings and parking structures and by demolishing most of the older buildings in the Square. Some citizens, however, saw beyond the deterioration of the existing buildings and recognized the historic integrity inherent in the district, which was filled with Romanesque Revival architecture. They launched an effort to save structures by establishing a designated historic district, an effort that succeeded in 1970 when Pioneer Square became both a local preservation district and a national historic district. But activists also were concerned about the needs of the city's transient population and wanted the neighborhood to continue serving them. In a most unusual coalition, the city responded by developing provisions in the city codes that encouraged the retention of the SRO (single-room occupancy) hotels and rooming houses and the establishment of social service agencies in the area. Entrepreneurs purchased and began improving the deteriorating buildings. This spurred other redevelopment in the area, and the older buildings became

Pioneer Square, Seattle.

desirable properties. As a result, the building valuations in the Pioneer Square area increased 600 percent in less than a decade. The district since has become a showcase of urban mixed-use development, with more than thirty fine art galleries, two hundred independently owned shops, and a lively nightlife.

Redevelopment Incentive

STATION SQUARE, PITTSBURGH

Under preservationist Arthur Ziegler's leadership, in the mid-1970s the Pittsburgh History and Landmarks Foundation tackled a much bigger project than any they had taken on before. The Pittsburgh and Lake Erie Railroad owned an unused station building with an intact, lavishly ornamented, Edwardian-era interior surrounded by forty acres of underutilized commercial buildings. The complex was across the river from downtown, and although it was only a short walk away, most investors saw the area as having little potential because of its rough

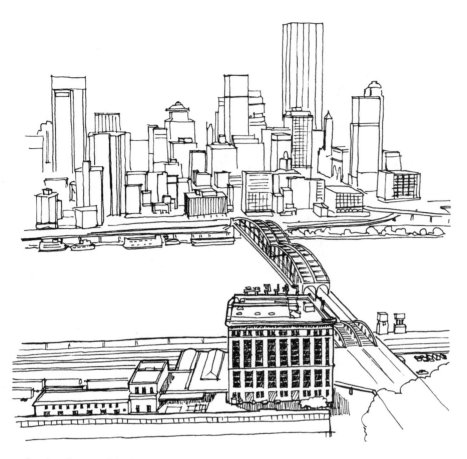

Station Square, Pittsburgh.

industrial appearance. But Ziegler envisioned the adaptive use of the structure as an upscale destination shopping area, with shops and restaurants trading on the historic theme and the marvelous interior spaces. He noted that "Pittsburgh's nearest fashionable shopping district was in Manhattan, and Pittsburgh's last tourist came in 1946."[1]

Although leery investors scoffed, the development, known as Station Square, moved ahead with a $5 million grant from the local Allegheny Foundation and $2 million from Chuck Muer, a restaurateur who established a 500-seat restaurant in the station's grand concourse. The project's success was immediate. Although the experts had projected a maximum annual gross of $300,000, the project instead earned $3 million in the first year and has remained a successful draw for both tourists and Pittsburgh residents.

"LoDo" area of Denver. Courtesy of Michael Ott.

Stabilization or Increase in Property Values

LOWER DOWNTOWN (LODO), DENVER

In the early 1980s, the Lower Downtown (LoDo) area of Denver was an older warehouse district on the fringe of the center city with no real prospects. It had a vacancy rate of 40 percent and fully 30 percent of the properties had been foreclosed. In response, in 1988 the Denver City Council created the Lower Downtown Historic District. The action was originally opposed by 75 percent of the area's property owners, who were concerned with the regulations and loss of property rights. They felt that the designation would lower their property values and send the area into further decline, but precisely the opposite occurred. By 1995, the number of vacancies had dropped to 10 percent and properties were in demand. The area became home to dozens of new restaurants and clubs, art galleries, and hundreds of converted residential units. Throughout most of the area property values doubled. What made these properties desirable, in addition to the character of the old warehouse spaces, was the fact that the historic district regulations stabilized the area and assured investors that properties surrounding theirs would not be allowed to be demolished or neglected. The city's original $2 million investment in public improvements had generated almost $100 million dollars in private investment in less than a decade.

Public Relations and Promotion

LOWELL, MASSACHUSETTS

In the mid- to late-nineteenth century, Lowell, Massachusetts, was at the center of New England's textile industry. When the textile industry moved to lower-cost, nonunion Southern states in the 1920s, Lowell and other similar older industrial cities were largely abandoned. Large, well-built mill buildings remained, but most were vacant, and they lined the rivers as ghosts of former times. Lowell was one of the largest of the textile towns and was hit hard by the changed economy.

Today, Lowell represents an important preservation success story. In 1978, the city's center was designated as a 137-acre preservation district under the National Historical Parks program of the National Park Service, the first such program of its kind. Since then, many of the textile buildings have been restored as residential units, and the Boott Cotton Mill Museum, the National Streetcar Museum, and New England Quilt Museum encourage tourism. A tourist center

Lowell, Massachusetts, historic industrial district.

was added in one of the vintage mill buildings. Lowell's National Historical Park is complete with two-and-a-half miles of trolley and canal boat tours. Lowell has traded successfully on the history of the textile industry as its primary historical and tourist attraction. The historic district is less an attempt to preserve a grouping of buildings than an effort to preserve the elements of an earlier local industry of national significance. As a spin-off from this base, Lowell's downtown has been revitalized, with many new shops, continuing renovation, and new employment opportunities. The city now attracts new industry, thereby boosting the entire local economy.

HISTORY IS NOT STATIC

One of the traps into which preservationists can fall is that of seeing a community's history as static. A high point in the community's history is often determined as the period to be preserved and protected—usually a period of economic growth and success. A historic district ordinance is enacted to try to preserve the look and feel of that period, possibly to eliminate by attrition conflicting evidence from other periods.

In *History in Urban Places*, author and urban historian David Hamer makes the case that all periods should be represented as part of the urban history of a place. He writes: "The concept of the historic district has to a large extent been based on a commitment to a representation of history as static, a series of points in time artificially frozen and then immunized to a substantial degree from the impacts of change. This is not only un- or even anti-historical. It is also profoundly anti-urban in the sense that it denies the diversity that is the very essence of urban life and the source of its greatest challenges and enjoyment. For change is the essential and only constant characteristic of the history of many American city districts."[2]

Occasionally there are examples of cities that have been "frozen in time." They have one significant point in time and serve almost as urban museums representing that given period. Examples include the mining towns of the West, shipping ports on the East Coast, canal/railroad villages throughout the nation, and lumber towns of the Midwest. But most cities have an evolving history representing many time periods, and historic districts should represent the full spectrum of a community's past, not simply a selected slice through it at one particular time period.

Georgetown

An example of an area representing a given time period is the Georgetown district of Washington, D.C. Georgetown was first settled in the late 1600s and incorporated as an independent town in 1751, when the United States was still a British colony. It thrived as a port for the Chesapeake and Ohio Canal, which delivered goods to boats docked on the Potomac River.

In 1871, Georgetown was formally annexed by the city of Washington, D.C. By that time, railroads were replacing canals as a primary form of shipping, and Georgetown became destitute. As a result, most of its early Federal period houses were largely ignored and remained relatively unchanged. The area came back to life in the 1950s, when then-Senator John F. Kennedy and his wife Jackie made Georgetown fashionable, hosting parties for many of the capitol's influential people. Since then, Georgetown has been the home of many members of Washington's elite. Over the past fifty years, residents have created an upscale

Georgetown district, Washington, D.C. Courtesy of Dennis Koomen.

neighborhood with the "Georgetown style" architecture, recalling the lifestyle of its original residents in an idealized way. Although structures throughout the district have been built at various time periods, most reflect the dense urban fabric of two- or three-story brick townhouses so common throughout the area, and although many were constructed during the mid- to late-nineteenth century, they represent the Federal style common to the original period and still define the character of the community into the twenty-first century.

Seton Hill, Baltimore

A contrasting case study involves the Seton Hill district near downtown Baltimore, because its many periods of significance make it difficult to define one period or era that is most representative of its history. Seton Hill was known as the French Quarter of Baltimore in the 1600s. In 1791 St. Mary's Seminary was established at this location as the nation's first Roman Catholic Seminary. A few years later the seminary founded St. Mary's College, the first university in Maryland. Sister Elizabeth Ann Seton opened the country's first parochial school for girls and led the first order of nuns in the United States, the Sisters of Charity. As a result of her work, in 1975 Mother Seton became the first American to be canonized as a saint.

As significant as the early period was, and despite the fact that almost every structure had been built by the mid-nineteenth century, the Seton Hill neighborhood continued to evolve through a number of other significant periods as well. The small low-ceiling two-story rowhouses adjacent to the seminary grounds served as residences for workers and slaves, with underground walkways connecting their basements to the seminary grounds. In the mid-nineteenth century, the popular Lexington Market, which still exists just south of Seton Hill, became the eastern terminus of the National Road, the country's first federally built highway. Numerous inns were located in the area for the many wagons that came to load or unload their goods.

With the decline of the seminary and the Baltimore and Ohio Railroad taking over the freight business, the district had to regenerate itself. In the 1910s and '20s its small houses served a new purpose as the speakeasy district for the downtown area. With the repeal of the Prohibition Act, Seton Hill became one of the city's "red light" districts, with the same small townhouses serving as centers of the business of prostitution. Gradually the neighborhood slipped into neglect,

Seton Hill rowhouses, Baltimore.

and inner city slums adjacent to the district greatly depressed the value of the properties.

In the late 1960s and '70s, the neighborhood attracted a gay community willing to invest in rehabilitation of the townhouses. With this impetus, a process of gentrification began, and young professionals recognized the inherent charm in the townhouses, and the convenience of the location, near downtown and the adjacent upscale Monument Street neighborhood. Many of these new residents stripped the interiors of the historic houses to their brick shells, reconstructing them with new room layouts, mechanical systems, and modern amenities. The charm of the exteriors remained, but the interiors were renewed as modern living spaces.

Given the many layers found in this Baltimore neighborhood over its four-hundred-year history, it is difficult to define its significance by limiting its historical consequence to one era. Each era had its own importance, seen through its impact on the Seton Hill neighborhood and the city of Baltimore, as well as in the larger patterns of urban growth throughout early eastern coastal cities.[3]

SETTING UP A HISTORIC DISTRICT COMMISSION

Historic district commissions, with their powers of regulation, can be established at the local level generally only after a municipality has been given this right by state government through enabling legislation. State enabling legislation, also called a state historic preservation act, encourages historic district ordinances and commissions to serve the following common purposes:

1. Safeguard the heritage of the local unit by preserving one or more historic districts that reflect elements of the unit's history, architecture, archeology, engineering, or culture.
2. Stabilize and improve property values in each district and the surrounding areas.
3. Foster civic beauty.
4. Strengthen the local economy.
5. Promote the use of historic districts for the education, pleasure, and welfare of the citizens of the local unit and of the state.

A regulatory historic preservation district normally is created when citizens petition the local legislative body (city council, township board, county commission) to establish an ordinance that delineates ways to identify, recognize, and protect local historic resources. The resulting ordinance normally follow the tenets of the state historic preservation legislation. Such legislation typically results in the following powers:

1. Establishment of local historic districts
2. A method for identifying historic resources (the historic inventory and survey)
3. Acquisition of certain resources for historic preservation purposes

4. Preservation of historic and nonhistoric resources within historic districts

5. Establishment of historic district commissions

6. Maintenance of publicly owned resources by local units

7. Certain types of assessments under certain circumstances

8. Procedures

9. Remedies and penalties

Factors to consider when establishing a district are described in the following sections.

ESTABLISHING HISTORIC DISTRICT BOUNDARIES

A historic district should be established when a grouping of historic structures is unified by spatial and architectural characteristics, and when the group of structures as a whole has more importance and significance than the structures do individually. To justify its creation, a district should have at least one unifying element or theme that ties together all or most of the structures within its boundaries. The establishment of a historic district may be justified when a concentrated assemblage of historic structures represents an architectural period or style. For instance, many downtown districts are formed around groupings of nineteenth- and early-twentieth-century brick commercial buildings. The ground levels of these buildings often have undergone many changes, but the structures retain historic integrity on their upper levels as well as in the consistent height, scale, setback, and exterior materials. By creating such a downtown district, property owners can institute guidelines, regulations, and incentives that encourage retention or restoration of the district's historic and architectural integrity.

A district can also be based on an important era in the community's history. If mining played a significant role in a town's development, a district may try to incorporate an assemblage of the remaining buildings that represent this industry. In some situations, a district may comprise noncontiguous sites or structures if they have a common theme. Perhaps structures representing early settlement, for example, are scattered across a city. In this case, trying to collect the significant buildings within one physical district would mean substantial contortion of the boundary lines, not unlike gerrymandering. A thematic district comprising non-contiguous elements would be the most appropriate approach, but this approach

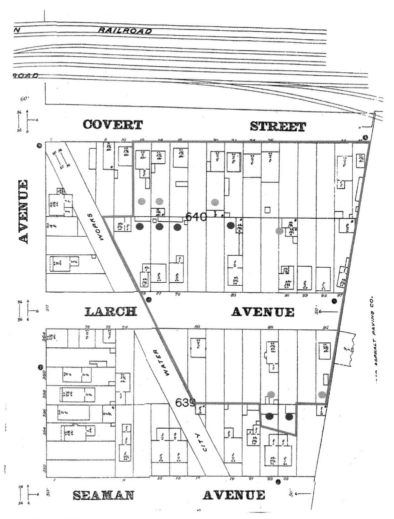

Covert/Larch Historic District, Jersey City, NJ. Courtesy of the New Jersey Department of Transportation.

is relatively rare because it does not capture the sense of place—one of the most important factors in a historic district—and is subject to challenge by owners who do not support the concept of control through a local ordinance.

By definition, boundaries differentiate between areas and to some degree separate them. This is also true with historic districts. As soon as boundaries are established for a historic district, the city begins a pattern of differentiating areas on both sides of those boundaries. The creation of boundaries, from the perspective of historical protection alone, is sometimes overly simplistic in how they are defined.[4] Where should boundaries be established?

The boundaries of a historic district may be defined by natural features and edges—logical boundaries that echo the images residents have of their community. A district may also be based on the early settlement patterns in a community. Although the logical edges of such a historic area may not be apparent, referring to early maps and descriptions may reveal important differentiations. Looking at city atlases and rural plat maps can provide a logical and defensible way to delimit boundaries. Such boundaries are based on the actual historical development of a community and are less subject to interpretation and challenge. With some designations, particularly of larger cultural landscapes such as heritage areas and corridors, communities have taken the approach that if a certain area identifies culturally with the heritage area, then it should be included within the boundaries.

Boundaries may also be established to protect a historic area from adjacent growth and development. Such boundaries should recognize the economic forces that create the need for development and try to accommodate growth and change in some areas while protecting the historic fabric in others. The local planning department and other groups concerned with development issues should be consulted when such districts are contemplated.

Establishing the boundaries of a district creates, by definition, one kind of area within and another without. In addition, the edges often acquire a distinctive pattern of change on their own. While the core of a district can grow and change within its defined environment, residents or property owners in the fringe area may feel the boundary restrictions most directly. These areas can become districts of their own, albeit with invisible and tacit boundaries. In some instances, communities recognize the important role of these buffer transition areas, even affording them a different level of designation and protection than the historic district itself.

In some states, proposed historic districts are considered for approval by the State Historic Preservation Office. The SHPO evaluates a proposed district based on the ratio of historic properties to nonhistoric properties, the rationale being that the higher the proportion of historic structures, the more likely the possibility the proposed district would be supported at higher levels of government. But this assumption may not be the most important factor. The integrity of the boundaries themselves also must be considered, and may be an even more significant aspect because the SHPO may look negatively on proposed districts whose boundaries are gerrymandered to achieve the highest ratio of historic properties possible. The cohesion and integrity of a proposed district's boundaries should be obvious.

Various studies have looked at the significance of boundaries. Kevin Lynch, in his seminal book on urban planning, *The Image of the City,*[5] considered how residents perceive their urban environments. He asked survey respondents to draw maps of their communities as they perceived them. In his home city of Boston he found, for example, that the clearer the edges of districts, the stronger the image of the district. He describes an exercise, called the Lynch Analysis, which was designed to help planners, and by extension preservationists, determine key design elements affecting all aspects of city functions, including historic districts. Through the use of "cognitive maps" drawn by residents, evaluators are able to determine perceived districts, nodes, edges, and landmarks that give a commu-

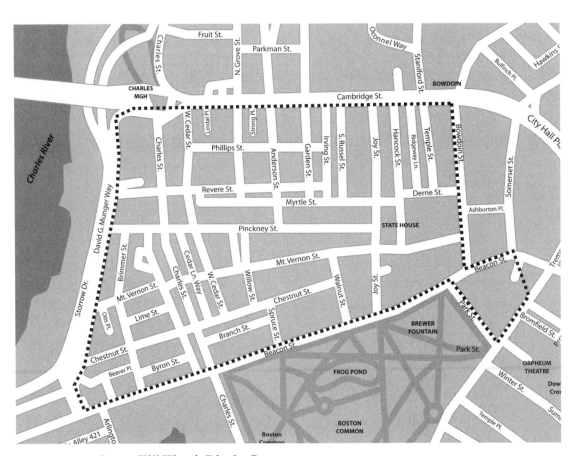

Beacon Hill Historic District, Boston.

nity its character. Many college and university courses about historic designation, preservation planning, and preserving community character benefit by use of the Lynch Analysis to address the historic district boundary question, and as a way of discovering what gives a neighborhood or area its sense of place and time.

In a study of Michigan cities,[6] the author Norman Tyler developed an index of downtown health based on surveys of business owners. One survey question asked respondents to draw what they considered to be the boundaries of their downtown. The findings indicated a significant correlation between how clearly defined the boundaries of the downtown district were and its health. A healthy downtown typically was perceived as having strongly defined boundaries. The Beacon Hill Historic District in Boston, the oldest historic district in Massachusetts, is a good example of a district with well-defined boundaries. Its western boundary is the Charles River and the southern edge is the large Boston Common park. To the east is Charles Bulfinch's magnificent Massachusetts Statehouse, built in 1795, and Cambridge Street, an artery crossing the river to Cambridge, defines the northern boundary. With its gaslit streets and nineteenth-century red-brick rowhouses, it is one of the oldest and most intact neighborhoods in Boston.

The establishment of a historic district is a useful tool, but the consideration of each district's boundaries must include a broader perspective of the city and the many forces and interactions that give that place its vitality.

THE WELL-WRITTEN ORDINANCE

A historic district ordinance must be able to withstand legal challenge, for owners who do not wish to abide by its restrictions may search it for weaknesses or loopholes. A good ordinance adheres to the provisions of its state enabling legislation but also includes sections providing for local concerns. For instance, the state may mandate that one member of a historic district commission be an architect. The local government may want to require an attorney as well, which it is free to do. However, each such additional provision tends to limit the flexibility of the city, and the makeup of the commission should be carefully considered before including such provisions.

An ordinance should be predictable in its application by the review agency (most often the Historic District, or Preservation, Commission). Clear, explicit criteria and standards should be used so that property owners can be fairly certain of how to gain approval when they petition to make changes. If approval by the commission is hard to predict, the ordinance is weak in either its formulation or application. Before drafting an ordinance, it is useful to review problems that other ordinances have typically engendered. Probably the most common problem is that an ordinance is too vague in its provisions and leaves too much to the discretion of the historic district commission or other review agencies. In such a case, decisions are based as much on the personal dynamics of commission members or political considerations as on objective, rational standards. Most State Historic Preservation Offices have on file examples of successful ordinances that have worked in their state.

To minimize misinterpretation or misapplication by local commissions, it is recommended that local ordinances refer to the standards and guidelines established in the Secretary of the Interior's *Standards for the Treatment of Historic Properties*. This document establishes nationally recognized criteria for determining the appropriate types of changes to historic buildings. (See Chapter 7 for more about these guidelines.) Historic District Commission members often have difficulty agreeing on aesthetic values. What appears visually compatible to one reviewer may be visually disruptive to another, and it is difficult to base such opinions on more than personal experience. To help overcome this problem, commissioners can refer to the Secretary of the Interior's standards, and by working together and reviewing previous cases, they can gradually develop a consensus viewpoint on what is appropriate design.

Problems often develop in ordinances when they attempt to define property maintenance provisions. If an owner neglects the maintenance of a property and it falls into serious disrepair, then the commission must take initiative and begin action against the owner. This concern was addressed in the 1975 case of *Maher v. City of New Orleans*. "Once it has been determined that the purpose of the Vieux Carré [historic district] legislation is a proper one, upkeep of buildings appears reasonably necessary to the accomplishment of the goals of the ordinance."[7] Because commissions rarely have power of enforcement, the city agency that enforces building codes should be responsible for enforcing the historic ordinance as well. If the commission is selective in its enforcement proceedings, an owner may claim that it singled him or her out unfairly, and that similar problems at other properties are not being addressed. This argument may be awkward for the commission or the city to counter, but courts generally defer to commissions as expert bodies, and failure to enforce it in one case is not a legal defense in another. As a rule, an ordinance should be applied uniformly throughout the specific historic district or the larger community, if it is applied to more than one district.

A well-written ordinance clearly describes how both "due diligence" and "due process" will be addressed by the commission. *Due diligence*, the legal term for "dotting the i's and crossing the t's," is a legally defensible approach to take. It refers to paying consistent and thorough attention to posting notices, awarding certificates of appropriateness, handling applicants, publishing meeting minutes, agendas, and notices, and generally following the prescribed operational measures to the letter of the law. Such diligence will rule out legal challenges based on procedural issues. A related term, *due process*, refers to the legal procedures that are available to all applicants, including the opportunity to address the commission, to object to or agree with a ruling, and to appeal a decision by the commission to a higher political or legal entity, as prescribed by local and state statute.

LEGAL CRITERIA

A historic district ordinance is a legal document and must follow requirements of state and local governments in its tenets. It should be evaluated according to three basic provisions. First, its purpose should be to *promote the public welfare*. The purpose of government is to protect and promote the welfare of its citizens in general, and an evaluation of the provisions of an ordinance must show that its primary purpose is to benefit the general community, rather than a group of individual property owners.

Second, the means specified in the ordinance should be *rational*. The ordinance provisions should be similar in character to other city ordinances in how they are applied, and not so convoluted that they lead to easy misinterpretation or misuse. For example, an ordinance requiring that all properties in the historic district have a green front door is irrational, for such a decree would not be based on historical precedent but rather created at the whim of the writers of the ordinance.

Third, the provisions of the ordinance should be *fair*—that is, not unduly onerous or burdensome—and should apply equally to everyone within a specified group. Indeed, if the ordinance is too restrictive on certain properties, their owners could argue that their property is subject to a legal "taking," and the city could be liable for compensation to those owners.

The vast majority of the applications for work on historic structures reviewed by a historic district commission are approved; unfortunately, what is often picked up by the media and by word-of-mouth are the projects in the remaining 5 percent that require additional review and revision, that are simply rejected, or that are subject to appeal. As a result, the public may be left with a negative impression of the review process. Public reaction to negative decisions can best be addressed through education and promotion of the benefits of historic designation and review.

THE NECESSARY ORDINANCE

To be effective, an ordinance must fill a need. In some situations, historic buildings are protected and maintained through other agencies and no local ordinance is needed, for it would be either redundant or ineffective in its application. In such an area, perhaps recognition by the municipality or protection through a preservation easement or other covenant that runs with the property is sufficient. Such historic structures can be recognized by way of special resolutions, markers, and signage.

Elsewhere, an ordinance may not be necessary because properties are not threatened, and the political tradeoffs in pushing through an ordinance would be detrimental in other ways. Historically significant houses may be found in stable residential areas where no pressure for change is foreseen. Rather than draft an ordinance that attempts to anticipate future needs, it might be preferable to hold off on the regulatory front. If the situation changes, the need for a protective ordinance can be more realistically assessed at the time. This is not to say that local ordinances should be put off until the last possible moment, when the threat is all too real and the response must be reactive. Preservationists should always let the community know which areas and structures they consider historically significant and how they best can be protected. Education should be a primary goal of historic preservation. How can the public know what is important if that information has not been disseminated? Historic home tours or neighborhood surveys are particularly useful in educating citizens. One strategy is to hold an "inventory day," when the public is asked to provide information, old photographs, and the

Historic district homes tour, Baltimore.

like, or post a "house of the week" article in the local newspaper. Efforts like these will engender interest and support for preservation efforts.

To be effective when reviewing proposals for additions or alterations to designated buildings, a commission must have the authority to deny a proposal. If it can only advise and recommend, then its powers and ability to protect are severely limited and depend more on the personal and moral persuasion of its members than on sound review criteria. In some cases, courts have invalidated designations because the criteria used were either too vague or absent entirely.[8] To determine whether designation is legally defensible, ask these questions: (1) Did the review body follow designation procedures (due process) as set forth by state and local laws? (2) Did owners receive legal notice of the proposed designation (due diligence)? (3) Were owners given an opportunity to challenge designation? (4) Did the local review body base its decision on the evidence before it?

THE APPROPRIATE ORDINANCE

A historic district or a landmarks ordinance typically controls the exterior alteration and demolition of designated structures (and sometimes, as in New York City, Boston, Seattle, and Washington, D.C., that of the interior). Ordinances may also include control over additions, maintenance, and repair. The extent of control is a decision made by the local community through its legislative body. Owners of designated properties must gain approval before making changes. The Certificate of Appropriateness (or other approval) obtained from the local historic district commission is based on criteria established in the ordinance.

The historic district ordinance should not conflict with either the local zoning ordinance or building department regulations, or the state's preservation enabling legislation. Sometimes property owners have made changes based on the approval of one city agency only to find that they are in conflict with another agency. Historic district ordinances may take precedence over other city ordinances, but this hierarchy must be explicitly stated in the law.

A boilerplate ordinance (one that simply copies another) should be avoided, for different communities have different needs and desires. For example, Alaska designates by state statute the establishment of historic districts with structures listed on the National Register of Historic Places, but supplements that by including districts "characteristic of the Russian–American period before 1867, the early territorial period before 1930, or early native heritage."[9] The Arkansas ordinance directs that exterior changes to historic properties be approved by a local commission prior to the building of any structure, including "stone walls, fences, light fixtures, steps and paving, or any outdoor advertising."[10] The District of Columbia code says that anyone who is in violation through demolition or alteration of a protected structure shall be required to "restore the building or structure and its site to its appearance prior to the violation."[11] An ordinance dealing with a specific area in Indianapolis encourages preservation of Meridian Street "to preserve significant tourist attractions of historical and economic value by limiting or restricting any use in the area that would be inconsistent with its character."[12] Each of these examples illustrates how ordinances can reflect local concerns and needs.

Concerns about Historic Districts

The proposed establishment of a historic district covered by an ordinance sometimes is met with opposition from groups with a variety of concerns. It is important to understand and address these concerns when putting the concept forward. Surprisingly, opposition also often comes from other agencies of local government. Such concern may be based on a general fear of losing power to another city agency, in this case, the local historic district commission. A historic district also may be opposed because it can mean additional work for some city officials; perhaps the building department will need to coordinate its approvals for building permits with the historic district commission, or the city planning department will need to wait for comments from the commission before making recommendations on projects awaiting planning commission approval.

Other concerns may be financial. The cost of administering historic district ordinances (staff, office costs, project fees, and contracts) may come out of another agency's budget, either directly or indirectly. Also, the provisions of an ordinance may inhibit capital improvements projects. For example, while the transportation department may want to widen a street to increase traffic flow, the historic district commission may not agree that it is in the city's best interests to do this in the protected district. All these concerns, and others, may arise when a historic district is proposed.

Institutions may not be in favor of historic districts, especially if they have a stake in a designated property. State institutions (colleges, universities, hospitals, etc.) typically are not subject to local ordinances and need respond only to state regulations. Universities frequently ignore local historic district commissions. Generally speaking, the larger the institution, the more it can disregard local pressure for its structures to be included in a historic district. Yet, in most cases, these institutions represent important elements of a community's history and heritage. Their lack of involvement in local historic designation efforts can cause serious discord in developing and meeting a community's historic preservation goals.

Finally, historic districts may be opposed by private citizens who assert their rights with the cry, "Don't tell me what I can and can't do with my own property!"

Local residents discussing a historic district ordinance

This attitude runs deep in the American psyche and represents a valid concern. However, legal precedents have already established the right of a city and its agencies to limit what people may and may not do with their property through zoning or building codes. Nevertheless, when historic districts are proposed, the concerns of many citizens may come to the forefront.

In general, opposition is based largely on the amount of control being imposed. The best way to divert this criticism is to focus on three areas. First, create an open, educative atmosphere by providing the public with an abundance of information about the historic district and its history and significance. Focusing on specific blocks, important structures, and buildings of unique or outstanding architectural interest are good ways to engender trust and support. Second, develop an ordinance that combines regulations with incentives. Finally, welcome discourse about the district and the ordinance, and be open to all decisions from the beginning. This process will both reveal the opposition and allow time to address, and hopefully mitigate, negative reactions.

The following concerns represent the most common points of opposition when historic districts are proposed. These concerns are heard especially when the designation of commercial buildings is proposed, because owners fear that the designation will limit their right to profit from their investment. The suggested replies provide reasonable answers to these concerns.

Concern: Designation will add another level of bureaucracy to the city's approval process.

Reply: When changes or additions are proposed to designated buildings, the review process of the historic district commission should be efficient, predictable, and integrated into the normal review of other city agencies. Approval or disapproval by the commission should be completed expeditiously (e.g., typically no more than sixty to ninety days from the time the application is submitted). The determination should be given in writing, listing the reasons for approval or disapproval. As owners become accustomed to this procedure, it should take no longer than other approvals.

Concern: Designation will cause unnecessary hardship to property owners.

Reply: The act of designation should not cause economic hardship. As a Virginia court found, the identification of an area as a historic district did not deprive the owners of any property rights.[13] Designation should be based solely on historical or architectural significance and not on economic impact. However, historic preservation has been shown in many communities to help spur economic revitalization. In residential areas, property values do not fall after such designation but rather stabilize, as designation implies more neighborhood stability and renewal. In commercial areas, designation has led to many new programs and revitalization proposals that have created a fresh image and new vitality for businesses.

If an economic hardship arises through inequitable property taxes or other regulations, it can be remedied by incentive programs described elsewhere (see Chapter 8). Owners who feel they are treated unfairly always have an appeals process, usually to the mayor, city council, or an appeals board.

Concern: Designation means I can't change or add on to my building.

Reply: This is probably the most misunderstood and surprising concern, since most ordinances permit alterations and additions. Indeed, it would be foolish not to allow alterations, because historic properties would be doomed to be museum pieces if they could not be updated.

Alterations and additions should be permitted if two conditions are met. First, the changes should not destroy the elements that give a property its historic integrity. For example, if the front façade is important as part of a district's streetscape, then an addition could be allowed at the rear. If the entire exterior is architecturally significant, then perhaps change can be made to the interior or an addition permitted if it is compatible with the original structure. The guidelines for making such changes are clearly described in the *Secretary of the Interior's Standards and Guidelines for Historic Rehabilitation* (see Chapter 3). The addition also could be designed so that it could be removed at a later date without damage to the historic structure. Second, alterations or additions should be subject to the review and approval of a historic district commission. This review ensures that the standards are applied appropriately and consistently.

Concern: Designation is mandatory. Shouldn't it be voluntary?

Reply: At first, this point seems a valid concern, for if ordinances allowed for voluntary designation, they would be acceptable to most property owners. In fact, over 330 local governments are believed to have established owner consent requirements as part of their designation procedures.[14] However, such ordinances are inherently weak from both preservation and legal viewpoints, for they give owners the right to determine whether or not their property is historically or architecturally significant; owners may not be the best informed to make this judgment. Some owners want to give high status to their property when its significance may be relatively insignificant, whereas others fear the restrictions that accompany designation and may insist that their important historic property not receive any form of designation.

This is not to say that an owner's rights are not important, but whether or not a structure is historically or architecturally significant should not hinge on whether or not the owner agrees. The determination of historic significance should be made by a qualified panel of experts; consistency in the designation process is important because historic buildings may have no other protection from demolition or destructive alterations. Owner consent also may be constitutionally invalid, for it fails to treat similar historic properties alike and regulates them in what could be considered an arbitrary manner.

Concern: It is unfair to designate my building, for there are no firm criteria for selection. The list of proposed buildings seems arbitrary and based on subjective judgments only.

Reply: The selection of properties and districts to be designated and subject to the regulations of a local ordinance should be made by an impartial panel of individuals knowledgeable about local history and architectural history and styles. Serving on the selection committee is no easy task, for the merits of individual structures can be argued from many perspectives and consensus achieved at times only through much debate and reconsideration. The final list should present the reasons for each selection and any exclusions.

Although selection is subjective to some degree, as it must be, legal precedents have established that such a process has lawful standing as long as (1) the selection decisions were made by qualified people and (2) selection criteria were established beforehand. The selection criteria need not rely on hard statistical logic but can be "soft"; complete objectivity is impossible when it comes to questions of historical significance. Courts have generally upheld the legality of such determinations and should not substitute a court's judgment for that of the expert selection committee.

Selection is ultimately based on two factors: historical or cultural significance and architectural significance. More specific criteria may be added, including such factors as age; rarity—that is, the number of buildings of a certain type extant in the community; listing on local, state, or federal registers; association with important local events; examples of fine craftsmanship, and so forth.

Concern: The ordinance has no sound legal basis and will be subject to lawsuits.

Reply: Any ordinance for designating and regulating historic buildings should be legally well founded. Many legal precedents uphold the right of local governments to enact preservation ordinances as a valid exercise of "police powers," including the well-known Penn Central case of 1978 (see Chapter 4). Such ordinances should also be compatible with state legislation. An ordinance should be scrutinized by legal counsel, whether the city attorney or private counsel, for it is a document with many legal as well as economic ramifications and may be challenged by a disgruntled owner or buyer.

With a sound basis in law, there is little reason to be concerned about the right to designate historic structures through a local ordinance. Over the past decades, the right of local jurisdictions to designate historic districts has become as accepted a practice as the creation of zoning ordinances, which were earlier subjected to similar scrutiny and challenge. Nevertheless, owners cannot be denied reasonable use of their property without the due process of law. Therefore, if a Historic District Commission is considering a property for designation, two steps should be included in the process: the owner should first be given adequate notice of the contemplated action (thirty- to sixty-day notice by registered mail is typical) and second, the owner should be given a chance to speak at a public hearing.

An Alternative Perspective on Designation

Often, historic designation is given to a building largely on the basis of age. But age is relative and, by definition, constantly changing. Consider, for example, the situation of Oak Park, Illinois. In the early 1900s, Oak Park was one of the most desirable suburbs of Chicago. Its tree-lined streets were fronted by stately Victorian-era homes, many in the ebullient Queen Anne style. The homes were tall, with steep roofs, turrets, and multiple gables. Into that setting Frank Lloyd Wright brought a new style for residential design, eventually known as the Prairie (or Wrightian) style, which was largely inspired by the broad Midwestern plains (see Chapter 3). Wright's houses were more horizontal than vertical, with low, sloped roofs and wide, overhanging eaves. There could not have been a sharper contrast to the Victorian-era houses in Oak Park than this new architectural style, as illustrated by comparing the dramatically horizontal form of Wright's Cheney House with its next-door neighbor.

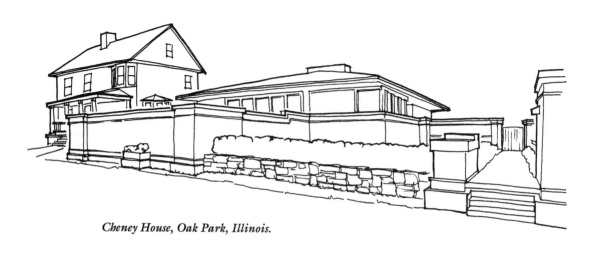

Cheney House, Oak Park, Illinois.

A question arises from this example. If Oak Park had had a historic district ordinance and had set up a historic district commission to review new construction, would Frank Lloyd Wright's designs have been approved? Or would the commissioners have denied the requests because the designs were incompatible with the residential character of the neighborhood? Today we recognize the brilliance of these early houses designed by Wright, which are among the nation's architectural treasures. Yet in 1910 or 1915 they were new, incompatible, controversial, and probably would have not been built if a strict review procedure had been required. A tragic loss for Oak Park and the nation would have been the result.

In the same vein, the question must be asked today whether historic district requirements prevent the building of innovative and important architecture. In our attempt to protect against the worst designs, are we also regulating out the best examples of new construction? Sometimes it is challenging to recognize significant architecture before it has had a chance to age; excellence must be nurtured and encouraged wherever it is found.

Running a Historic District Commission Meeting

One potential source of conflict between a historic district commission and property owners who petition the commission for approval of work is in the conduct of the meeting. Many commissioners are citizen appointees who have had little experience in conducting official business. An agenda that is consistent and predictable in format and fair to all parties can minimize conflicts.

The process begins with the petitioner's application for approval of proposed changes. (Such an approval is often referred to as a certificate of appropriateness, or COA.) The application should be simple to understand and clearly list information required for the commission to make a decision. For more efficiency, some commissions empower a designated staff person to make administrative approvals of predefined types of work that do not require the commission's time in public session. An example would be a simple handrail or a type of roof previously approved. Such administrative approvals should regularly be reviewed by the commission's chair and reported in the minutes so that they become part of the public record.

A formal application should include basic information about the property and can be prepared jointly by the petitioner and the staff person. It should include sufficient information about proposed changes to make clear the effect of those changes on the historic property. This information could include drawings, photographs, manufacturer's literature, or any other source needed to fully describe the proposed changes.

To encourage a smooth procedure, a staff person, commission chair, or other designated commissioner should contact petitioners prior to the meeting to review the application. Each property to be reviewed could be visited by one or two commissioners and/or staff prior to the meeting, since firsthand impressions can be important in a determination.

To accommodate petitioners, hearings should occur early in the agenda of commission meetings. Applicants should be encouraged to attend to present their case and to answer any questions that may arise. Agendas and related material should be readily and obviously available when entering the room. For many petitioners, especially first-time applicants, such a meeting can seem daunting. Commissioners should be courteous, welcoming, attentive, and refrain from talking among themselves during the presentations. Even the room layout can cause apprehension, especially if a council chambers or other raised-dais type of setting is used; a personal approach by commissioners and staff can be extremely useful in establishing a positive atmosphere.

Individual hearings can be conducted in a variety of formats. The following sequence allows both the petitioner and the commission to discuss the application in an orderly way:

1. The chair calls the case.
2. A staff member or commissioner presents the case.
3. The applicant presents his or her case, if any.
4. The floor is opened to audience participation (important for controversial applications).
5. The applicant responds.
6. Commissioners ask questions, if needed.
7. The hearing is closed and the commission discusses the issues and takes action.
8. A commissioner or staff is appointed to monitor approved projects.

It is helpful if commissions conduct meetings according to *Robert's Rules of Order*.[15] Robert's Rules is used by more local governments than any other procedure for conducting meetings. Adopting such rules can easily be accomplished by inserting the following statement into the commission's bylaws:

> The rules contained in the current edition of *Robert's Rules of Order, Newly Revised,* shall govern in all cases to which they are applicable and in which they are not inconsistent with these bylaws, any special rules of order the commission may adopt, and the laws and rules adopted by local or state government.

Other Activities of a Historic District Commission

Although the review process described above is the most important responsibility of a historic district commission, it also can be involved in many activities relating to local history and preservation. The powers given to commissions are granted by local government and state law, although commissions often become involved in activities other than those specifically given through the ordinance. The following list, from *A Handbook on Historic Preservation Law,*[16] describes other powers or activities:

- To survey and identify historically and architecturally significant structures and areas.
- To require affirmative maintenance of historic structures.
- To make recommendations regarding zoning amendments and to make comments on updates to the local comprehensive plan.
- To undertake educational programs and activities.
- To establish standards and procedures for designation and development review.
- To accept funds from federal, state, and private sources.
- To buy, sell, or accept donations of property.
- To exercise the power of eminent domain.
- To accept easements and other less-than-fee interests in property.

Certified Local Governments

The National Historic Preservation Act was amended in 1980 to allow local communities to request their state government to give them the status of certified local government (CLG). This designation ties the local government more closely with the State Historic Preservation Office in administering preservation programs, and makes it eligible for certain types of grants. To be eligible for CLG status, the local government must give evidence of having established a historic preservation commission that is able and willing to conduct reviews and to enforce state and local preservation ordinances. It also should have a system of surveying historic properties tied to state office procedures.

CLG status involves the local agency in the historic nomination review process, and the local commission must give preliminary approval for all historic nominations sent on to the state office. CLG status also conveys priority eligibility and staff support for federal and state preservation grants to conduct surveys and inventories of historic areas and archeological sites. CLGs can also receive funding to prepare and review National Register nominations, develop published design guidelines, write or amend preservation ordinances, as well as preparing and publishing exhibits and brochures and sponsoring special events. CLG grants also now may be used for bricks-and-mortar work, such as the restoration or renovation of historic buildings owned by the local government.

Chapter Seven

INTERVENTION APPROACHES, DOCUMENTATION, AND TECHNOLOGY

◄━━◆━━►

WHAT IS PRESERVATION TECHNOLOGY?

Preservation technology is defined by the methods and materials used to protect and conserve our historic buildings, sites, and artifacts. It deals principally with the conservation of building materials: identifying them, determining their condition, evaluating treatment options, and making work recommendations. Preservation technology requires a broad and deep knowledge of construction, gained through experience in working with older buildings. Indeed, much of the historic integrity of a structure can be lost through inappropriate work, even when the goal is restoration.

Work in the field of preservation technology is multidisciplinary, involving architects, engineers, planners, archeologists, architectural and object conservators, curators, educators, managers, tradespeople, historians, contractors, technicians, and students. A working knowledge of preservation technology along with an understanding of historic building materials is important to preservationists of many types. There are currently more projects involving the adaptive use of older buildings than there are new construction projects, and the resulting demand for architectural conservators will continue to grow. Expertise in newer building materials such as plastics, glass, high-strength steel, and concrete will be in particular demand, for little attention has been paid to their long-term conservation.

Training in preservation technology can be pursued from many directions including architecture, construction, and conservation. Training in architecture and construction imparts knowledge in design and methods of construction.

Architect checking steeple from "cherry picker" lift.

Programs offering a focus in conservation emphasize knowledge of the decay of materials and methods of mitigation. Training in any of these areas contributes to good preparation for this specialization. Also required, however, is a particular knowledge of historic building practices and interest in working directly on older buildings. With that interest, many avenues of appropriate education and training may be pursued.

Opportunities to gain expertise in preservation technology are numerous and varied. The Association for Preservation Technology (APT) International is a multi-disciplinary organization focusing on the practical application of technology to conservation of the built environment. Its publications, in particular the *APT Bulletin*, describe building conservation techniques and case studies of projects throughout the world with an emphasis on the United States and Canada. Field schools provide opportunities for individuals to gain firsthand experience in preservation technology or special conservation methods. Examples of established schools include the Campbell Center for Historic Preservation Studies in Illinois, RESTORE in New York City (and various other parts of the country), the National Park Service's Historic Preservation Training Center, and the Preservation Education Institute in Historic Windsor, Vermont (see also the National Park Service's annual cultural resource training directory).

The best and most common way of gaining expertise, however, is by working directly with someone skilled in the field. Whether working under a restoration architect, a materials conservator, or a master carpenter, a student of preservation technology can acquire practical experience not possible in a formal academic setting.

As the general level of sophistication increases in the preservation community, the need for better technical advice and construction skills becomes increasingly important. Through apprenticeships, training centers, and organizations such as the Association for Preservation Technology, more opportunities are available for individuals to develop skills in preservation technology, and these skills are increasingly desired and requested by others, including architects, building contractors, and preservation administrators.

TYPES OF INTERVENTION

As described in chapter 1, Viollet-le-Duc, Ruskin, and others who followed them presented divergent approaches to treating historic resources. Over time, consideration of the more extreme viewpoints was tempered and refined and a general consensus formed as to appropriate "intervention" strategies, that is, what should be done in the conservation of a building. The National Park Service has developed definitions of treatment standards and guidelines that are now generally accepted. Each type of intervention—preservation, restoration, reconstruction, and conservation—has a special meaning appropriate for a particular situation. A review of these, with examples of their applications, points out differences as well as similarities.[1]

Preservation

The term *preservation* refers to the maintenance of a property without significant alteration to its current condition. This approach should be taken when it is appropriate to maintain a building or structure as is. A structure changes over its lifetime and each change represents a part of its history and integrity. The "preservation" of a historic building accepts those changes but maintains its historic integrity and as much of the original fabric and features as possible. According to the Secretary of the Interior's *Standards*, the definitive source for appropriate building intervention techniques, changes which may have taken place in the course of time are evidence of the history and development of a building, structure, or site and its environment. These changes may have acquired significance in their own right, and this significance should be recognized and respected. When preservation is the appropriate strategy, the only intervention is normal maintenance or special work needed to protect the structure against further damage.

Seattle's Pike Place Market is an example of an innovative preservation approach. This old city market was threatened with demolition to make way for an urban renewal project. However, the residents of Seattle considered the market an important part of their city's life and culture and wanted to preserve it. A citywide ballot proposal provided clear evidence that most people wanted the market saved, and the decision was made to keep the downtown facility. Soon city

Pike Place Market, Seattle.

Pike Place Market interior.

planners perceived a new problem. They recognized that Pike Place might be so popular and successful that its character would change into that of a boutique-type shopping center, in the process losing its original character as a somewhat scruffy everyday market run by local farmers and small-scale entrepreneurs. To prevent this kind of alteration, the city developed a preservation ordinance that not only protected the structures from demolition but also from becoming trendy in their appearance and operation. This protective ordinance addresses two primary considerations. The first part states that structures must remain common, or ordinary, in their construction materials. If any structural material deteriorates, it should be repaired if possible. If it must be replaced, the replacement material may not be of a quality different from the original. In other words, a solid wood beam cannot be replaced by a wood box beam or steel beam—only by another solid wood beam. Second, the ordinance provides protection via the market's management techniques by specifying that all vendors either make or grow their own products. This stipulation prevents upscale franchises from becoming the primary market tenants. The Pike Place Market area has kept its unique historical character intact through use of these unusual preservation measures, retaining the character residents first recognized and loved—and then protected.

Restoration

Restoration refers to the process of returning a building to its condition at a specific time period, often to its original condition. Restoration of a building is appropriate when portions of a structure's historic integrity are lost or where its importance at a particular historic time period was particularly significant. The decision to restore should be made carefully, however, for it means ignoring the natural evolution of a building and recreating a former time period. However, if a building has a past of great significance, then restoration may be justified.

Frank Lloyd Wright's home and studio in Oak Park, Illinois is an example. Over the decades, the structure was modified many times and eventually split into apartments. A foundation established to preserve the Wright home and studio

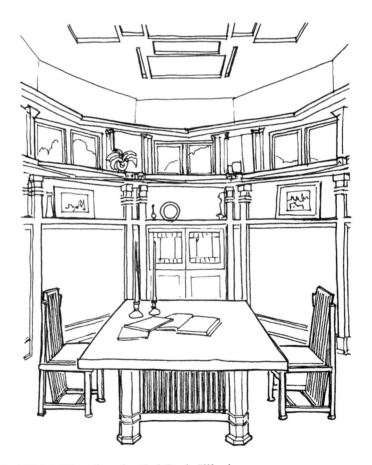

Frank Lloyd Wright House interior, Oak Park, Illinois.

purchased the property. A program of restoration was begun, but restoration architects and conservationists faced a problem. Wright had lived in the home for many years and had continually added to and modified the structure. Beginning as a small, modest home, the property gradually became an elaborate complex with wings and additions. The decision to restore made it necessary to choose a specific time period; restoring it to one period meant excluding elements from other periods. After intensive study and discussion, the decision was made to restore the property to the year 1913, Wright's last year there. The foundation undertook an extensive study of the original plans, photographs, and other archival material to determine what elements remained from that period and which had to be reconstructed. Changes made after 1913 were removed.

A guiding principle of good restoration practice is that an original element, even if in poor condition, is preferable to a replicated element. Historical conjecture is especially discouraged. If documentation does not show an original element, then generally it is better to leave it out or, if necessary, replace it with a compatible contemporary element. Restoration work should not be based on guesses about what a historical element might have been (as Viollet-le-Duc did), but should work from actual evidence, even if limited. As stated in the Secretary of the Interior's *Standards*, repair or replacement of missing architectural features should be based on accurate duplication of features, substantiated by historic, physical, or pictorial evidence, rather than on conjectural designs or the availability of different architectural elements from other buildings or structures."

Reconstruction

The term *reconstruction* indicates the rebuilding of a structure. This approach is taken when a historic structure needs to be physically in place for contextual reasons, even though it no longer exists. For example, when the Rockefeller family sponsored the restoration of Colonial Williamsburg, Virginia, most of the town's historic buildings remained. However, nothing remained of the Governor's Palace, which was the focus of the town's original layout until it was destroyed by fire in 1781. Planners decided to reconstruct this building since the original no longer remained. The original plans were not available, but after extensive research, in 1929 an engraved copperplate showing the structure was found at the Bodleian Library at Oxford University in England. This Bodleian plate provided enough information for the building's reconstruction. Some aspects of the rebuilding were

Governor's Palace, Williamsburg, Virginia.

Restored barn with superimposed line drawing, Mount Vernon.

necessarily conjectural, but the discovery of this much documentation provided sufficient information to maximize authenticity of the reconstruction.

Another example is the reconstructed treading barn at Mount Vernon. George Washington kept meticulous records of his purchases, particularly for his various farm enterprises and outbuildings. Referring to an archive of his handwritten lists and receipts, the quantity of bricks, beams, and windows provided an accurate base from which to "reconstruct" the original building. The only physical evidence of the actual structure was a nineteenth century photograph. Computer enhancement of this image revealed the angle of the beams, the thickness of the brick walls, and the configuration of the windows. Using these two resources, it was possible to create accurate drawings to reconstruct the barn and restore this important contextual site, which included the barn and flanking corncribs, as part of the Mount Vernon Estate and Gardens.

Rehabilitation (Adaptive Use)

For historic buildings needing repair, alterations, or an addition, the most flexible intervention strategy is *rehabilitation*, which preserves those portions or features that convey the structure's historical, cultural, or architectural values while making compatible use of the property possible. Because this approach involves the freedom to assign a new use to the historic property, it is also referred to as *adaptive use*. Rehabilitation describes a suitable approach when existing historic features are damaged or deteriorated, or modifications are made to update portions of the structure. Generally, the changes are most radical on the interior, where more latitude may be taken, such as adding new mechanical systems or handicapped-accessible features. Exterior changes are generally minimal, however, to maintain the building's historic integrity.

A large and successful adaptive use project is the rehabilitation of Union Station in St. Louis, Missouri. Union Station was built in the 1890s during the height of the railroad era. The station was very large, serving more than a hundred thousand rail passengers a day. The Romanesque-style station included a Grand Hall, with sweeping archways, fresco and gold-leaf detailing, mosaics, and an elaborate Tiffany window. The Victorian-inspired train shed, the largest ever constructed, covered more than eleven acres and could shelter thirty-two trains.

By the 1980s, the station complex was no longer needed for trains and sat underutilized in its center city location, awaiting demolition. Instead, it under-

Union Station, St. Louis, Missouri.

went a $150 million rehabilitation. The station building was adapted to many new uses, including a sophisticated restaurant in its fully restored Grand Hall. The large train shed houses a new shopping center, complete with chain store retail, independent small shops, numerous restaurants, a new hotel, and even a pond and small park area, lighted by the shed's large roof windows. Adaptive use of these structures has been very successful, and Union Station now is the most visited site in St. Louis.

When rehabilitation is chosen as the appropriate intervention, alterations and additions can be made, but they should be done in a way that avoids confusion with original historic elements. The rehabilitation standards are intended to guide project decisions so that alterations, additions, and related new construction are compatible with and protect the integrity of the historic property and surrounding context.

Each of the four types of intervention, as codified in the Secretary of the Interior's Standards, has its place, and owners and architects should carefully consider the appropriateness of an approach on a case-by-case basis. Projects are often a combination of approaches, but the overarching theme of one guides decisions for the entire project. Although the Union Station project in St. Louis is generally considered a rehabilitation project, it includes restoration treatment of the highly significant architectural spaces, such as the Grand Hall. Rehabilitation that makes its use as a restaurant possible involved adapting less significant spaces for supporting uses such as a commercial kitchen and mechanical equipment. New construction expanded and enclosed the train sheds for covered retail and dining uses in a style that was distinctly new yet compatible with the original train shed construction. (See chapter 3 for more discussion of contextual design issues.)

Conservation

The term *conservation* refers to the preservation of specific materials and the management of cultural property for the future. Conservation applies careful scientific analysis to understand the details of specific problems and justify appropriate solutions. Conservation activities include examination, documentation, and treatment and preventive care, supported by research and education. The professional conservator is responsible for the care and treatment of historic buildings and artifacts. Standards for professional conduct, scientific investigation, preventive conservation, treatment, documentation, and emergency situations have been established by the American Institute for Conservation of Historic and Artistic Works (AIC). Since 1972, when the AIC was organized, the field of conservation has grown to encompass diverse arenas in education, highly specialized practice, laboratory testing and research, and history and archives management.

One example of a conservation technique is the evaluation of colors used for historic structures. Research on which colors would have been applied historically to embellish buildings or artifacts is translated, through careful sampling and laboratory work, into a color palette that confirms the original treatment. This color palette is presented as an *accurate*, rather than speculative, record to guide future maintenance and restoration. Although it is still necessary to make an educated interpretation of the information, the resulting recommendations are ideally based on sound conservation guidelines.

An example of the ongoing use of research data for conservation purposes is the paint color and coatings analysis performed at Fallingwater, Frank Lloyd

Fallingwater, Mill Run, Pennsylvania.

Wright's home for the Kaufmann family at Mill Run, Pennsylvania. To begin, paint was sampled from various locations on both the concrete and metal elements of the structure. The samples were analyzed in a microscopy laboratory and the colors matched to the Munsell color system. Concurrent with taking the samples, selected areas of the paint coatings were scraped to expose the layers of previous coatings for a visual comparison and confirmation of the scientific analysis. During this on-site investigation, storage areas in the building and elsewhere on the grounds were inspected, and several cans of original paint materials were found that confirmed both the original color and material of the first concrete paint finish. Finally, historic research investigated Wright's intention for the original appearance of both colors, several options that he considered, and natural materials that provided his inspiration. Ultimately, custom colors were matched,

Paint sampling, Fallingwater.

using the Munsell color system, to serve as an objective reference for ongoing restoration projects, returning the interior and exterior finishes to their original, Wright-designed appearance.[3]

Conservators often step from objective analysis directly into application of the restorative work, following professional guidelines for treatment or intervention. Treatments require a thorough knowledge of material technology, both historical and contemporary. The most basic decision is whether to follow a literal application of historic construction methodology or to revise the treatment by adapting modern technology in an appropriate and sensitive manner. Sometimes a compromise approach is deemed to be the wisest course of action.

Cements used for masonry restoration are a case in point. Before 1871, Portland cement was largely unavailable, so most nineteenth-century and older buildings were constructed without the use of any modern cements. Instead, builders relied on natural cements or hydraulic lime of various sources for the cementing properties of mortar. Today, so many modern materials for repointing and reconstruction are used that it is important to first understand the properties of the masonry units, particularly their compressive strength, before initiating repairs.

The composition of historic mortar can be confirmed by laboratory analysis, resulting in a recommendation for a compatible repair mortar that will ensure repairs do not harm the masonry units. Too often, readily available bagged cements are used for convenience, resulting in damage to softer masonry units found in historic masonry walls. The primary guideline is to use mortar that is softer (in compressive strength) than the masonry units in which the mortar is applied. Aesthetic matching of cementing material color, sand/aggregate color and size, and tooling of the joints is also specified. The conservator or preservation professional makes detailed recommendations to achieve this aesthetic match, in addition to writing the technical specifications for the mortar recipe for masonry repairs.

RESEARCH AND DOCUMENTATION OF HISTORIC PROPERTIES

Researching historic properties is both a craft and an art. The craft is in piecing together information on a property from disparate sources; the art is in its interpretation. This research process is fundamental to historic preservation and demands investigative prowess, good writing skills, the ability to follow directions, and sometimes a touch of luck.

The Literature/Resource Search

Whether designation or treatment is desired, the first step is to research and document a property. A good place to begin is with the current or former owner of the property. Either may have photographs, old news clippings about the site, or even plans from the original construction or from a later construction project that include information about original conditions. The architectural or construction firm that designed or built the building may still be in business, and their files may include valuable materials. The records in the local building or engineering department may provide important information, including the title history and key dates for changes made to a property. Building permits and records of sewer and/or water taps may be valuable dating tools.

Information also may be found in the local history section of a nearby library or historical society. Collections of local archival information are often stored there, and, although they may be difficult to search through, they may yield material well worth the effort. Old city directories provide perhaps the richest source for building-specific data. If a specific date is known, newspapers can be searched, usually on microfilm or microfiche. County courthouses may have important information relating to property ownership and disposition. Abstracts of Title, which document the chain of title/ownership, may have been filed with the court for cases involving disputed ownership. Probate courts often have wills and property inventories that can be especially useful in determining the character of a property at the time of death of a previous owner.

Most counties and states, and some cities, have compiled and published their own histories. These works usually are available at local or state libraries, though many are becoming quite rare and rate placement in the "reserve" section of the library, meaning that they cannot be checked out. Sometimes a book is written about a historic structure to commemorate its construction and dedication; such a volume may contain copies of old photographs and stories about important personages from the period of construction. The date of construction can also be used as a guide in searching vintage professional architecture and construction journals, such as *Inland Architect.* Builder's catalogs, too, may have pertinent information. For example, a marketing brochure from the Cleveland Quarry, dated 1909, included photographs and data about several buildings using their stone. In researching materials used at the Milwaukee City Hall for a Historic Structure Report, this brochure essentially confirmed the type and cost of stone, making it possible to specify a match for repairs and replacement. State libraries and archives may be useful, especially for deciphering the larger historical context of the property. Genealogical societies, U.S. Census data, and university archives are often fruitful sources of historical information. For a significant historic property, the Library of Congress, including the HABS, HAER, and HALS files, may be a useful resource.

Maps and City Lithographs (Bird's-Eye Perspectives)

Plat maps, vintage atlases and gazetteers, and other historic maps are invaluable graphic resources. Many types of historic maps can provide a wealth of land division, ownership, and individual property information. Among the most useful are the nineteenth- and early-twentieth-century large format atlases that were published by many counties throughout the nation. These often have beautiful lithographic images of both rural and urban scenes that include highly detailed views

1902 lithograph of Pittsburgh, Pennsylvania. Reproduced with permission from the Historical Society of Western Pennsylvania, Pittsburgh.

of specific places. Such atlases were most often sold by subscription, so only those property owners who paid a fee had their property view included, but those that were shown are a veritable smorgasbord of cultural information.

In the mid- to late nineteenth century, a group of traveling artists made their living by drawing detailed "bird's-eye" perspectives of the towns in which they stayed. They then sold copies of these lithographs to residents. Though not technically maps, these very detailed perspective drawings showed the streets and roads, natural features, railroads, and structures. They were carefully prepared because their sales potential depended on accurate depictions, from which residents could pick out views of their own homes and businesses and those of their neighbors. A good-quality lithograph, suitable for framing, sold for only two to five dollars, so many were purchased. Even now, they are readily found in local archival repositories and often found among personal household memorabilia. The drawing and selling of city lithographs flourished from the 1850s until the end of the nineteenth century. For historians and preservationists, they are rich documents that accurately portray a city or town during a particular time period.

Excellent collections of city lithographs have been assembled by urban historian John Reps in his *Views and Viewmakers of Urban America* and *Bird's Eye Views: Historic Lithographs of North American Cities*.[4] Originals can be purchased from book or ephemera dealers, and quality reproductions are available through the company Reps founded in 1964, Historic Urban Plans.

Sanborn Fire Insurance Maps

A related and equally valuable source of historical information is the Sanborn Fire Insurance Map series. Published by the Sanborn Map Company from the mid-1800s to the present day, they show, in very accurate detail, the street layout and existing buildings in approximately twelve thousand U.S. cities. Building information includes size, type of construction, condition and use, and an indication of how far from a water source a building is located. Elements of building

Sanborn Insurance Map, Uniontown, Pennsylvania.
Copyright 1872 Sanborn Map Company, EDR Sanborn, Inc. (This Sanborn Map^{TM} is reproduced with permission from EDR Sanborn, Inc. All further reproductions are prohibited without prior written permission from EDR Sanborn, Inc.)

construction are shown by color: yellow indicates wood frame construction, pink indicates brick, blue indicates stone or concrete, etc. Other symbols identify the roofing style, placement of windows, thickness of walls, height of buildings, and distance from sidewalks.

Although developed primarily for insurance purposes, these maps have become important historical documents. Their publication dates vary from city to city; during certain periods they were released almost annually, whereas during other periods ten or twenty years passed between dates of publication. In many cases updates were pasted directly over the previous map, making it difficult to evaluate the earlier version.

Sanborn maps are indispensable for studying the changes of urbanized areas over decades. They may be used in combination with census information, archival photographs, old city directories and gazetteers, and other research materials to identify buildings and neighborhoods at various periods in history, examine local businesses and view changes in a city's business and industrial base, study the development of water, rail, and highway transportation in urban areas, and understand the frequency of types of building materials used for different building types·

EDR, Inc., the copyright holder of all Sanborn maps, owns the largest extant collection in microfilm format and takes its fiduciary responsibilities and ownership seriously. Copies of Sanborn maps can be purchased directly from EDR, or institutional digital access may be available through its agent, ProQuest LLC. Caveats include the fact that digital access is primarily in black and white, and that copyright permission is required to reproduce the maps.

Oral Traditions

Researchers often overlook the wealth of information held by people who have lived for many years in or near a historic property. Much can be gained by asking property owners, tenants, and neighbors for information. Sometimes the best way is simply to ask them to tell the stories they know about the place, who lived there, and what happened there.

Workers and contractors, if they can be found, can also provide useful information on techniques of original construction or changes made over time. They may provide a historical context for construction methods appropriate to a period and help establish when work was completed. They may also describe the significance of craftsmanship techniques found at a property and give weight to

Oral interview.

arguments for the property's designation. Good guides for conducting oral histories can be found readily on the Internet. It is not as easy as it may seem to interview one of these "experts," so time spent preparing for an interview is time well spent.

Reading the Building

The building or structure itself is a valuable source of information. In a process we call "reading the building," students of preservation can be trained to look not only at the basic structure but also for architectural changes and discontinuities. Blocked-in doors and windows, scarfed beams, or breaks in molding may indicate a previous iteration of a structure. Residential structures are more difficult to "read" because of frequency of changes by homeowners, whereas public and commercial buildings often have more visible clues to their history. Other details include a cornerstone, upper-level date or name plaque, ghost images of a previous use or material, or a cast-iron column with the foundry name and location in raised letters. Some cultural resource management and architectural restoration firms specialize in these investigations, which can result in reports on historic structure or condition assessment. *Preservation Briefs*, published by Technical Preservation Services of the National Park Service, particularly Numbers 17 and 35, provide many suggestions for identifying the visual character and significant

Ghosted feature from Lincoln Tallman House outbuilding, Janesville, Wisconsin.

features of a historic building. Preserving and protecting the materials and features that convey the historic significance of a place begin with careful architectural investigations, as well as historical research and focused documentation of the resource.

Documenting with Measured Drawings

The documentation of structures can be accomplished through preparation of field-measured drawings. Such drawings allow the documenter to record notes and sketches based on direct observation. If done in an orderly manner, these field drawings provide the basis for preparation of hard-line architectural drawings and may become part of a comprehensive Historic American Buildings Survey (HABS) documentation or a component of a Historic Structure Report. The level of detail and quantity of sketches are dependent on the intended use and time available in the field.

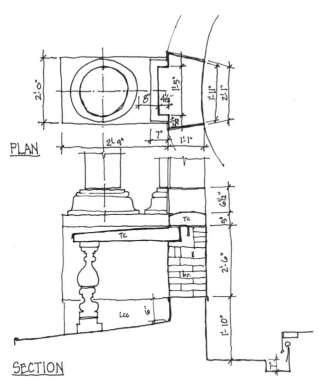

PLAN

SECTION

Copy of a "field-measured drawing," First Church of Christ, Scientist, Boston, Massachusetts.

Measured drawings are prepared in two steps. First, sketches are made at the site, including floor plans, elevations, and as many architectural details as can be reasonably sketched during the field visit. It is highly recommended that field sketches be drawn on graph paper with a grid of one-eighth-inch squares, within a larger one-inch grid, using a clipboard "desk." Each square of the grid can represent a given scaled area; for plans and elevations, a common scale is one square equals one square foot, or one-eighth-inch equals one foot.

Care must be taken to record information clearly, neatly, accurately, and unambiguously. Guidelines established by HABS should generally be followed, particularly if the ultimate product will be submitted to HABS. These outline field sketching methods, describe several drafting techniques, and allow for uniformity of documents as well as clear reproduction capability.

When collecting dimensions for measured drawings, the most effective approach is for a team of two or three people to work together at the site. One person prepares the sketch drawings and one or two assistants read dimensions

Reese Grist Mill, Greene County, Pennsylvania.

Drawings of Reese Grist Mill.

from a tape measure. Measurements should be read off as running dimensions—that is, a long (hundred-foot) tape measure should be held at one corner of the structure and distances to doors, windows, and other elements on one wall read without moving the tape. This technique avoids the compilation of errors that would likely occur if the tape were shifted for each measurement. Dimensions are placed on the sketches; using an alternate (red) color for dimensions makes the lines and numbers easier to distinguish from the line drawings. Materials and conditions, possibly in an alternate (blue) color, are also noted right on the sketches.

The second step is creating hard-line drawings from the field sketches. Traditional HABS drawings are still created by hand, drawing in ink on Mylar drafting film. Standards can be found on the HABS Web site and should be followed explicitly if the ultimate goal is to submit the drawings to the archival collection in the Library of Congress. In recent years, HABS standards have been expanded to include computer-generated drawings, referencing the same standards for detail and appearance. Views generally include floor plans, elevations, architectural details, and construction elements, depending on the complexity and significance of the building. (Note: Refer also to the later section in this chapter on Physical Investigation and Field Survey.)

Photographic Techniques

Digital photography has become an accepted standard in photographing existing conditions for historic resources of all types. A rule-of-thumb is to use the highest available image quality setting in a .jpg format, so that details are viewable when using the zoom feature. (A suggested image quality minimum is at the "fine" level with a 5 megapixel camera.) Digital photography allows photos to be directly downloaded to computers. The digital images can be incorporated into computer drawings (computer-assisted drawing, or CAD) and replace or supplement drawn details. Digital photos can also be used as part of the construction drawings, with arrows, notes, and dimensions applied directly to them.

The use of digital cameras combined with notebook computers enables architects to work on CAD drawings directly at a project site, saving time and increasing the accuracy of their work. The resulting computer drawings can be sent instantaneously as .dwg or .pdf files to offices anywhere in the world and returned in the same format. The primary limitation of this technique is the battery life of the camera and the computer.

Rectified photography is another relatively simple technique. Targets are placed on a structure at a set distance apart when photos are taken. The targets define the scale when used on a photograph of the structure and provide reference points for a superimposed grid. With this grid drawn over a photograph, measurements of a structure can be derived for any elevation perpendicular to the camera directly from the photo rather than from laborious on-site measuring. Obviously, such derived measurements are not as accurate as actual site measurements, but in many instances they are sufficiently precise for the intended purpose. To measure some features, such as large flat walls with repetitive punched openings, the technique actually may be preferable because of the difficulty of measuring repetitive building details that are out of reach. A drawback of rectified photography is that it can be used accurately only on flat elevations. Recesses or projections change in scale, and angled surfaces are distorted unless photographed separately with the camera perpendicular to the angled surface.

Some architects and contractors use radar to locate building materials that cannot be seen by eye. For example, radar can detect the location of metal anchors within masonry walls. Infrared sensing is a method of identifying energy performance of buildings, particularly with respect to areas of heat loss or water infiltration. Although a method of illustrating conditions, this system is not used to create background drawings.

High definition survey (HDS) is an emerging photographic tool used to create accurate computer drawings of existing conditions. Also known as 3D laser scanning, HDS uses a special digital camera to capture existing conditions of the built and natural environment in minute detail. Instead of registering photographic data on film, laser beams travel to an object and back to the scanner. The actual 3D location of the 'hit' is registered in a database. Multiple hits can occur within a small distance, giving an actual point contour of the surface. This results in a "cloud of points" that map out a complete surface; multiple laser scans can be combined to generate a 3D cloud showing all sides or even sections through the building. With minor conversions to the digitally collected data, the point cloud is referenced into engineering design software, such as AutoCAD or MicroStation, and used as backgrounds for design work. Special software applications, such as the CloudWorx plug-in, allow the point cloud to be turned on or off, filtered, or its resolution adjusted or clipped to focus on an object or area of interest. Thus it is possible to trace information in the point cloud images and create detailed as-built drawings. The information is dimensionally accurate in all

HDS scan converted to AutoCAD drawing.

three dimensions, and images can be rotated to any angle for views not available by flat camera images alone.

HISTORIC STRUCTURE REPORTS

A historic structure report (HSR) guides the restoration of a historic building, much as a roadmap guides the traveler to his or her destination. Its general content is a two-fold narrative of the structure's developmental history and recommendations for its treatment and use. A third component, rarely incorporated into the actual HSR, addresses work that has been carried out. Far more important is establishing the basis on which the work can be executed with accuracy, integrity, and respect for the structure's historic and cultural significance. Supplemental information, such as a bibliography, references, field survey data, measured drawings, photographs, materials testing reports, and copies of relevant historic documents, is placed in appendices, which are as important as the body of the report itself.

The first HSR in the United States, *The Moore House: The Site of the Surrender—Yorktown*, was written by Charles E. Peterson for the National Park Service in 1935. Since this HSR *followed* the restoration of the site, it established a practice of providing a "completion report" describing the work that was carried out and including attached drawings and specifications, fiscal information, comments on new information or additional research, and statements detailing where the work may have deviated from the information in the recommendations section. This form of documenting historic buildings has become increasingly standardized, culminating in 2004 in the publication of *Preservation Brief No. 43: The Preparation and Use of Historic Structure Reports*, written for the National Park Service. This was the first time basic information about the HSR process, accompanied by a sample outline, was made readily accessible to the public. Although a complex task, this diagram simplifies the understanding with a graphic representation of the parts essential to an HSR.

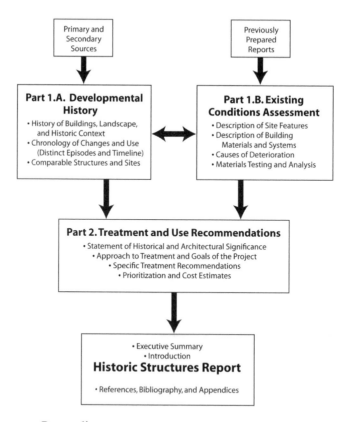

Historic Structure Report diagram.

Chronology, Timeline, and Episode Descriptions

A useful component of the HSR is the Chronology of Development and Use, which describes dates of original construction, modifications, and changes in use. Making it into a graphic expression of historical events associated with the building enhances the chronology statement and provides a tool for defining key "episodes" in the development of the site. In turn, these episodes provide a framework for placing key features of a building in one period or another, thereby guiding the decision of how to treat those features.

In the HSR for the Milwaukee City Hall, for example, it became pivotal to determine the dates associated with changes to the historic clock tower. Because of severe damage following a fire in 1929, the clock faces were entirely blackened and unreadable. The clock tower was partially rebuilt and the clock faces entirely

Milwaukee City Hall clock tower. Courtesy of Eric Oxendorf.

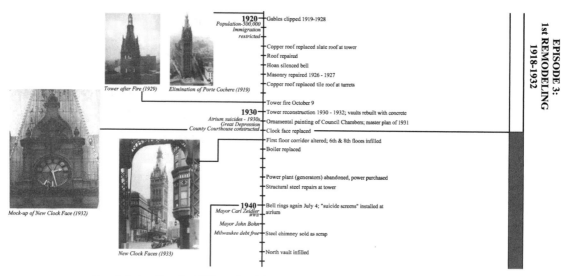

Partial timeline for Milwaukee City Hall HSR.

reworked, altering their appearance from the street by switching from a white face with black tick marks and clock hands to a black clock face with white painted tick marks and hands. Returning the clock faces to their original appearance was not only feasible, but would complement and support restoration of the building's exterior appearance to the earlier episode.[5]

Physical Investigation and Field Survey

Field surveys are an important part of the physical investigation for an HSR and for documenting existing conditions in other preservation projects. This is when the researcher is able to use all of his or her senses to "read" the building and absorb any subliminal messages gleaned from the site.

When performing such a physical investigation, the following key steps typically are included:

1. Make mental and written notes of the building's key elements—its overall features and details—that contribute to the building's historic significance, from the exterior as well as the interior. A previously prepared survey worksheet is an immensely helpful tool for recording key materials, features, and their condition.

2. Assess the building's structural condition (first, is it safe?) and consider the integrity of the basic structure and materials that give the building its form and finished appearance. Note what appears unsafe, changed, or out-of-synch with the prototypical building type or era of construction.

3. Search for evidence of modifications and additions and attempt to confirm the date of original construction and sequence of changes. Ghosting from missing or moved elements, obvious infill areas, as well as changes in the exterior skin all provide clues to changes over time.

4. Using basic grid paper, sketch primary building façades and floor plans as a base for notations and measurements. Drawings need not be to scale as long as the essential information is captured. Assign room numbers and window and door numbers to create a logical system for an inventory of conditions. Record some of the information separately from the drawings, using lists or schedules to organize it.

5. Measure the overall building footprint to obtain basic information for scaling or estimating the cost of recommended work. Measure openings to consider modifications that may be required to meet building and accessibility requirements. Measure or estimate heights of overall building façades, prominent features (such as a tower), and interior ceilings.

6. Photograph the building in context, overall exterior elevations, key and typical details, and areas where further consideration may be required. Photograph interiors, room by room, from diagonally opposing corners, as well as selected interior details. Use a photolog and/or sketch plans to identify photo locations for future reference. Methodical notations in the field take time but are invaluable back in the office.

7. Conduct a room-by-room survey of interior conditions using previously prepared survey worksheets. Make sure each worksheet is labeled correctly with room name and/or number, date, surveyor's name, and building name.

8. Inventory the structural system (e.g., balloon frame or masonry bearing walls), mechanical systems (e.g., radiators or ductwork), electrical system (e.g., wiring and light fixtures), and other systems (e.g., elevators or intercom) that may be relevant to the historic building. Consultants who specialize in these disciplines also may be part of the survey team, and these tasks can be delegated to them.

Drawings illustrating the structure at various periods in its history can be used in conjunction with episode descriptions. Along with narrative descriptions, these episode drawings make the developmental history easier to understand. Showing the original construction plans with black lines, subsequent changes are shown in a contrasting (red) color, with uncertain speculative conditions illustrated in a third (blue) color. Such episode drawings are included as an appendix to the HSR.

CULTURAL LANDSCAPE REPORTS

Like the HSR, a cultural landscape report (CLR) provides a guide for treating the historically important "cultural landscape" (see Chapter 11) and is the primary tool for its long-term management. Initially incorporated into the HSR, the CLR took on more importance when the National Park Service established the need for "Historic Grounds Reports" in the 1960s as a stand-alone document for cultural sites that were not otherwise being considered as historic and documented in an HSR.[6]

Organized like the HSR, the CLR presents the developmental history and recommendations for treatment and use. Because the CLR is generally written in advance of performing the recommended work, a supplemental record of treatment may be completed at a later date. Supplemental information for the appendix is similar to that for an HSR and includes a bibliography, references, field survey data, maps, photographs, technical reports, and copies of relevant historic documents.

Cultural Resource Management Guideline, NPS-28[7] serves as the guide for cultural landscape management. Initially released in 1981, it has been updated several times and sets the standard for preparing the CLR. In addition, *Preservation Brief 36: Protecting Cultural Landscapes: Planning, Treatment, and Management of Historic Landscapes* provides a step-by-step process for documenting historic designed and vernacular landscapes.[8]

THE ROLE OF ARCHEOLOGY

Archeology represents another important aspect of preservation research. This field deals with the physical remains of past human activities and yields information important to both prehistory and history. Prehistoric studies focus on the Native American past prior to contact with Europeans; historic archeology generally includes the period from the time of European contact to the present. Archeologists study past human behavior through the examination of remaining material culture of previous human societies. Archeologists identify the information content and determine its importance to scientific and scholarly research. Artifacts often yield information that can be put into one of three categories: historical documentation, material culture/commodities, or ideas. Historical documentation may provide information about the use of artifacts at various time periods and the technologies associated with them, such as early tools. For example, archeological research has revealed information on how the earliest colonial settlers at Jamestown, Virginia, traded glass beads for food with the Native Americans.

Artifacts used as commodities provide information on consumer behavior at different time periods and can represent differences in socioeconomic status. For instance, unearthed pottery shards may include names or registry marks that indicate the manufacturer and date. Artifacts can also convey implicit information about the ideas of groups or cultures being analyzed because they represent what

Archaeological excavation, Lower Colorado Region. Courtesy U.S. Department of the Interior, Bureau of Reclamation, Lower Colorado Region Resources Management Office.

is most important to those cultures. Religious symbols can provide meaningful clues of the spiritual side of a culture or community.

In the United States, the most practiced branch of archeology is referred to as cultural resource management (CRM). This approach is largely based on the requirements of the National Historic Preservation Act of 1966, which mandated that no construction project on public land or involving public funds could proceed if it damaged an unstudied or suspected archeological site. The steps involved begin with a cursory review of a site to determine if there are any significant archeological areas that would be affected by construction. If any exist, time and money must be allocated for their excavation. If the site is determined to have extraordinary significance, construction may be prohibited entirely, though this scenario is rare.

Some archeological excavations, although useful for historical and scientific reasons, have elicited protests from some Native American populations that consider the practice to be a desecration of sacred ancestral burial sites. For many years, archeologists removed and stored burial remains for further study. In a native perspective, however, history is seen as cyclical rather than linear, and disturbing the past by digging it up, removing it, and storing it can have dire consequences for the present. An attempt to resolve this conflict was addressed through the Native American Graves Protection and Repatriation Act (NAGPRA, 1990), which has encouraged a dialogue between the scientists and native peoples, and has resulted in the return of many human remains and funerary objects by some of the most prestigious museums in the nation to bona fide Native American claimants.

A further examination of the role of archeology is based on recognition that many native peoples see natural features, such as lakes and mountains, as sacred sites with great cultural significance that should be protected. One of the most well-known examples involves the Aborigines in Australia. The incredibly beautiful and magnificent rock in the center of the continent known as *Uluru* (formerly known by the British as Ayers Rock) is an important totem to the Aboriginal culture, representing the essence and spirit that had its beginning in "Dreamtime," the source of all life forces. Representatives of the Aborigines have demanded that tourists no longer climb the sacred rock, out of respect for its cultural significance and because the climbing route crosses an important "dreaming track." Similarly, in the United States the Sangre de Cristo Mountains in New Mexico and Colorado hold a place of reverence for some Native American populations.

TECHNOLOGY OF BUILDING SYSTEMS

Roofs

Water is the enemy. Roof materials provide the first line of defense in keeping water out and protect the structure and historic fabric below the roof. Therefore, this system is critical to structural integrity. Roof materials may also contribute to the historic significance of the structure, however, so it is important to identify the status of the original materials, whether they are extant or deteriorated, because it is necessary to determine the cause of failure (i.e., leaks). Careful inspection of conditions can begin from the ground, but eventually close access using ladders or lifts may be required, especially if there is no roof hatch to provide access.

Walking on the surface of a flat roof or leaning out of dormers or hatches allows you to probe for wetness below the membrane surface, observe torn or blistered membranes, mold and moss growth, broken tiles/slates, or cracked flashing, and to consider how many layers of roofing may have been placed over the original materials. Sometimes a probe or cut, which should then be patched, is required to confirm this information. It is also important to look at the underside of the roof structure to check for wet spots, staining from current or old leaks, visibly rotted materials, or efflorescence. This observation helps develop an understanding of original construction methods, which may also have contributed to failure of the roof system. Poorly drained roofing results in ponding on flat roofs, and inadequate flashing may allow water to penetrate behind the roofing into the structural framing.

All materials have an estimated useful life (usually expressed in a range of years from minimal to optimal). When exposed to weathering conditions, asphalt shingles and built-up bituminous roofing, for instance, can be expected to perform adequately for fifteen to thirty years, whereas slate and tile roofing, if properly installed and maintained, can last from eighty to one hundred years. If the underlying structure is protected by a watertight roof system, then the structural frame should last indefinitely. If there has been radical change over the lifetime of the building, then recommendations will have to accommodate conditions at the time of inspection.

The Old Courthouse in St. Louis, Missouri, housed thirteen courtrooms that were in use from 1845 until 1930, and served as a public gathering place for pioneers planning their westward trek across the plains. The courthouse dome,

Old Courthouse, St. Louis, Missouri.

which dominated the city's skyline until the turn of the twentieth century, was the first to use a cast-iron structural frame, even before the national Capitol. Both the cast-iron dome and the heavy timber-framed lower structure were clad in copper.

By the time the National Park Service took over the property in the 1930s, the building had suffered years of neglect. The entire roof structure was rebuilt with structural steel, sheathed with gypsum deck, and clad in lead-coated copper. These changes to the roof structure affected the building's design, slightly raising the parapet and eliminating the external downspouts. This system has been maintained until the present time, when gradually deteriorating conditions warranted study and documentation for replacement. The parapet and drainage system could not be reversed to pre-1940s state, but the metal roof is able to be replaced in copper, allowing the natural patina to develop to match the green dome. The seams, valleys, and other features of the roof are designed to match the 1940s design, which in itself was designed to match the original, pre-1940s historic metal roof.

Roof materials are usually considered "sacrificial" due to their exposure and their protective function. They must be replaced, because they cannot be restored, in all practicality, even if the materials themselves are highly significant to the structure. Replication of an original roofing system can be very expensive, and consideration may be given to substituting modern materials. Aesthetically and historically, this is not the preferred route. Most traditional roofing materials are readily available, and there are skilled roofing tradespeople willing to perform the work. Quality assurance is critical for this work, and references and examples of prior experience should be requested to evaluate qualifications of the construction team. Using a mockup installation provides another checkpoint at which to approve the overall system before proceeding with the entire project, and inspections should be conducted at regular intervals during the work.

Windows

Windows contribute in two primary ways: by providing natural light and ventilation to the interior of a building. How well they serve these two purposes depends on their condition and the use of the building. The openings are functionally important, but they are also significant to a building's historic style and integrity. Due to heavy use and weather exposure, they are a frequent casualty in a restoration project, as owners will consider their windows expendable in their concern about costs and energy conservation.

The Secretary of the Interior's *Standards for Rehabilitation (No. 6)* states that repair is preferable to replacement, and that efforts should be made to repair existing windows (and doors), if possible. When the severity of deterioration requires replacement, then new windows should match the old in design, color, texture, and material that is substantiated by documentary and physical evidence. Use of newer materials changes the original design and must be weighed against the loss of integrity of the original fabric.

Vinyl windows are a controversial case in point. With promises of a lifetime warranty, extravagant energy savings, and no maintenance, marketing has been

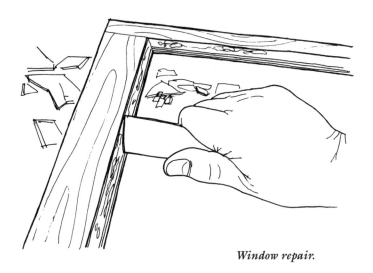

Window repair.

aggressive and highly successful in replacing old wood sash with new, extruded vinyl replacement sash. This change removes historic fabric and results in a reduced glass area with a markedly different profile. Typically, tax credits are denied by the National Park Service for projects that use vinyl replacement windows.

Several manufacturers offer more compatible replacement options, using wood for wood, or steel for steel, or even aluminum that approximates either the wood or original steel sash. The most difficult feature to match is the glass. Thickness of insulated glass is inherently greater for two panes, plus the airspace, than for the original single pane. If the sash is thick enough, then replacement glass can be accommodated with no overall change—except that the stops holding the glass in place will no longer be traditional putty but either wood or aluminum. Once painted, the replacement sash should closely match the original.

This is easiest to accomplish for sashes that have no internal muntins dividing the lights within the frame, but are one large pane of glass filling an entire sash. To replicate divided lights, it is best to use a single insulated panel for the sash and apply muntins to both exterior and interior faces, making sure that there are spacers within the insulated panel that exactly correspond to the muntin pattern. Requesting a darker bronze spacer will improve the appearance of double glazing.

Conservation of existing sashes and frames should be given careful consideration, because doing so is often cost-effective when compared to full replacement with comparable value units. Remember that old-growth wood is far more durable and resistant to rot and damage than newer material. Consider also the contribution of the original windows to the overall significance of the property. The wood may be fine with a new coat of paint, new weatherstripping, and reglazing. Replacement with insulated glass, discussed above, may be an option for thicker sash; typically a minimum thickness of 1¾ inch is required for routing a wood sash deep enough to accept insulated glass. It is especially important that the row stops achieve an adequate bite to fully cover and conceal the spacer; that is the most vulnerable component of the insulated glass assembly, and increasing the bite protects it from harsh UV light.

Exterior Walls

Exterior walls keep out the weather and hold up the roof. Keeping exterior walls in good condition is therefore essential to the integrity of the structure. Although there may be an interior structural system, the exterior cladding defines the character of the building at its public face and can only perform as well as it is constructed and maintained.

Masonry walls are composed of multiple units that, when stacked and mortared together, form a composite wall system that both resists water penetration and bears the weight of the roof, wind, and any other forces. Maintenance

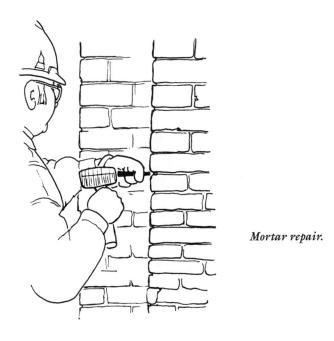

Mortar repair.

addresses both the masonry units themselves and the mortar between them. If these two components perform adequately, then the interior finishes are protected.

There is also the aesthetic quality or character of masonry walls to be considered. The type of masonry, profiles and details of individual units and the finished face are all important details that contribute to the significance and overall integrity of a historic building. Rough masonry surfaces attract dirt in a number of ways—from airborne pollutants, pigeons, human hands, and as the result of contact with metals. Masonry also suffers attack from acids in rain, the stress of moisture freezing and thawing in the walls, and impact damage caused by people and machines. Conservation efforts address these problems separately. Repairs are typically executed before cleaning the walls to eliminate moisture penetration

Disassembly and repair of masonry cornice.

and further damage. Repair options include repointing open and eroded mortar joints, replacing broken and damaged masonry, injecting epoxies at cracks, and patching with a cementitious compound tinted to match the adjacent masonry. Repaired walls are then cleaned using the "gentlest means possible" to remove disfiguring stains and deposits without damaging the masonry.

Before work is carried out, cleaning materials and methods should be tested for both their effectiveness *and* affect on the structure. General cleaning using a low-pressure spray application of water to soften the dirt and rinse it away may be sufficient. If not, chemical cleaners of increasing strength can be tested and applied according to manufacturer's instructions. An approved test panel is used to compare and approve results of the cleaning operation. Special cleaning may be needed for deeply embedded stains caused by bird repellent chemicals or runoff from copper flashing. Products that aggressively draw out these stains are usually applied as a poultice, but they must be used with caution and then neutralized and rinsed off thoroughly.

Additional treatments to consider include consolidants that penetrate and strengthen the masonry and water repellents to reduce water absorption or maintain a cleaner surface. These are extreme measures and should be used only with the utmost caution and knowledge of expected results based on pretesting. Abrasive cleaning is used only in rare instances, and is generally prohibited unless all other methods are found ineffective.

CASE STUDY: THE FIRST CHURCH OF CHRIST, SCIENTIST, BOSTON

The First Church of Christ, Scientist, was founded on the teachings of Mary Baker Eddy in the latter part of the nineteenth century. When membership grew and meeting in members' homes was no longer feasible, a church was constructed in 1895 with seating for fifteen hundred. Before the doors had even opened, membership had outgrown the Romanesque-style rustic granite building, and plans were underway to construct an addition. The extension was completed less than ten years later with seating for five thousand in a classical style with elaborately carved granite and limestone walls topped with domes and a cupola of white glazed terra cotta.

Maintenance on this structure has been diligent and sensitive over the years. In the 1950s, the steel framework of the central dome was repaired and the terra

First Church of Christ, Scientist, Boston. Courtesy of Stephen Graham.

cotta replaced. Even so, the building had never been cleaned properly. Many exterior materials had deteriorated and required intervention and comprehensive treatment to restore the church's appearance. A comprehensive preservation plan was implemented over a period of ten years. Blackened with carbon deposits, the building's carved limestone detailing of column capitals and large cornices was especially encrusted. Granite surfaces were eroding and flaking. The exterior conditions were evaluated and the various stone materials used in the façade tested because the cause of erosion was unknown. Materials for cleaning and consolidating the stone were also tested, both in the laboratory and on site.

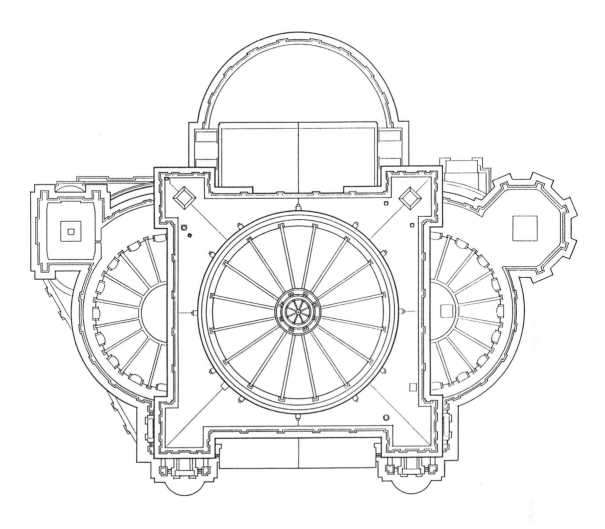

Roof plan of First Church of Christ, Scientist.

The information gained from these tests was put to use in a complex program of cleaning and renewal. No harsh chemicals were required to remove the carbon crusts; they were simply softened and washed away with water. Specially formulated chemicals removed stubborn stains caused by pigeon repellents, copper and iron deposits, and mildew. As work progressed, adjustments were made in the chemicals, in their concentration or dilution, in the amount of their dwell time on the stone surfaces, and in the number of cycles or applications of the chemical that obtained the best results with the least effect on the stone.

Abrasive cleaning methods, for example, sandblasting, were not used to remove soil, as this would have also removed the fragile stone surface and detail. Acid rain was already visibly affecting some limestone areas. After the stone was carefully scraped with hand tools to remove larger flakes and delamination of the granite, abrasive materials were used to smooth and feather the rough edges.

To protect cleaned surfaces, a water repellent with consolidant was applied over the limestone walls. In addition to keeping the stone surfaces cleaner, the repellent prevents salts from leaching out of the limestone and washing over the granite surfaces below. Restorers determined that the granite was not of the most durable quality; it was susceptible to erosion and flaking due to a chemical reaction with the runoff from the limestone. Underneath the repellent, a stone consolidant was applied to the granite to strengthen and reinforce the cellular structure of the stone. Repairs at the exterior masonry also included patching deteriorated stone, replacing selected damaged stones, and repointing eroded and open mortar joints. Sealants were used only on horizontal or sky-facing joints of parapet capstones and wide horizontal ledges.

CONCRETE

Although typically viewed as a "modern" material, concrete has been used for millennia, dating to the Roman use of "pozzolanic" concrete for both mortar and cast-in-place concrete. After centuries of being ignored or forgotten, concrete regained popular use in the nineteenth century after the development of Portland cement, which improved quality control and strength of the finished material.

Architectural use of concrete is a twentieth-century phenomenon, and nowhere is it more celebrated than in the accurate, full-scale replica of the Parthenon built in Nashville, Tennessee. John J. Earley was a pioneer in the use of concrete to create beautiful buildings that took advantage of its inherent attributes. By carefully selecting aggregates, Earley designed a concrete mix for the Nashville Parthenon. Its appearance was a result of buff-colored aggregates used in the mix to simulate the warm-toned masonry of the original structures at the Greek Acropolis. Scoring the poured concrete to simulate actual stone joints enhanced the perception of the building as masonry, rather than as a monolithic concrete structure.

Parthenon, Nashville. Courtesy of Gary Layda.

Restoration of the local landmark was accomplished by a team of experts that included preservation architects, architectural conservators, materials engineers, historians, and contractors. The team also included artists to model the pediment and metope sculptures, skilled craftsmen to replicate the ornamental trim, and decorative painters to restore the colorful peristyle plasterwork.[9]

CONSTRUCTION CODES AND REGULATORY CONCERNS

Most of the existing designated historic buildings were constructed long before the establishment of modern building regulations. When they undergo rehabilitation, therefore, they are likely to be subject to more restrictive building code requirements than were in effect when they were built. Some of these regulations create hardship for owners of historic properties. It is important to understand these potential problems before proceeding with rehabilitation.

Fire and Life Safety Codes

In the past, a fire in one structure could result in entire blocks of downtown buildings being lost. As a result, over the decades stricter fire safety regulations have been enacted. Although these regulations help protect property, their primary purpose is to allow for the safe exit of occupants.

TWO MEANS OF EGRESS

The primary goal of modern safety regulations is to provide for alternate means of egress (exit) for occupants of a building in case of fire. That is, a building needs to provide two ways of getting out from each level. Older buildings often had just one stairway connecting floors. When these buildings are updated, a second "fire-separated" stair must be added. The exception to this rule is small two-story buildings with few occupants, the uses of which do not include the assembly of large numbers of people, and which therefore may require only one stairway.

Older commercial buildings (e.g., stores and hotels) often had a large open staircase leading to upper floors. Such a stair opening can draw fire rapidly upward like a chimney. Fire code regulations typically insist on the enclosure of such open stairs, which often substantially changes the character of a historic interior. These open stairs typically do not count toward providing the required two means of egress.

SPRINKLER SYSTEMS

In older buildings, fire codes allow for some deviation from their strictest provisions if developers install a sprinkler system—a thermally activated system of sprinkler heads that spray water when temperatures in a room reach a certain level. However, these systems can add considerable cost to a small rehabilitation project and may also require the installation of a new main water supply line as well as new piping throughout the building.

Other fire and panic code regulations may also apply, depending on how spaces are used and their occupancy level. Several state building codes recently have addressed the problems that can be unique to historic buildings and other older structures with the introduction of rehabilitation building codes. These codes define levels of treatment for repairs, alterations, and additions. However, all regulations should be interpreted by an architect or code official.

Accessibility Codes

A movement to provide easier access to buildings for people with disabilities arose in the 1970s. People in wheelchairs and with other physical limitations often were unable to enter public buildings, restaurants, offices, and residential units. Accessibility (barrier-free) codes were adopted by many states, based on the principle that all persons should have full access to buildings that are open to the public. With the passage of the Americans with Disabilities Act (ADA) of 1990, access to properties open to the public is now a civil right, and both new and rehabilitated buildings must meet these requirements.

New buildings readily allow for universal access in their initial designs, but barrier-free regulations often make the rehabilitation of older structures challenging. A common requirement is to provide a ramp for wheelchair access to an entry located a few steps above grade. Because older buildings often feature raised entrances with stairs, the construction of ramps has become a common necessity on historic buildings. The maximum permissible slope of such a ramp is one foot vertical for every twelve feet horizontal if a handrail is used (without a handrail, the maximum slope is one foot vertical for every twenty feet horizontal). For example,

Access ramp.

an entrance three steps (twenty-one inches) above grade may require a ramp as long as twenty-one or more feet. Obviously, maintaining the historic character of the front entrance while adding such a prominent feature is a significant design challenge for architects and owners of historic properties.

To provide universal access to all floors inside, the installation of elevators is often necessary. This can be an expensive proposition, sometimes prohibitively so, especially if no section of the older building allows for the vertical shaft required for an elevator. One solution is to include elevators in an addition to the building that allows for such space. Sometimes, however, rehabilitation of a historic building is constrained by the difficulty of satisfying access requirements.

Barrier-free codes also require more spacious restroom facilities, with toilet stalls and open space large enough for a 5-foot turning radius of a wheelchair. New buildings can be designed to accommodate these spatial needs, but the facilities of older buildings are usually much too tight, often requiring workers to tear out walls and existing plumbing fixtures and install new ones.

To the greatest extent possible, historic buildings must be made as accessible as nonhistoric or new buildings, but without threatening or destroying their significance. State Historic Preservation Offices can be helpful in determining whether full accessibility requirements would threaten or destroy a structure's significance and in finding acceptable alternatives. If full compliance is not possible, then the following alternative requirements may be utilized (as described in the Americans with Disabilities Act Accessibility Guidelines, ADAAG):

- Site Accessible Route: At least one accessible route must be provided from a site access point to an accessible entrance.
- Ramps: A ramp may be used as part of an accessible route to an entrance.
- Entrances: At least one accessible entrance which is used by the public must be provided. Access must be provided to all levels of a building and facility whenever practicable.
- Toilet Rooms: If toilets are provided, then at least one toilet facility, which may be unisex in design, must be provided on an accessible route.
- Displays: Displays and written information should be located so as to be seen by a seated person.

Although compliance is always the desired objective, sometimes it is not possible to comply fully wth accessibility standards for rehabilitation work. To encourage creative solutions to accessibility, the ADA includes a provision, known as "equivalent facilitation," which allows for alternative design and technology to create substantially equivalent, or greater, access to a property as specified in the ADA Accessibility Guidelines. Tax incentives may be available to help absorb the costs of accessibility alterations.

Technology and design alterations can provide for an alternative experience that substitutes, to some degree, for lack of physical access. If the upper floors of a historic museum building are inaccessible to individuals in wheelchairs or with other disabilities, the experience of this space can be presented in a video that is shown regularly in an accessible area, together with a display of artifacts from the inaccessible portions of the building.

As a specific example, the National Park Service and its partners make every effort to accommodate visitors to the Old Courthouse and the Gateway Arch complex in St. Louis. Both sites have special exhibits and features for visitors with disabilities; however, historical and architectural features make visiting the top levels of both sites unreachable for visitors in wheelchairs, scooters, and strollers. For visitors who cannot visit the top levels of the Old Courthouse and the top of the Gateway Arch, there are accessibility kiosks at both locations where visitors can take a virtual tour. Those visitors who venture to the top of the Arch will encounter approximately ninety steps and considerable standing, but the rest of the Gateway Arch complex, such as the lobby, Museum of Westward Expansion, theaters, and museum stores are all accessible by ramps. For hearing-impaired visitors, audio enhancement devices are available.

Visitors to the Old Courthouse enter the building by using a wheelchair lift. Pressing the bell will alert a National Park Service Ranger to provide assistance. The museum galleries and rest rooms on the first floor of the Old Courthouse are fully accessible. Due to the historic nature of the building, the upper levels of the Old Courthouse, however, are not wheelchair accessible. The theater at the Old Courthouse has audio enhancement, and special audio-taped tours of the Old Courthouse are available.

Having a historic building is not an excuse for not providing access to the disabled, and every effort should be made to ensure a rich and satisfying experience for all individuals.

Chapter Eight

PRESERVATION ECONOMICS

———◆———

Preservation often comes down to a question of dollars and cents. Preservationists cannot expect the private sector to save older buildings if it results in a financial loss. Likewise, the public sector, with its limited resources, should not be expected to invest in older buildings unless it makes sense from a cost–benefit perspective or is of such significance that public subsidy is appropriate. The bottom line is, unless preservation makes financial sense, it may not get support from either the public or private sectors.

The good news is that, from a community perspective, preservation *does* make financial sense. Many economic advantages accrue from historic preservation—too many to list here. They are thoroughly documented, however, by a recognized expert on this topic, Donovan Rypkema of PlaceEconomics in Washington, D.C. He has listed and described one hundred financial advantages in his book *The Economics of Historic Preservation: A Community Leader's Guide.*[1] In a presentation in New York, Rypkema gave an abridged list of reasons why preservation benefits both economics and "Smart Growth," which included the following:[2]

- Almost without exception historic buildings are located where public infrastructure already exists. This can save both the community and the investor on the costs of new water lines, sewer lines, streets, curbs, and gutters.

- Municipalities need financial resources if they are going to grow smart. Vacant, unused, and underused historic buildings brought back to life are also brought back as tax-generating assets for a community.

- An element in the drive to encourage human movement by means other than the automobile is the interconnection of uses. Based on the foolishness of post–World War II planning and development patterns, uses have been sharply separated. Historic neighborhoods were built from the beginning with a mix of uses in close proximity. Cities with the foresight to readjust their zoning ordinances to encourage integration of uses are seeing that interconnectivity reemerging in historic areas.

- In many places . . . people are moving "back to the city." But almost nowhere is it back to the city in general. In nearly every instance it is back to the historic neighborhoods and historic buildings within the city. We need to pay attention to market patterns, and if it is back to historic neighborhoods to which people are moving, we need to keep those neighborhoods viable for that to happen.

- Business districts are sustainably successful where there is a diversity of businesses. And that diverse business mix requires a diverse range of rental rates. Only in downtowns and older commercial neighborhoods is there such diversity. Try finding any rental-rate diversity in the regional shopping center or the so-called office park. There ain't none.

- As a general rule, new construction is 50 percent labor and 50 percent materials. Rehabilitation, on the other hand, is 60–70 percent labor. While we buy an HVAC system from Ohio, sheetrock from Texas, and timber from Oregon, we buy services of the carpenter and plumber, painter, and electrician from across the street. They subsequently spend that paycheck for a haircut, membership in the local Y, and a new car, resulting in a significantly greater local economic impact, dollar for dollar, than new construction.

- Solid waste landfill is expensive in both dollars and environmental quality: 60–65 percent of most landfill sites are made up of construction debris. And much of that waste comes from the razing of existing structures. Preserving instead of demolishing our inventory of historic buildings reduces that construction waste.

- Reinvigorating historic neighborhoods reinforces existing schools and allows them to recapture their important educational, social, and cultural role on a community level.

- No new land is consumed when rehabilitating a historic building. The conversion of a historic warehouse into forty residential units reduces the demand for ten acres of farmland. The economic revitalization of Main Street reduces the demand for another strip center. The restoration of an empty 1920s skyscraper reduces the demand for another glass and chrome building at the office park.

Actually calculating the economic benefits of historic preservation, however, can be challenging, given how much emotion may be involved in these efforts. In his 2005 research report for the Brookings Institution, titled "Economics and Historic Preservation: A Guide and Review of the Literature," Professor Randall Mason of the University of Pennsylvania examined the literature on the economics of historic preservation and offered an excellent review of the theories, practices and resources available. His report put into perspective many case studies and reports, including Donovan Rypkema's work, and ended with a conclusion that underscored the often difficult nature of quantifying and applying lessons learned in practice. Mason stated: "While conclusive, scientifically verifiable answers to preservation economics questions are elusive at best, a number of

Demolition of historic Frieze Building, Ann Arbor, Michigan.

reasonable conclusions can be drawn about the economic benefits of historic preservation on the basis of the literature reviewed here. Historic preservation has important economic values and produces certain economic benefits for both the private sector and the public at large. Preservation projects can be profitable, and preservation policies do make sound fiscal sense.[3]

THE ECONOMICS OF REHABILITATION

There are drawbacks to "rehabbing" older structures; spaces may not be easily adaptable to current needs, deterioration may not be apparent at the beginning of work, and there might be difficulty in finding appropriate construction materials. However, older structures also have inherent advantages. They typically have better and more marketable amenities, including good locations, more spacious interiors, higher-quality and more interesting detailing, and a more marketable image. Rehabilitation often saves a developer time and money by bypassing a lengthy development review process, local neighborhood opposition, and regulatory approval delays. As a result, in many cases, rehabilitation costs can be significantly less than new construction costs.

Rehabilitation might even save money compared to new construction. A recent study found that in Chicago, where the public school system is spending $2.5 billion to upgrade facilities, bare-bones new construction is costing $155 per square foot, but renovation of existing buildings in established neighborhoods is costing just $130.[4] Updating existing schools in existing neighborhoods not only makes sense from the perspective of community vitality, it also makes good economic sense.

The costs of rehabilitation can be seen in other ways as well. A government study found that rehabilitation construction uses 23 percent less energy than new construction, because the work is more labor intensive and less material intensive, depleting fewer natural resources.[5] "Conservation of the Urban Environment," a report prepared by the Office of Archaeology and Historic Preservation in the Department of the Interior, explained this point in more detail. The reliance on labor-intensive work "is important not only in terms of the employment potential of historic preservation, but also in terms of an individual project's multiplier impact on a local economy. Dependent on the size and sophistication of a locality, a higher proportion of construction materials will come from outside the area than will construction labor. For funds that are spent in a local economy, a higher percentage of funds remains as a stimulant in that locality from projects that are labor intensive. Thus, funds utilized in historic preservation projects have greater impact on employment than funds used in the construction of new buildings such as hospitals, schools, and office buildings because of (1) the greater labor intensity of preservation projects, and (2) through this labor intensity multiplier."[6] Testimony by the General Services Administration indicated that rehabilitation creates two to five times as many jobs as new construction, and that this advantage was especially important because older buildings are often found in areas of the city that have the highest rates of unemployment and underemployment.[7]

Another government agency, the Advisory Council on Historic Preservation (ACHP), has accumulated a profusion of reports and studies on the issues involved in the economics of preservation. Their Web site (www.achp.gov/economicstudies.html) is an easily accessible resource and offers a menu of topics addressing the

Building rehabilitation.

following areas: General Studies, Statewide Studies, General Community Studies, Impacts of Historic Designation, Impacts on Property Values, and Impacts of Preservation Tax Credits. The section on statewide studies makes available fifteen separate state-based case studies, most published within the last decade.

One major consideration that is just now being recognized is "embodied energy." This concept is rapidly becoming a *cause célèbre* within the architectural and preservation communities. Recently, at a "green" conference held for participants interested in the issues of sustainability and green design, only one speaker represented the field of historic preservation. Not one of the audience members, comprised of designers, environmentalists, architects, contractors, goods suppliers, and academics, had even considered the act of reusing an older building as energy efficient. They were so focused on *green design* and developing new, more "earth friendly" materials and methods of constructing new buildings that they had lost sight of the most energy retaining act of all—that of reusing existing structures.[8] There is increasing recognition that reusing existing buildings is one of the "greenest," or energy-sensitive, approaches available to a world just beginning to understand the term "sustainability."

TAX ASSESSMENTS FOR HISTORIC PROPERTIES

Owners of designated historic properties often complain that they are taxed unfairly. Local tax assessors may evaluate a historic property in a commercial area based on the property's potential for development. Thus, an owner who restores a two-story residence in a prime area may have to pay a property tax rate comparable to that of a newer and larger commercial building. It is unfair to penalize the owner of a historic property for maintaining it rather than replacing it with a building that would create a more intensive use.

Steps can be taken by local governments to mitigate the disincentive of higher assessments. Some cities are empowered to defer tax increases, often called abatements, for a number of years; this power can be invoked when the restoration of a historic property is completed. Some preservation ordinances allow for a reduction in property taxes for designated historic properties.[9] These tax rebates, which may be tied to ordinances regulating the right to demolish or alter the exterior of a property, compensate owners by recognizing the potential inequity of owning a historic property. In some communities, local lending institutions have agreed to jointly offer a program of below-market-rate or guaranteed loans to owners of historic commercial properties who wish to restore or rehabilitate their buildings. Through such programs, historic districts are better able to withstand the pressures for development and demolition.

EASEMENTS ON HISTORIC PROPERTIES

A method for easing the financial responsibilities of owning a historic building is the provision of historic easements. Under an easement provision, an owner retains use of the entire property, but agrees to relinquish part of the "bundle of rights" (the various rights of ownership inherent in a property; some of these rights may be given away, sold off, or usurped through regulation) inherent to property ownership in return for favorable tax treatment. Though increasingly subject to governmental scrutiny, easements can potentially be a valuable means to both protect historic buildings and provide value to their owners. For example, the owner of a property with an architecturally significant façade can agree to give up the right to change the façade in perpetuity in exchange for a property easement. The administration of the easement is given to a qualifying organization, which must be tax-exempt under Section 501(c)(3) of the Internal Revenue Code. Such an organization, typically an established local or statewide historical organization, is responsible for monitoring the condition of the property regularly to ensure that it continues to satisfy the provisions of the easement. The current owner and all future owners are bound by the easement provisions. In return, the current owner can claim the value of the easement as a charitable donation for income tax purposes. A qualified appraiser who has had experience with similar appraisals should determine the fair market value of the easement.[10] This may be beneficial to the owner if the current use value is lower than the fair market value without the easement.

A case study property in a historic district provides a good example. The property includes a significant historic house and carriage house (shown in solid black in the sketch on the next page). Assume that the two structures and land had a total market value of $400,000. However, a developer offered $1.5 million for the property, subject to approval, to build eighteen townhouses, as shown. The owner wanted to sell, but the local historic district commission would not approve such intensive development of the property. The owner felt

Easements diagram.

he was being treated unfairly and said that he should be compensated by the city for the $1.1 million loss of potential profit resulting solely from the historic district commission's designation. The courts, however, have consistently upheld a community's right to deny inappropriate development of historic properties, as long as owners continue to get a "reasonable return" on their property, even if it isn't the highest and best return. (Refer to the precedent-setting Penn Central decision discussed in Chapter 4.)

In this case, however, the owner was able to recoup some of his loss of potential income by donating a real property easement. An agreement in perpetuity attached to the property title said that the property would remain undeveloped. In return, the owner could claim a one-time personal income tax deduction for the $1.1 million difference. (This deduction could be spread over a number of years.) Depending on the owner's tax bracket, this could be a substantial benefit and would serve as considerable compensation for not being able to develop.[11]

The decision to enact an easement can be complicated, and is one reason why this method is not more readily utilized. The program is good in theory, but less so in practice. A Government Accountability Office (GAO) study found that easements were typically overvalued by appraisers, often at 200 percent or more of their actual value,[12] because a high appraisal value typically is in the owner's interest. Few appraisers are experienced in evaluating easements and therefore do not have comparable information from which to extrapolate values. This lack of experience is one reason for the intense scrutiny to which easements may be subjected. Owners also may find it difficult to identify not-for-profit associations willing to hold an easement, especially if this responsibility is taken without compensation. The easement has a great potential to create problems for the accepting body, but it offers little in the way of reward. Most receiving organizations require endowments, often substantial, with the easement to defray the cost of administering and possibly defending it.

When properly set up and administered, easements are a good way to maintain a property's historic and architectural integrity. They permit a community to hold onto important elements of its heritage while benefiting a property owner, who earns tax breaks for ensuring that the property is protected for posterity.

TRANSFER OF DEVELOPMENT RIGHTS

In densely developed urban areas, smaller historic buildings can be threatened by economic forces. The demolition of a historic structure permits a property to be redeveloped to its highest economic use. Owners of these older properties may feel limited by historic designation, which can prohibit them from realizing higher profits from their property. A Transfer of Development Rights (TDR) provision, if established by a city, may help alleviate this financial inequity.

A TDR program allows owners of buildings in zoned districts where more intense development is permitted to sell that development potential to owners of other sites. As shown in the diagram on the next page, development rights are literally purchased for use on a second site.

The city of Philadelphia has a TDR program that came about when an ordinance was passed to prevent the demolition of a downtown landmark building. At the same time, a longstanding "gentleman's agreement" not to build a downtown building higher than the hat on the sculpture of William Penn atop City Hall was broken by a developer wishing to build a high-rise structure. It was recognized by city officials that development could be encouraged while also preserving the historic character of the downtown district through use of a TDR

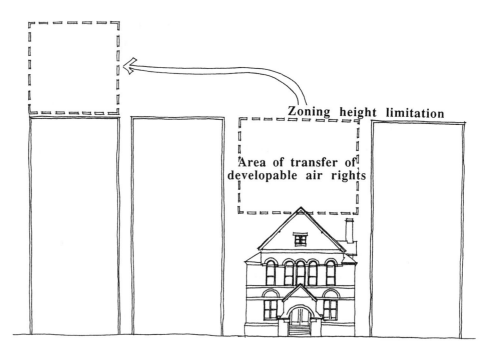

Zoning height limitation

Area of transfer of
developable air rights

Transfer of Development Rights diagram.

program. The Philadelphia TDR program had three goals when it was first established: (1) to provide an economic incentive for rehabilitation of locally designated landmarks; (2) to protect the 1984 local historic preservation ordinance from
court challenge by offering relief to city-certified property owners on land zoned
for more profitable use; and (3) to establish an innovative incentive for nonprofit
owners of historic properties to maintain and rehabilitate their buildings.[13] More
than two hundred owners of historic structures were eligible to sell development
rights through the TDR option. This incentive was combined with two other
development programs: an enhanced real estate tax abatement program that
included historic properties, and a large revolving loan fund.

San Francisco also considered a TDR program as a way to encourage preservation, described in *A Preservation Strategy for Downtown San Francisco,* which
proposed the following recommendations for the use of TDRs:[14]

- Permit transfer of development rights only from significant buildings.
- Permit transfers within the same zoning district at 1 to 1 ratio and in special
  development districts at a 1.5–2 to 1 ratio.

- Allow an automatic right to use TDRs on eligible receiving sites up to the maximum permissible floor area ratio (FAR) or maximum achievable FAR under height and volume limits.
- Require valid occupancy or current use as a condition for transfers.
- Permit a bonus transfer for restoration.
- Record a permanent reduction in development potential and maintenance agreement in the city's favor upon transfer.
- Encourage city support in organizing a trust to create an initial bank that would ensure an active market in TDRs.
- Prohibit the demolition or significant alteration of the highest-rated buildings except in restricted, special circumstances. (The study highlighted this protection as a critical component of the proposed TDR program.)

PURCHASE OF DEVELOPMENT RIGHTS

An allied program, the Purchase of Development Rights (PDR), is often used in rural areas or anyplace where agricultural landscapes, scenic views, and open countryside are highly valued by the local populace. PDR programs are a response to community concern that valuable farmland is increasingly being commercially developed. A public policy was needed to provide financial incentives for farmers to continue their operations, rather than cash in on the handsome prices developers were paying for their large parcels on the urban fringe, as well as to preserve scenic beauty, wildlife habitat, watershed areas, and recreational opportunities. To protect this land in perpetuity, the public provides a cash payment, sometimes quite large, to a landowner in exchange for a deed restriction on the property preventing development as real estate; other uses may continue. The advantage for the community is that the land is conserved by the owner, rather than through continuing public expenditures.

Such an easement allows continued use of the land as it is currently, but restricts more intense use. The value of such an easement is calculated as the difference between the fair market value of the land without the easement and its value as restricted by the easement, as determined through an impartial appraisal. For example, land may be worth $50,000 per acre if developable, but only $5,000 per acre as agricultural land with the easement as part of the property's "bundle of rights." Compensation for the PDR should reflect this $45,000 per acre difference, and serve as a guide for negotiating fair payment to the property owner.

PDR programs have met with success in many areas, but are very closely tied to local sentiment and recognition of the importance of open space and agricultural usage. They often are funded through the passage of a local tax levy, and therefore have been criticized as nothing more than an additional tax that devalues property and affects only a select number of properties. As with all tax levies, however, the decision is in the hands of the local electorate. Approximately one-third of the states have passed enabling legislation authorizing the local use of PDRs. As of 2004, state PDR programs had protected about 1.4 million acres nationally, at a cost of about $1,400 per acre, or $1.9 billion.

An example of a significant PDR program is found in Carroll County, Maryland. Located between the sprawling Washington, D.C. and Baltimore metropolitan areas, the pressure in this area to sell underutilized land for redevelopment has been great for decades. In the 1970s, the county established a PDR program with the goal of protecting up to a hundred thousand acres of farmland in Carroll County. A major problem with the program was that it was not able to respond quickly enough when an owner of a prime parcel received a purchase offer from a developer. In response, the county, in cooperation with the state, created a "Critical Farms Program." This program guarantees a minimum easement value for farms being transferred to a protected state agricultural district, thus assuring property owners at least a minimum value for giving an easement. Based on an appraisal of the potential value of an easement, the county offers a payment of 75 percent of its value for a five-year option to acquire the easement. If the option is exercised within five years, the state reimburses the local government for the initial payment. If the state does not accept the easement, the owner may either accept the local easement or repay the county for termination of the agreement.

TAX BENEFITS

Although the federal government laid much of the groundwork for preservation efforts through the National Historic Preservation Act of 1966, little was done up to that time to offer financial incentives for preservation. Without financial incentives, preservation often was seen as an idealistic pursuit, removed from the mainstream of development. Indeed, at that time developers were given an income tax deduction for expenses incurred in the demolition of older buildings—essentially a disincentive for preservation. This deduction was given without prior determination whether the structure had historic significance and should be protected.

These types of tax deductions, combined with federal and state programs such as Model Cities and Urban Renewal, encouraged the wholesale demolition of many older urban places, including fringe areas of downtowns and inner city neighborhoods. Entire large districts were destroyed, one after another, under the guise of such programs. Many sites were torn down to make way for new development that did not materialize, leaving behind the eyesore of vacant lots, sometimes quite large in scale. Urban renewal programs also generated the construction of limited-access highways in the city's core, allowing suburbanites speedy access to downtown offices. "Superblocks" brought in a new order of high-rise apartments that replaced the smaller block sizes of traditional urban neighborhoods comprising two- and three-story rowhouses and single-family residences.

When the horrors of urban renewal projects of the 1960s, '70s, and '80s became apparent, the federal government responded in a limited way. The Tax Reform Act of 1976 was a first step in recognizing the inadequacies of legislation protecting existing neighborhoods and historic structures.[15] The Act stated that developers could no longer consider the cost of demolition for historically certified structures as a deductible business expense; previously, developers essentially were reimbursed for demolition. The Act also permitted a tax advantage of accelerated depreciation for substantial rehabilitation of historic structures, allowing owners to take greater tax deductions in the early years of a project.

The 1978 Tax Act went further by establishing a tax credit program for rehabilitating older buildings.[16] The Rehabilitation Investment Tax Credit (RITC) program allowed developers a 10 percent tax credit for the costs of rehabilitating a historic structure used in a trade or business or held for income-producing purposes. This credit gave a reasonable incentive, for unlike a tax deduction, which is a reduction from gross income claimed on the tax form, a tax credit is subtracted directly from the amount of tax owed and represents a much higher savings (more on this topic later).

Because the new RITC could be taken only for rehabilitation work on historic structures, a procedure was needed for determining what structures qualified as historic. To accommodate this, the National Park Service assumed primary responsibility for review and approval of eligibility for Certified Historic Structure (CHS) status. This status became a rehabilitated structure's mark of eligibility for the new tax credits, provided its rehabilitation was certified by the National Park Service as complying with the Secretary of the Interior's *Standards for Rehabilitation.* The RITC program was an immediate success. A 1979 study showed that $1.3 million in tax credits had generated $27 million in rehabilitation work. Between 1976 and 1986, nearly 17,000 projects, valued at $11 billion, took advantage of the program.[17] The focus of urban projects shifted dramatically from demolition to rehabilitation. Speaking for the success of this program during that time frame, Missouri Congressman Richard Gephardt referred to the tax credits as "the most important feature for urban redevelopment and urban renewal" in the 1980s.[18] Another preservation stalwart, Nellie Longsworth, recently retired president of Preservation Action, concurred, explaining the significance of the credits in revitalizing downtowns: "All kinds of things have been tried to stop the deterioration of downtowns. The first program that ever really worked was the investment tax credit."[19]

Because of the success and increased public support, the federal government expanded the RITC program in 1981 as part of the Economic Recovery Tax Act (ERTA). It has continued to evolve since that time. Various tax acts have led to the creation of many new historic districts, for through this device, structures that had not been recognized as historically significant on their own could qualify for substantial tax credits as "contributing" structures. The tax credit program's purpose was not to restore significant older buildings as museum pieces, but to return their use to meet current housing, retail, industrial, and commercial needs. Even developers with no previous interest in historic preservation wanted to become involved because of the financial incentives. This stimulation of private investment through a public program was unparalleled by many other government programs.

The tax credit program made some strange bedfellows. Whereas "old-line" preservationists previously had opposed proposals presented by developers, now preservationists and developers both supported such proposals, the former because it saved historic buildings and the latter largely because it was profitable. The biggest financial beneficiaries were high-tax-bracket investors looking for ways to decrease their tax burdens.

USING THE REHABILITATION INVESTMENT TAX CREDITS

The Federal Historic Preservation Tax Incentives program is one of the federal government's most successful and cost-effective community revitalization programs. The RITC program has done much to stimulate interest in rehabilitating older structures, but has changed considerably since its inception. Current tax incentives for preservation were established by the Tax Reform Act of 1986 (PL 99-514; Internal Revenue Code Section 47 [formerly Section 48(g)]). The current program operates according to the following provisions.[20]

Which Buildings Qualify?

Buildings can qualify for RITCs either as historic or nonhistoric. To be considered historic, a building must be a Certified Historic Structure (listed in, or "eligible" for, the National Register), or be certified as a contributing structure in a historic district recognized by the Secretary of the Interior. A 20 percent credit is available for income-producing properties rehabilitated for commercial,

An income-producing property.

industrial, agricultural, or rental residential purposes, but it is not available for properties used exclusively as an owner's private residence. A nonhistoric, nonresidential building built before 1936 is eligible for a 10 percent credit.

Qualified Expenditures

Expenditures that qualify for RITCs are essentially those connected with the rehabilitation or restoration of the structure. The Secretary of the Interior must certify that the work is consistent with the historic architectural character of the building; this approval is conveyed by the National Park Service. If the work is incompatible or inappropriate, the project may be denied certification for a tax credit.

Examples of qualified expenditures:

- Rehabilitation costs
- Construction interest and taxes
- Architectural and engineering fees
- Legal and professional fees
- Developers' fees
- General and administrative costs

The cost of other work, such as additions to the structure or construction not related to rehabilitation or restoration, does not qualify as a certified expenditure. Examples of nonqualified expenditures:

- Acquisition costs
- Enlargement costs; expansion of either the building footprint or volume
- Acquisition interest and taxes
- Realtors' fees
- Paving and landscaping costs
- Sales and marketing costs.[21]

Substantial Rehabilitation Requirement

Other provisions must be met for rehab expenses to qualify for a RITC. First, the work done must be considered "substantial rehabilitation." To satisfy this requirement, the work must exceed the value of the adjusted basis cost of the building, or $5,000, whichever is greater. The adjusted basis of the building is the owner's cost of the property (less the value of the land) plus the cost of any capital improvements less depreciation taken.

Consider a commercial building for which the owner paid $1,000,000 five years ago. If the value of the land alone is $250,000 of that figure, the owner has made $100,000 in improvements, and has depreciated the property at $60,000 per year, the adjusted basis would equal:

Cost of property	$1,000,000
Less value of land	−250,000
	750,000
Plus improvements	+100,000
	850,000
Depreciation (5 years @ 60,000)	−300,000
Adjusted basis	$550,000

The rehab expenditures must exceed $550,000 to qualify, as it is the greater of $5,000 or the value of the adjusted basis.

Prior Use Requirement

To be eligible, a structure must have been used as a building prior to its rehabilitation. For example, requests have been made to include a caboose or grain silo converted to use as a habitable building; these were not approved.

Wall Retention Requirement

If the rehabilitated building is a qualified nonhistoric structure (qualified because it was built prior to 1936 and is not located in a historic district), it must also meet the wall retention requirement. To satisfy this requirement, a certain proportion of the exterior walls and framework must be retained, as follows:

- At least 75 percent of the external walls must be retained either as external or internal walls.
- At least 50 percent of the external walls must be retained as external walls.
- At least 75 percent of the internal structural framework must be retained.

Financial Methods

An important incentive of the RITC program is the use of tax credits rather than tax deductions. Tax credits provide a dollar-for-dollar direct reduction in income tax owed, whereas deductions reduce taxes based on an individual's percentage tax bracket. As an example, assume the rehab cost for a project is $100,000, with an incentive of 20 percent or $20,000. As a credit, the owner could reduce the amount of federal income tax owed by $20,000; this is a savings of the full $20,000. However, as a deduction, the actual savings would be $20,000 times the individual's tax bracket (e.g., $20,000 x 28% tax bracket = $5,600). This illustrates the significant advantage to the tax *credit.*

Another example illustrates the important tax advantages of the RITC program to a property investor. Assume $1 million is invested in the construction of a new building. With straight-line depreciation over thirty-one and a half years (the standard rate), the accrued tax benefits would be $80,638. For comparison, assume an investor purchases a historic property for $250,000 and spends $750,000 to rehabilitate it. The same total amount of money is spent on this property as on the new construction. However, with the resulting 20 percent credit for rehab and a similar depreciation rate, the tax benefits would total $204,906, yielding more than two and a half times the benefits. (Both examples give present value of the tax benefits, assuming a 10 percent discount and 28 percent tax rate.)

Conditions of Use for Rehab Tax Credits

To be eligible for the tax credit, the work on a rehab project must be certified by the National Park Service. This certification can be arranged by completing an application filed with the appropriate State Historic Preservation Office (SHPO). This application is reviewed by the SHPO and then forwarded with recommendations to the National Park Service for approval or denial. The rehab certification decision of the National Park Service is the final one, though the Internal Revenue Service holds the final say as to the actual granting of the credit. If a tax credit is denied, an appeal is always allowed.

The application is submitted in three parts:

> *Part I—Evaluation of Significance.* This part usually contains a narrative describing
> the history and/or architecture of the building so that the National Park Service

can determine if the building contributes to the historic district within which it is located. (Buildings listed in the National Register individually are automatically certified historic structures.)

Part II—Description of Rehabilitation. This part is intended to provide both the SHPO and the National Park Service with a narrative, images that outline the architectural and historical features of the building as they currently exist, and a description of the proposed work to be undertaken. It is recommended that both Parts I and II be filed before work is started on the project.

Part III—Request for Certification of Completed Work. This final part of the application process is intended to notify the state and the National Park Service that the project is completed and that the owners are requesting that the project be reviewed for certification. It includes images of the completed rehabilitation. In some cases, the building is subject to an on-site visit by the SHPO or the National Park Service.[22]

If the building is sold, exchanged, or converted to personal use within five years of the credit being taken, the tax credit must be repaid at a recapture rate of 20 percent for every year under the five-year minimum. For example, if the building is sold after three years, the owner must repay 40 percent of the credit taken. The new owner is ineligible for any portion of the credit.

It is important to realize that the tax credit program is complicated and subject to change. The description here is only a general overview of the major provisions. Before work is actually begun on any such project, owners should review current tax law, obtain the advice of a reliable financial advisor, and contact their SHPO office; all SHPO offices have staff assigned specifically to aid owners in qualifying for the tax credits.

Homeowner Tax Credits

Since the mid-1990s, efforts have been directed at establishing a rehabilitation tax credit for homeowners. Because they do not have income-generating property, they have been unable to benefit from the federal tax credit program, although many would argue that their contribution to preservation is just as important as that of other owners. However, such homeowner-based tax credits now are found in many state tax incentive programs. By 2007, twenty-eight states had enacted some form of income tax incentive that applies to the rehabilitation of historic

"Designated" house, Mountain View, California.

properties, with twenty-five of those, plus the District of Columbia, offering some level of homeowner tax credit. (Nine states do not tax income, so a tax credit is not possible, and the others have a state income tax, but do not offer historic property tax credits at this time.)

Some states have established alternate programs of tax incentives for owners of historic properties. For example, in 1972 California passed the Mills Act, which allows qualifying private owners to receive a reduction in their property tax if they own an existing designated historic structure or a contributing structure in a designated historic district. In return, the owner agrees to maintain and preserve the structure in accordance with the U.S. Secretary of the Interior's *Standards for Rehabilitation*. Eligibility is limited to single-family homes with a current property tax assessment of $500,000 or less and commercial/industrial/multifamily properties with a current property tax assessment of $1.5 million or less, although some selected areas are exempt from the assessment limits. Property taxes recalculated using the special Mills Act assessment method can be reduced 50 percent or more. A formal agreement, generally known as a Mills Act or Historical Property Contract, is executed between the local government and the property owner for a minimum ten-year term. Contracts are automatically renewed each year and are transferred to new owners when the property is sold. Periodic inspections by city or county officials ensure proper maintenance of the property.

FINANCIAL ANALYSIS TECHNIQUES

Pro Forma Analysis

Many variables pertain to the financial feasibility of rehabilitating an older commercial building. How can these variables be systematically accommodated so as to calculate a project's potential? *Pro forma analysis* is a technique commonly used for projecting the financial future of a project for a given number of years. It calculates dollars taken in versus dollars going out. This bottom-line comparison must be favorable for an investor to consider a rehab project. Pro forma analysis begins with a baseline year, usually the current year, and considers how the financial status of a project will change over three, five, or even ten years, based on certain assumptions made by the analyst. Five years is the most common time span, long enough for the project to "settle in," to recover most start-up costs, and to develop a normal occupancy rate, yet not so long that projections are too hypothetical.

Case Study: Rehab of an Older Commercial Structure

To illustrate the elements of a pro forma analysis, the following case study examines a typical three-story, late-nineteenth-century commercial building. The property is for sale at an asking price of $395,000. Located on Main Street in the downtown, it is in an area with good potential for growth for offices, stores, or residences. The property has not been improved in more than forty years.

The following analysis assesses the feasibility of investing in the rehab of this property and presents, item by item, the factors to consider. The financial data sheet gives a detailed overview of this analysis.

Typical historic downtown commercial building.

FINAL PRICE

The first piece of information needed about the project is how much it will cost to purchase. If the asking price for the property is $395,000, it is possible that a seller may accept less. For this analysis, we will assume an offer of 5–7 percent below the asking price will be acceptable. Therefore, the final price will be $365,000.

COSTS OF REHABILITATION

The costs of rehabilitation can be calculated in a number of ways. Initially, a project architect gives preliminary estimates based on prices from similar projects and figures from cost-estimating books. (Contractors' bids provide more accurate estimates, but are difficult to obtain until the project is actually designed and plans and specifications available—a process that follows, rather than precedes, the feasibility analysis.) Typically, a preliminary cost estimate of an overall dollar-per-square-foot value is calculated based on comparable work. This "quick and easy" approach generalizes many of the project details—one factor may be estimated low, another high—but if good comparables are used, the result should be reasonable. An estimated square-foot cost can also be obtained by talking with builders or realtors in the area, who can provide a reasonable estimate based on their experience with similar projects.

Rehabilitation construction costs can be grouped into three general categories. Level 1 work is basic cleaning and fix-up of the structure in its current condition. It would have the same or similar use(s) on each floor, with similar floor arrangements. An example of the cost for this level of work would be $60–100 per square foot. For instance, a 1,000-square-foot structure with few changes, estimated at $80 per square foot, would cost $80,000 to rehabilitate.

Level 2 rehabilitation might include more comprehensive work to update the structure. In this instance, the heating, plumbing, and electrical systems are updated to meet current codes, an enclosed stair added to meet fire safety codes, and an elevator, an entrance ramp, and handicapped restrooms added to satisfy accessibility guidelines. A rule-of-thumb cost for this work would be in the range of $120–160 per square foot.

Level 3 rehabilitation would be more inclusive, adding significant structural work to the above work, including major repairs, possible areas of reconstruction, and changes to the floor plan. The costs for this extent of work could range from $160 to $200 per square foot. With a three-story structure with floors of 2,000 square feet each, and an estimated construction cost of $180 per square foot, the total project construction costs would be just over $1 million. For comparison, the cost of a new structure could be approximately $200 per square foot. For each of these estimates, additional costs are incurred for items such as architect and attorney fees (soft costs) and general administrative costs. These may add 10–12 percent to the basic construction costs.

For this case study, a preliminary cost estimate was established at $120 per square foot for Level 2 rehab on each of the three floors. As shown on the spreadsheet, this gives the project's "hard" costs at $730,000. Add to this the soft and administrative costs, and the total cost for rehabilitation is $839,751.

The "soft" costs for the project include nonconstruction elements—professional fees for the architect, appraiser, and attorney; costs of the mortgage during construction (assumed to be six months); closing costs, permits, and start-up

PRO FORMA for Building Rehabilitation
Projected Typical Year

A Cost of Rehab			a Soft Costs		
INITIAL AMOUNTS		a Soft costs	92,751	Architect (6% of constr.)	43,200
Purchase price	365,000	b Hard Costs	730,000	Appraisal	2,000
A Cost of rehabilitation	839,751	c Rent-up Costs	17,000	Attorney's fees	3,000
Total Project Cost	1,204,751	Sub-total	839,751	Debt service (6 mo.)	36,551
				Closing costs	2,000
Loan to Value Ratio (LTV)	80%	**B Gross Rent**		Permits	2,000
Mortgage Amount	963,801	Leaseable SF (1st Fl.)	2,000	Constr. startup costs	4,000
Cash Investment	240,950	Rent/SF (1st Fl.)	$26.00	Sub-total	92,751
		Rental Income (1st Fl.)	52,000		
ANNUALIZED AMOUNTS		Leaseable SF (2nd Fl.)	2,000	b Hard Costs	
INCOME		Rent/SF (2nd Fl.)	$22.00	Demolition	10,000
B Total Gross Rent	140,000	Rental Income (2nd Fl.)	44,000	Construction	720,000
less assumed 5% vacancy	7,000	Leaseable SF (3rd Fl.)	2,000	Sub-total	730,000
Gross Effective Income	133,000	Rent/SF (3rd Fl.)	$22.00		
C less Operating Expenses	47,514	Rental Income (3rd Fl.)	44,000	Construction	
D less annual Debt Service	73,103	Total Gross Rent	140,000	Total SF Rehabbed	6,000
ROI #1 Before Tax Cash Flow	12,383			Cost per SF	120
ROI #1 (percent)	5.1%	**C Operating Expenses**			
		Taxes	28,914	c Administrative Costs	
E ROI #2 Return on Taxes	7,932	Insurance	1,800	Advertising	4,000
ROI #2 (percent)	3.3%	Mgt. (3% Gross Rent)	4,200	Office Costs	4,000
ROI #2 w/ Historic Tax Credit	16.7%	Legal/ Accounting	2,800	Cleaning	2,000
		Leaseup Fee	2,800	Realtor Leasing Fee	7,000
F ROI #3 Appreciation	36,143	Repair/Maintenance	7,000	Sub-total	17,000
ROI #3 (percent)	15.0%	Sub-total	47,514		
TOTAL ANNUAL ROI (1, 2, 3)	23.4%	**D Debt Service**			
		Mortgage	963,801		
TOTAL ROI with Hist. Credit	36.9%	Interest Rate (%)	6.5%		
		Number of years	30		
Debt coverage ratio	1.17	Monthly Payment	6,092		

(Annual net income/Annual debt service)

Abbreviations:
ROI: Return on Investment
SF: Square Feet

E Return on Taxes				
Without Rehab Tax Credit			**With Rehab Tax Credit**	
Total Property Value	1,204,751		Rehab Tax Credit (%)	20%
less Value of Land	100,000		Total Value	167,950
Depreciable base	1,104,751		Depreciable base	936,801
Number of years	39.0		No. of years	39.0
Annual depreciation	28,327		Annual depreciation	24,021
Tax bracket	28%		Tax bracket	28%
Return on taxes	7,932		Normal Return on Taxes	6,726
			Tax Credit (over 5 yrs)	33,590
			Total return on taxes	40,316
			ROI #2	16.7%

F Appreciation	
Property Value	1,204,751
Annual Appreciation	3%
Sub-total	36,143

Sample Pro forma spreadsheet.

costs. For this project, these total $92,751. Administrative costs, which include advertising, marketing, and office expenses in finding initial tenants, amount to $17,000. Adding all these costs to the original purchase cost gives a total project cost of just over $1.2 million.

To raise the $1.2 million total project amount, two investment sources were used—the investment made by the owner, and the loan/mortgage amount from a lending agency. *Investors* are individuals willing to put up their own money in the hope of a significant return or for tax advantages. *Lenders* are institutions, such as banks, that lend money as a business.

Banks and other lenders generally are unwilling to put up all the money for a real estate venture. They require that some funds be developed through other resources, so that if the project fails they will recoup enough in building value to cover their portion of the investment. The percentage of the total costs a lender is willing to risk is established as the loan-to-value (LTV) ratio. Typically, this is 75–90 percent of the project's value if the project is determined to have a sound financial basis. This determination is decided on the basis of a feasibility analysis, such as this example. Based on an LTV ratio of 80 percent, the case study project could expect a mortgage from the bank of $963,801, requiring $240,950 in cash from investors.

This means that although the total project costs over $1.2 million, the owner's cost is approximately $241,000. In other words, the owner is purchasing $1.2 million worth of real estate for $241,000 of his or her own money. The remainder is the mortgage, and its cost will be covered as part of the project's annual income and expenses.

ANNUALIZED INCOME AND EXPENDITURES

Calculations of ongoing income and expenditures must now be added to the analysis. Their impact must be determined on an annual basis (referred to as *annualizing*)—that is, converting all information into an income or expenditure over a one-year span.

Total Gross Rent

The annual rental income derived from the project is projected based on market data figures for the local area. For this case study community, the typical rate for ground-floor commercial space in the downtown area is currently $16–$28 per square foot per year. Because the property is located just off the main shopping street, a rate of $26 per square foot is assumed for ground-floor rental. The second and third floors could be leased for offices at an estimated $22 per square foot (the basement is assumed to have no rental value). Based on the square footages for each floor, as shown in the pro forma spreadsheet, a total gross rent (annualized) of $140,000 is anticipated.

Projected Vacancy Rate

Not all of a project's space can be leased all the time, even in a very good market. Initially it takes months or years to come up to full occupancy at full market rates. An average vacancy rate of 5 percent is assumed, subtracting $7,000 annually from the potential gross rent. By reducing the gross rent figures by the projected vacancy rate, the expected annual income, called the *gross effective income*, is shown as $133,000.

Operating Expenses

Balanced against the gross effective income are ongoing project expenses. These include taxes, insurance, project management costs, legal and accounting fees, and normal repair and maintenance. The cost of utilities may either be included as a project expense or passed along to tenants if the lease so specifies. (The case study assumes the tenant pays for utilities.) Annual operating expenses are projected at $47,514 for a typical year.

Debt Service

The annual debt service is based on the total mortgage amount (in this case, $963,801), the mortgage interest rate, and the number of years of payments. This case study uses an interest percentage rate of 6.5 percent paid over thirty years, or 360 months. A monthly payment is derived using an amortization calculation and then converted to an annual payment. Such calculations can be done quickly by a bank loan officer or by one of many uncomplicated computer programs now available. This monthly payment is converted to an annual payment by multiplying by twelve, which in this example totals $73,103.

Return on Investment (ROI)

The whole purpose of a pro forma analysis is to determine how much an investor can expect to get as a return on an initial investment. This is referred to as return on investment (ROI). Will it be as much as could be expected from other types of investments, such as the stock market or a money market bank account? Is the return high enough to be worth the extra risk involved, especially if the money may be tied up for an extended period? What are the local market conditions?

How are they likely to change over the course of three, five, or ten years? Changes in some of these factors can dramatically alter the financial outlook of a project, whereas others will have surprisingly little impact on the total return. Thus, there is always some element of financial risk, however minimal it may be.

A rewarding aspect of investing in real estate is that there are three ways to make a return on the initial investment. The three types of ROI found in real estate are cash flow, return on taxes, and appreciation. Together, these three types of ROI can add up to a significant total return—one that justifies the greater risk and involvement.

Before-Tax Cash Flow (ROI #1)

Cash flow is the amount returned annually to an investor as cash. It represents the most direct type of return, although it is typically lowest in the early years of a project. It initially may even be negative, meaning additional cash must be put into the project over the short term.

Cash flow is determined by deducting the annual amounts for operating expenses and debt service from the annual gross effective income. In this case, the annual cash flow is $12,383, not a lot for an initial investment of $240,950, but at least a positive, rather than negative amount.

ROIs can be evaluated better if converted to a percentage. To determine the percentage return for ROI #1, the annual cash flow return ($12,383) is divided by the amount of the original cash investment, which was $240,950. This represents a return of 5.1 percent. (Note that the mortgage amount is not included as part of the cash investment, because this was not part of the investor's capital and was previously accommodated in the calculations under debt service.) Is this amount satisfactory? One rule-of-thumb is that the cash return should be at least double the percentage that could be earned in a bank savings account, so the cash return for this example is minimal. But also remember that there are two additional returns on investment to add to this amount.

Return on Taxes (ROI #2)

Many investors, especially those in high tax brackets, are less concerned with cash return than they are with the tax advantages of real estate investment. For them, historic building rehabilitation provides some of the best tax opportunities available.

The calculation of the return on taxes is shown on the data sheet in Box E. Annual tax return is based on the depreciable value of a property. The depreciable value is the total value of the property less the value of the land (a basic assumption of tax law is that a building depreciates [decreases] in value over time, but the land it is on does not). With a land market value of $100,000 (established through local appraisal), the case study example has a depreciable base value of $1,104,751. A building's value, under current tax law, can be depreciated over thirty-nine years. This allows an annual depreciation of $28,327 in this example.

To calculate the investor's actual return on taxes, this annual depreciable amount ($28,327) is multiplied by the individual's tax bracket. We assume here that the total state and federal tax is 28 percent, giving an annual tax return of $7,932. As with ROI #1, this amount is compared to the initial cash investment of $240,950, for an ROI #2 of 3.3 percent annually.

In addition, the rehabilitation costs of a historic building designated as a Certified Historic Structure (CHS) or contributing in a Certified Historic District (see Chapter 5 for a description of Certified Historic Structures) can be partially recovered through the Rehabilitation Investment Tax Credit (RITC) provisions. The rehabilitation of such a building could make investors eligible for a tax credit totaling 20 percent of the rehab costs. Assuming the case study building is a CHS, there is an additional total credit of $167,000 (20 percent of the rehabilitation cost of $839,751). Because most individuals don't need this much of a credit on their personal federal taxes in one year, the credit can be spread over multiple years. In this example, it is taken over a five-year time span, with an annual RITC credit of $33,590. This amount is added to the previously calculated tax return based on depreciation (now calculated less the rehab credit), which is $6,726, for a total of $40,316 for each of five years. For ROI #2, the annual return is now 16.7 percent instead of the previously calculated 3.3 percent return without the historic tax credit. In addition, some states provide additional state tax incentives to complement the federal tax credit, adding even greater tax benefits. As is shown here, there is a direct and significant financial gain possible through the use of the rehab tax credit program.

Appreciation (ROI #3)

The greatest return on investment is typically from the continuing appreciation of the property's value. If properly maintained and regularly updated, properties increase significantly in market value over time. This assumption initially seems contradictory, given the explanation that tax law assumes a decrease in the value of property over time, but depreciation is a theoretical assumption, whereas appreciation represents the true market value over time.

The amount of increase based on appreciation varies with local and regional market conditions. The case example assumes an annual increase in the total value of the property of 3 percent. Thus, if the project is worth $1,204,751 upon completion, its value one year later will be $1,240,894, or a 3 percent increase of $36,143. Although the appreciation increase is based on the total value of the property, ROI #3 compares this increase in value only to the cash investment made by the investor (e.g., $36,143 divided by $240,950 initial cash investment), showing ROI #3 to be 15 percent annually. In other words, the investor gains the value of appreciation not only on his or her own money (the initial $240,950), but on the bank's money (the $963,801 mortgage) as well. Certainly this is a beneficial situation, since it effectively converts a 3 percent gain into one of 15 percent!

This relatively high ROI due to appreciation represents one of the primary reasons for investing in real estate. However, this return is realized only on the sale of the property, and is dependent on investors' willingness to tie up their own money for an extended period. In summary, real estate investment is not for those who need a regular, predictable return, but it can be rewarding for investors who can commit relatively large amounts and wait for favorable market conditions.

OTHER FUNDING SOURCES

A historic rehab project also may benefit financially by taking advantage of external sources of funding. A variety of sources at the federal level can be considered for funding preservation projects. Among them are:

U.S. Department of the Interior

Historic Preservation Fund: The Department of the Interior's Historic Preservation Fund (HPF) was established as part of the 1966 National Historic Preservation Act. Its purpose is to support the acquisition, stabilization, and development of historic resources and the identification and protection of historic and archeological properties.

Land and Water Conservation Fund: Under this program, funds are distributed for parks, trails, and other recreation sites. Occasionally, these sites tie in with historic resources.

Bureau of Land Management (BLM): Challenge Cost Share Funds provide matching funds to local communities for projects on or adjacent to BLM land.

U.S. Department of Commerce

Economic Development Administration (EDA): The EDA provides funds for technical assistance, planning, and development of projects that create new employment. This may include projects using historic resources.

U.S. Department of Housing and Urban Development (HUD)

Community Development Block Grants (CDBG): Block grants make many millions of dollars available for housing, infrastructure improvements, and economic development. Projects associated with historic properties typically must be reviewed by the SHPO.

Low-Income Housing Tax Credit: Often called Section 8 credits, this program can be used in conjunction with the RITC to create affordable housing in historic districts.

U.S. Department of Treasury

New Market Tax Credits (NMTC): A tax credit program designed to make investment capital available to for-profit community development entities (CDE) in qualifying low-income communities. A nonprofit entity may apply for a NMTC allocation with the intention of transferring the allocation to a for-profit subsidiary CDE through a limited partnership corporation. The NMTC and the rehabilitation investment tax credit (RITC) are natural allies.

Local Initiatives Support Corporation (LISC)

LISC is a national development organization that, since its founding in 1980, has generated more than $7.8 billion from over three thousand investors, lenders, and donors to create or rehabilitate more than 215,000 affordable homes and 30 million square feet of retail, community, and educational space in urban neighborhoods and rural communities nationwide.

Neighborhood Housing Services of America (NHSA)

NHSA is a national nonprofit that, since 1974, has helped to revitalize neighborhoods and strengthen communities by serving as a provider of secondary market capital for community development efforts that support its mission of providing affordable single-family and multifamily residential properties.

U.S. Department of Transportation (USDOT)

Since 1991, the well-funded Transportation Fund has diverted considerable money from highway construction and maintenance into its Enhancements Fund, established to provide flexible funding for transportation-related projects. Many historic preservation projects receive funding by showing a historical tie to transportation (e.g., historic railway stations, rails-to-trails, roadside inns, highway commercial buildings, bridges).

Institute of Museum Services (IMS)

IMS is an independent agency within the executive branch that provides assessment and operating funding to historical museums, whose purpose is to conserve American cultural, historic, and scientific heritage.

Save America's Treasures

Established in 1998 by the Office of the President in anticipation of the Millennium, Save America's Treasures is a national effort to protect "America's threatened cultural treasures, including historic structures, collections, works of art, maps and journals that document and illuminate the history and culture of the United States." Created by Executive Order, Save America's Treasures is a public–private partnership that includes the White House, the National Park Service, and the National Trust for Historic Preservation; it strives to recognize and rescue "enduring symbols of American tradition that define us as a nation."

Preserve America

Another White House initiative, Preserve America, was founded in 2003 and provides grants to selected communities. In collaboration with multiple federal agencies, Preserve America recognition awards have been used for a wide variety of preservation efforts. It does not fund bricks-and-mortar projects, but rather complements the Save America's Treasures grant program by helping local communities develop sustainable resource management strategies and sound business practices for the continued preservation and use of heritage assets.

Chapter Nine

PRESERVATION PLANNING

———•◆•———

INTEGRATING HISTORIC PRESERVATION WITH MASTER PLANS

The goals of city planners and preservationists sometimes appear to conflict with each other. It often is said that planners are pro-development, whereas preservationists are anti-development. Planners look for ways to encourage growth in their community, whereas preservationists are out in front of bulldozers trying to stop new development. However, this should not be, and does not need to be, the case. Preservationists are not against development; they are against *bad* development. They are opposed to development that is insensitive to the existing context of a community and its significant resources and heritage. They are in favor of development that blends new and old in a compatible way that strengthens both.

Decades have passed since the National Historic Preservation Act of 1966 defined historic preservation as a tool of community planning. Since then, hundreds of communities have adopted ordinances and designated local landmarks and historic districts. The National Alliance of Preservation Commissions estimates there are now more than 2,400 regulated historic districts in the United States. Their procedures are well established, and their power to protect historic properties against inappropriate changes has been confirmed in the courts, including the U.S. Supreme Court.

Preservation of our built environment is an important tool of land use planning, and many communities have revitalized older neighborhoods and districts through historic preservation. For example, Baltimore's Federal Hill Historic District contains several hundred eighteenth- and nineteeth-century rowhouses

Federal Hill district, Baltimore. Courtesy of the City of Baltimore.

dramatically overlooking the city's inner harbor area. The historic character of the district's main street helps maintain property values. Its nineteenth-century Cross Street Market has become a primary commercial and social hub for residents. Active neighborhood and business associations bring life to the district through their many activities. Through the protection of its historic character, Federal Hill has retained the sense of a complete community, with healthy residential, commercial, industrial, recreational, and educational uses.

Despite such successful examples, many planners view historic preservation as ancillary to the process of comprehensive planning. They refer to historic districts as "overlay zones," meaning that they are not fully integrated with either the community's zoning code or its master plan. Based on this perspective, a set of relevant questions comes to mind. What is a historic preservation "plan" and what should it contain? Should it be separate from, or integrated with, the comprehensive plan? The American Planning Association's report, *Preparing a Historic Preservation Plan*,[1] suggests ten components of a historic preservation plan. They are:

1. Statement of the goals of preservation in the community, and the purpose of the preservation plan.
2. Definitions of the historic character of the state, region, community, or neighborhood.
3. Summary of past and current efforts to preserve the community's or neighborhood's character.
4. A survey of historic resources in the community or neighborhood, or a definition of the type of survey that should be conducted in communities that have not yet completed a survey.
5. Explanation of the legal basis for protection of historic resources in the state and community.
6. Statement of the relationship between historic preservation and other local land-use and growth management authority, such as the zoning ordinance.
7. Statement of the public sector's responsibilities towards city-owned historic resources, such as public buildings, parks, streets, etc., and for ensuring that public actions do not adversely affect historic resources.
8. Statement of incentives that are, or should be, available to assist in the preservation of the community's historic resources.
9. Statement of the relationship between historic preservation and the community's educational system and program.
10. A precise statement of goals and policies, including a specific agenda for future action to accomplish those goals.

When local preservationists are asked if their community has a historic preservation plan, they typically say yes. But their concept of a plan differs from that of a planner. They may view it as consisting of the surveying and documentation of historic resources in a community or district. From the planner's perspective, such a document is limited in scope and has little to do with a community's broadly based comprehensive plan. However, this perceived disconnect between planning and historic preservation as functions of city government is inappropriate, based on component #6 from the list shown above. Historic preservation will

take its full role in local government only when it becomes an integral part of a community's comprehensive plan.

In 2005, a national survey of State Historic Preservation Offices was conducted.[2] The survey contained a single primary question: "Does your state legislation mandate a historic preservation element in local comprehensive plans?" Responses came from twenty-eight public officials from every geographical region in the United States.[3] The survey indicated that several states—Pennsylvania, Massachusetts, Rhode Island, and South Carolina—clearly mandated a historic preservation component in local comprehensive plans. As an example, Pennsylvania's Planning Code reads as follows:[4]

Section 301 (a) The municipal, multi-municipal, or county comprehensive plan, consisting of maps, charts and textual matter, shall include, but not be limited to the following basic elements

(6) A plan for the protection of natural and historic resources to the extent not preempted by federal or state law. . . .

(7) In addition to any other requirements of this act, a county comprehensive plan shall . . .

(iv) identify a plan for historic preservation.

Map of states with mandates for preservation plans.

A follow-up question asked whether local planners comply with these legislative mandates. Respondents indicated that local governments may follow the mandate, but the level of compliance varies significantly from one community to another.

In other states, legislation *encourages* preservation to be included as an element in comprehensive plans, but 70 percent of the respondents indicated that this approach yields only minimal compliance by local units of government. Two primary reasons emerged for this lack of compliance. The most widespread and common factor is simply a lack of political support. Historic designation is seen as an unwanted encumbrance on property ownership, even though it is a logical extension of local governments' responsibilities for protecting the public welfare. The respondent from the Colorado SHPO's office was representative of a broader opinion when he explained: "There is no mandate in Colorado law. With the possible exception of Boulder and Denver, this is an extremely conservative state. Property rights are paramount, and preservation is basically accomplished through incentives rather than regulation."

This factor merges with a second reason—the cost of producing a historic preservation plan. Done properly, preparation of a historic preservation plan may be time consuming and require specialists not available locally. Many local officials might view this proposed plan as another unfunded state mandate, and the limited number of trained preservationists in the community could result in a substantial cost to realize the survey portion of the plan.

Robert E. Stipe, who studied the legal and governmental aspects of historic preservation for 45 years, clearly argued in his article "What Is a Local Preservation Plan?" that a preservation plan should be part of the comprehensive plan and be given the same official status as any other planning element.[5] This opinion is elaborated in Kelly and Becker's *Community Planning: An Introduction to the Comprehensive Plan*: "Where preservation planning focuses on individual buildings, it is far more narrow in scope. . . . Where it focuses on preservation of a downtown, a neighborhood, or a context within which one or more historic buildings exist, it is much like comprehensive planning. Most effective preservation plans exist in the context of a comprehensive plan, with the comprehensive plan providing the land-use and other contextual items for the preservation plan."[6]

It is important for all communities, urban and rural, to recognize the value of preserving their physical heritage through historic preservation, which can provide economic and social benefits and give residents a sense of place. Historic resources need to be included as integral components of a comprehensive plan. Ideally, historic preservation plans should go beyond research and inventory to include planning elements. The adoption of historic district ordinances should use much more of the structure cited in the American Planning Association's report, described above. State planning enabling legislation should be amended as necessary in order to include a historic preservation component.

Downtown Planning and Preservation

In the last decade or two, many older downtowns have made significant comebacks. In large and small cities, some of the traditional core functions of downtown have been replaced with a new emphasis. Clothing and hardware stores may have moved to the suburbs, but restaurants, gift shops, and entertainment businesses have filled the voids. Local officials and business people have had to adjust to new realities, and the role of the traditional downtown has had to shift significantly to remain viable.

However, downtowns still provide an important focus to cities of all scales and sizes. Their health should not be ignored, since they play a prominent role in

Downtown Huntington, West Virginia.

their communities, and their revitalization can serve many purposes, including the following:

Existing infrastructure. Downtowns have streets, sewer and water lines and other utilities, and a central location. It is wasteful to discard this built-up infrastructure and pay to duplicate it at a city's perimeter. From both an economic and an environmental standpoint, ignoring downtowns is a poor decision for our society. The recycling of downtowns through renovation and redevelopment is a much more sustainable approach.

Community focus. Downtowns traditionally provided a focus for local communities, giving a sense of identity to their residents. Associating their historic downtown with the concept of community did much to create a common sense of purpose among residents, making it easier to raise support for local projects and activities. The need for a place with which to identify is increasingly important in a mobile society. With the loss of downtown fabric comes the loss of a community's center. To borrow Gertrude Stein's words describing Oakland, California, "There is no there there." Downtown provides a "there" much better than a suburban shopping mall.

Functional diversity. Downtowns are characterized by a greater functional diversity than many of the newer centers built on a city's fringe. They serve as a

Menger Hotel, San Antonio, Texas.

locus for a whole range of financial institutions, public agencies and local government offices, public transportation, historic areas, and cultural and educational institutions. This diversity comes in varying degrees but invariably gives downtowns an inherent and lasting strength. By contrast, fringe developments often are unifunctional, devoted only to specialty retailing, quick-stop shopping, or single-size residential, and are therefore more vulnerable to changing times—and indeed may become obsolete. Because of this lack of functional diversity, many suburban developments from the 1950s and 1960s have already been abandoned, to be replaced with newer fringe developments.

Employment. Downtowns can serve as incubators for new businesses, providing a supportive environment for nascent entrepreneurial companies. Research

Quincy Market, Boston.

shows that the highest proportion of new jobs comes from small, start-up businesses, the kind that flourish downtown. A study conducted at the Massachusetts Institute of Technology revealed that 50 percent of all new jobs are generated from expansion of existing small businesses. Such businesses can thrive in the environment of an older downtown, where structures do not have expensive mortgages, rents can be relatively inexpensive, and there are diverse support services available. The retention and prosperity of such businesses are vital to the economic stability and growth of any community. Older buildings respond to changes in economy through adaptive use, providing flexible, incremental, and sometimes inexpensive space for start-up businesses. In contrast, new buildings often are designed as single-use spaces and don't provide such flexibility.

Sprawl reduction. Keeping retail functions in a centralized location may lessen the tendency toward suburban sprawl. Centralization allows better utilization of land, infrastructure, services, and transportation systems.

Historic character. When the inherent historic character of an older downtown is preserved, it can become a tourist attraction, enhancing both the local economy and the sense of community pride. A Travel Industry of America study found that "heritage tourists" stay longer than other tourists and spend more money. For example, it also found 66 percent of midwestern tourists visited a historic place, and historic downtowns were the prime draw. Local economic development specialists are increasingly discovering that historic preservation is good for business. Quincy Market in Boston, redeveloped in the 1970s, is considered the prototype for urban commercial development, and still is a major draw for shoppers, tourists, and economic vitality into the center of the city.

Elements of Downtown Health

Preservationists traditionally have worked to save historic buildings. Yet a program intent only on saving downtown buildings is not enough, for the issue is not just the deterioration of the physical environment of the downtown, but also the decline of its economic and social environment.

After many years spent researching the issues of downtown revitalization by investigating the downtown health in sixteen small cities, Norman Tyler determined which factors have the greatest impact.[7] He found that the preservation of a downtown's physical elements, including its older buildings, historic façades, and streetscape, was important, but only in combination with maintaining functional aspects of the downtown environment.[8] For example, preservation of an old downtown drugstore building should be combined with an attempt to preserve the drugstore business itself, or, if not that specific function, a similar customer-oriented business. These functions (the "verbs" described in Chapter 1) are what define downtown as a focus of community life, not simply the physical groupings of buildings (the "nouns"). Downtown preservation efforts need to have goals beyond the physical preservation of buildings. Revitalization efforts, for example, should encourage existing businesses to remain downtown, for many residents associate specific businesses with a downtown's viability as a commercial district. Many are family-owned businesses that have not changed in years. Tactics should be found to update their operations, to make them vital and competitive in a changing market, without losing the historic integrity of the structures in which they are located.

Downtown redevelopment professionals and preservationists should recognize the need to bring new businesses to older downtowns. These core areas should not be seen as museums where time stands still but as organisms that continually evolve into new forms. The continuity of such districts relies on their ability to change over time. Because they are composed of commercial establishments, they need to change much more than other types of historic districts. A common conflict is encountered when preservationists encourage the restoration of downtown façades and storefronts. Such restoration advocates may fail to recognize that good promotional strategies for a retail establishment may include the need to periodically update its image and present a fresh face. It is generally accepted that retail stores should have a new image every five to ten years. The restoration of the storefront can provide a new and positive image; a historic image is marketable and well accepted by the public. Thus, restoration or rehabilitation of a storefront can, by itself, draw customers. The problem arises when, five or ten years later, the business is ready for another new image. What does the preservationist suggest then? This issue is unique to downtown preservation efforts, and flexibility must be the key. Whereas the goal in residential and institutional restorations is to retain and restore as much of the original structure as possible, the goal of many commercial projects is to retain the basic historical integrity of the structure while allowing the freedom to change, to provide for the image needs of the current business.

THE MAIN STREET PROGRAM

In 1980, the National Trust for Historic Preservation established the Main Street Program. National Trust leaders felt there was too much focus on saving individual landmark buildings and not enough on the more complex problems of downtown districts. Many preservationists at that time viewed downtown revitalization as a problem for others because it involved issues of marketing, economic development, and urban infrastructure, not necessarily within their realm.

The original concept for the Main Street Program was to challenge this assumption because many historic downtown commercial buildings were being either defaced or demolished in attempts to revitalize. The Main Street Program

Madison, Indiana, an original Main Street community.

was established to explore how rehabilitation of older commercial buildings could be an important part of downtown revitalization efforts. Initially, there were three pilot projects—in Galesburg, Illinois; Hot Springs, South Dakota; and Madison, Indiana. Revitalization experts were placed in each of these communities for three years to develop strategies for using preservation as a tool of downtown revitalization. What these early Main Street experts found was that preservation is inextricably linked to economic development and promotion, and the goals for downtown business owners and local preservationists were closely aligned.

The Main Street Program's Four-Point Approach

The Main Street Program's approach to downtown revitalization is based on four key ingredients that provide a commonsense way to address the variety of issues and problems facing traditional downtowns and other older business districts.

The underlying premise is to promote economic development through historic preservation, relying on traditional commercial values such as self-reliance, distinctive architecture, personal service, and local empowerment. The program's distinguishing four-point approach includes the following:

1. *Organization.* Perhaps the most difficult aspect of any revitalization effort is to create the organizational framework that brings together interest groups and individuals. Each comes to the table with its own agenda and sphere of interest. The merchants' association may be interested in the promotion of retail sales, the Chamber of Commerce in job creation, and city government in providing municipal services. Without coordination, these efforts may not be mutually supportive and in some cases may be at odds. The Main Street Program's project manager brings such groups together under an umbrella organization that deals directly and exclusively with the concerns of downtown.

2. *Promotion.* In many communities, the downtown is largely overlooked by citizens who regularly shift their consumer shopping patterns. To counter this, downtown needs to compete by promoting itself and presenting an attractive new image. Promotions are considered critical to attracting people downtown. By selecting various targeted groups (e.g., families with children, young professionals, tourists), the creation of sales and special events establishes downtown as a place of activity where something new and interesting is constantly occurring.

3. *Design.* Although physical improvements alone are not enough to revitalize an area, storefront rehabilitation and streetscape improvements provide visual proof that something is happening in a downtown. The design aspect of the Main Street Program is important because it provides evidence of revitalization activity in the course of creating a more desirable environment.

4. *Economic restructuring.* Financial support for a revitalization program is the last critical component in the Main Street Program approach. This effort attempts to find financial resources for revitalization work. A typical strategy may enlist local banks in a revolving loan program that funds rehabilitation work. In the past, downtowns were largely ignored by local lending institutions that saw little business potential there. But when local banks are convinced to give their support jointly, no one would feel greatly exposed to risk.

The four-point approach works most effectively when combined with eight principles as guides to developing revitalization strategies:

1. *Comprehensiveness.* A single project cannot revitalize a downtown or commercial neighborhood. An ongoing series of initiatives is vital to build community support and create lasting progress.

2. *Incremental approach.* Small projects make a big difference. They demonstrate that a downtown is alive, but also hone the skills and confidence of program supporters to tackle more complex problems.

3. *Self-help.* Although the National Main Street Center can provide valuable direction and hands-on technical assistance, only local leadership can initiate long-term success by fostering and demonstrating community involvement and commitment to the revitalization effort.

4. *Public–private partnership.* Every local program needs the support and expertise of both the public and private sectors. For an effective partnership, each must recognize the strengths of the other.

5. *Identification of, and capitalization on, existing assets.* A key goal of the program is to help communities recognize and make the best use of their unique offerings. Local assets provide the solid foundation for a successful Main Street initiative.

6. *Quality.* From storefront design to promotional campaigns to special events, high quality must be the main goal in all activities.

7. *Change.* Changing community attitudes and habits is essential to bringing about a commercial district renaissance. A carefully planned Main Street program helps to shift public perceptions and practices to support and sustain the revitalization process.

8. *Action orientation.* Frequent, visible changes in the look and activities of the commercial district reinforce the perception of positive change. Small but dramatic improvements early in the process remind the community that the revitalization effort is underway.[9]

According to data collected by the Main Street Center in Washington, D.C., since the program's inception the total public and private reinvestment in communities that have established a Main Street Program has been over $41 billion, with the average investment per community over $11 million. The program has led to the rehabilitation of 186,000 buildings and 350,000 resulting new jobs, with $25 reinvested for every $1 spent on program administration.[10]

In addition to its community offices, the center serves as a national clearinghouse for information and resources for communities following the Main Street approach. It provides resources to local officials and downtown development managers and coordinates regular National Town Meeting conferences, which communicate a wealth of how-to techniques. The positive results of this program are evident.

HISTORIC PRESERVATION AND THE "EXPERIENCE ECONOMY"

Local economic development as a tool of planning can happen through many types of approaches. For example, it can result from new industries, commercial growth, the new marketing of existing businesses, tourism, or even job training. These more traditional approaches to economic development can provide a stable base for a local economy. But there are new approaches to economic development as well, representing new American lifestyles in many ways. In a society no longer based primarily on agriculture and manufacturing, but rather on information technology, where much of our environment is global and even virtual, new approaches to economic development must reflect these new attitudes and interests.

One such new approach is referred to as the "experience economy"—an economy based not on commodities but on the sale of experiences. As stated by Joseph Pine and James Gilmore in *The Experience Economy*, "Recognizing experiences as a distinct economic offering provides the key to future economic growth."[11] One of their examples illustrates this point clearly. The cost of coffee beans when harvested is approximately 50¢ per pound; the cost of those same beans when sold as premium drinks at a Starbucks is about $230 per pound. This is a startling multiplier based on the concept of value added. The true genius and success of Starbucks is that they have taken that common cup of coffee, converted it into a specialty drink known as a Cinnamon Dolce Latte or White Chocolate Mocha Frappuccino, and then sold it in a shop with comfortable chairs and pleasant surroundings, wireless Internet connections, and an air of "cool." As a result, they are able to charge double or triple the going rate for a simple cup of coffee. It is clear they are selling more than the coffee; they are also selling a special experience.

Communities can learn from the Starbucks success, for they can also benefit by marketing themselves as part of the experience economy. Today, people want to buy more than commodities and goods; they even want to buy more than service. They are willing to spend more to purchase experiences.

Starbucks coffee shop.

Experiences involving historic preservation, often referred to as cultural heritage tourism, can be important to such an economic development program. A study conducted in Virginia recently found that heritage visitors stay longer, visit twice as many places, and on a per-trip basis spend two-and-a-half times more money than other visitors.[12] Wherever heritage tourism has been evaluated, this basic tendency is observed: heritage visitors stay longer, spend more per day and, therefore, have a significantly greater per-trip economic impact.

Across the nation, historic places are incorporating experiences into their sites. Marketing vintage sites as new experiences is increasingly common, as are interactive kiosks and touch-screen stations, bar-code-based responses, holographic or robotic-based interpretation, and more hands-on experiences. Some of this is being fueled by an interest in keeping up with the "edutainment" nature of many places such as zoos and even libraries, and, of course, the Disney parks.

Theaters as Part of the Experience Economy

Theaters can serve an important role in the experience economy and aid urban revitalization. The reincarnation of a vacant, derelict theater located in the heart of a struggling downtown district means more than fixing up a building and hanging out a banner saying "OPEN" again. It also means that the theater needs to be a viable member of its business community, partnering with its stores and restaurants and other businesses to create the vitality that was once part of a historic downtown.

Theaters provide more than a commodity; they also provide a regular series of experiences. This is especially true with historic theaters, which provide a setting that appeals to all the senses. Historic "atmospheric theaters," with their fantasy landscapes and colorful lighting, tap into the visual sense very strongly.

Civic Theater interior, Akron, Ohio. Courtesy of Wilson Butler Architects, Boston, Massachusetts/Robert Benson Photography, Hartford, Connecticut.

The sense of sound is also an important part of the theater experience. Whether a live musical performance or the high-definition soundtrack of a new movie, sound is central to the experience. At some theaters, restored organs are played before the showing of a movie, reminding patrons of the enjoyment of an audio component as part of the experience. Similarly, the sense of smell comes from the always-present popcorn machine, and whether one is hungry or not, this smell satisfies the sense of taste as part of the movie experience. Finally, the sense of touch is served by comfortable upholstered theater seating. A theater can appeal to all the senses in a satisfying way.

Theaters provide a way of reaching out and touching other members of a community as an alternative to the isolated experience of sitting at home and watching a movie on the television or DVD player. Theaters can be the focus of community activities. In a survey of members of the League of Historic American Theaters (LHAT),[13] respondents described many ways in which theaters have provided entertainment for the larger community. Schools often use local historic theaters for performances, recitals, and graduation ceremonies, involving students as volunteers. Local libraries link to theater activities by disseminating information and scripts about upcoming performances, as a venue for relevant book and author series, for tour programs, and even giving tickets as prizes for summer reading programs. Cultural arts programs may use the theater lobby as an art gallery space, rent the space as a dance studio, utilize it for special arts festivals, and even make it available on Sunday mornings for religious services. Local organizations may use a historic theater as a venue for fundraising events or political functions, as well as for swearing-in and other special civic ceremonies. Lastly, theaters may be rented for private special events such as weddings, birthdays, and anniversaries.

In the LHAT survey, local business owners said that a theater could have a significant impact on their nearby businesses beyond the activities that take place in the theater. The theater, with its evening hours, boosts downtown dining revenues, increases pedestrian traffic both before and after performances, serves as an important amenity when trying to attract new businesses and investment, and can be a keystone to revitalization efforts. As one downtown business owner stated, "A theater is probably the closest thing most downtowns have to an anchor store."

In smaller cities across the country, many downtowns "roll up the sidewalk" at 5:30 in the afternoon. "Mom-and-Pop"-type business owners don't like to spend their evenings in their store after spending the day there, and the scale of the businesses often doesn't allow them to take on the costs associated with expanded evening hours. However, daytime hours are convenient only for the unemployed. Even if one or two merchants stayed open later, their small numbers would not encourage additional shoppers. As a result, residents have made a habit of frequenting the stores at local malls, where businesses must stay open for extended hours. In contrast, theaters, restaurants, and other service and entertainment businesses fill downtown sidewalks with patrons during evening hours. These hours offer great potential for economic growth in the local economy. Studies have shown that with the proper mix of functions, street activity can remain almost at daytime levels through 11:00 P.M., and in some situations (e.g., larger cities, university towns) can remain at about half that level from 11:00 P.M until 3:00 A.M.[14]

Case Study: City Opera House, Traverse City, Michigan

The Traverse City Opera House was built in the nineteenth century, when a theater building had to fulfill many functional requirements. Although called an opera house, the space was more typically used for traveling vaudeville shows, local school performances, weddings, and community events. The space was as much a meeting hall as a theater. Also typical was its location on the second and third floors of a building, leaving important retail operations on the first floor.

City officials in Traverse City made a commitment to the vision that a restored City Opera House would both contribute to, and benefit from, Traverse City's growing reputation as a "destination" resort and regional commercial center. A planning study in 1995 generated plans for reuse of the building and provided strong graphic documents to illustrate and sell the idea to the community.

The Opera House's rehabilitation project was designed to retain the structure's historic integrity while catering to modern needs. The need for a larger backstage area led to the construction of a second-floor "crossover addition" to a building on the other side of the alley. This addition created new space for dressing rooms, set construction, an elevator, and a green room. Space at the front of house was filled with offices, antiquated restrooms, and an entry stair from the street that left no space for patrons during intermission, restricting its use. This problem was alleviated by utilizing an adjacent building for a new and wider stair, commodious restrooms, offices, and rehearsal rooms, giving more space at the front of the house for gathering functions and a much larger lobby. These changes updated the historic theater with elements necessary for a modern facility. The rear

City Opera House, Traverse City, Michigan. Courtesy of Quinn Evans Architects.

entrance now accommodates its service functions, while the enhanced entrance on Main Street keeps the theater's patrons on the sidewalk, where they pass stores and restaurants on their way to the theater.

The Traverse City Opera House is not only a beautifully restored structure, but its successful restoration also reinforced its partnership in the economic revitalization of downtown Traverse City. The project has had significant cultural and financial impact on the downtown, adding customers to many businesses. It has been estimated that the project generates $5,000 per seat per year, or an annual yield of $3,600,000 into the downtown community.

VARYING PERSPECTIVES ON COMMUNITY PLANNING AND PRESERVATION

Preservationists have a special interest in their community that is expressed in the protection of its historic heritage. However, each community's citizens may have diverse interests, goals, and agendas, and preservation may or may not be one of them. Preservationists can better understand how to protect their community's heritage by integrating that process with the natural and inevitable course of change and development that is an important part of any contemporary community. Sometimes the goals of citizens support preservation, and sometimes they may seem to be counter to preservation goals. Understanding the perspectives of others helps preservationists better deal with the full range of concerns as they arise.

City or Municipal Council Members

The municipal council is composed of elected representatives who are responsible to their constituents throughout the community. The council's actions often may be based on political expedience. Whereas other city agencies follow policy, the city council makes and implements policy. Most actions of a local historic commission are subject, in some form or other, to review by the council, as commission members are typically appointed either by the mayor or council. Historic ordinances also are subject to review and approval by the council, as is the designation of new districts or individual historic structures. Therefore, council support for the work of a historic study committee or historic district commission is necessary, and it cannot be taken for granted. Some council members may be fully aware of the importance of historic districts and the work of the commission, but others may not be. They may view the commission's work as extraneous and unnecessary, or even as an impediment to the community's ability to grow and prosper.

Because council giveth, council can also taketh away, at least to the extent that it is empowered to do so. It is therefore incumbent on preservation activists and historic district commission members to regularly educate and inform council members on preservation issues. This is important not only when a big vote is scheduled on a specific project. Rather, such an effort should also consist of a program that fosters regular awareness by, for example, an annual preservation awards program, the provision of printed updates on preservation issues, and the release of news features on historically significant structures.

Planning Commission and Planning Department

Although lumped together for purposes of discussion here, a city's planning department and its planning commission are different bodies. Each fulfills a function of planning for community growth, but from differing perspectives. The planning commission, consisting of residents appointed by council, represents the interests of the community at large, and its meetings include time for residents to voice their opinions on proposals. The planning department, in contrast, is composed of professional planners, not necessarily from the community, who are responsible for providing the technical and professional backup essential for planning commissioners and city council members to make determinations.

The underlying purpose of both the planning commission and planning department staff is to review development proposals and (1) verify if the plans satisfy regulations and are in the best interests of the community, (2) recommend approval or disapproval of plans as submitted, and (3) advise the city council of their determinations. As such, the commission and department provide an important overview function and can recognize how each proposed project fits within the long-range goals of the community. If preservation and downtown revitalization are defined as important goals, then planners can do much to encourage preservation by approving compatible development and discouraging inappropriate proposals.

Downtown Development Authorities

Downtown Development Authorities (DDAs) were instituted in the 1970s as a way to deal with the special needs of older downtowns. Many states also offer legislation allowing Business Improvement Districts (BIDs), where the private sector delivers services for revitalization beyond what the local government can reasonably be expected to provide. State enabling legislation allowed communities to establish DDAs with the twin goals of preventing downtown deterioration and promoting economic growth and revitalization. In many communities, DDAs are closely tied to downtown preservation efforts. In some cases, the DDA office serves also as the Main Street program office, with overlapping activities and personnel. DDAs are essentially revenue allocation authorities that encourage public and private development activities in downtowns. They can be very effective in providing funding for public improvements in historic districts.

DDAs are limited in the ways they can use their revenues. Projects are financed as public improvements and are intended to encourage private investment, but they must not directly benefit private individuals. For instance, street and sidewalk improvements within the downtown are an appropriate use of DDA funds, but improvements to individual structures generally are not, unless they are part of a general program available to all, such as a façade improvement program. Often DDAs work in conjunction with local banks, the DDA paying for public improvements and banks establishing a loan fund pool for individual property owners.

A typical financial basis for DDA funding is tax increment financing (TIF). Simply stated, TIF financing derives revenues through increases in district property values. First, the city determines the initial assessed value of properties within a defined downtown district for a specified year (the base year). This level of tax revenues from the base year continues to go into general municipal fund revenues. However, each year thereafter, the treasurer transmits to the DDA authority all monies that exceed this base amount within the district. This so-called "captured" assessed value is the tax increment revenue, which the DDA board can use within the district to encourage redevelopment. With TIF, any increase in the base amount created by renovations, rehabilitations, or new development within the downtown district is allocated exclusively to the DDA for use on designated projects within its boundaries. DDAs may also create a second source of revenue from the sale of municipal bonds based on the new increment financing.

Developers and Investors

Developers are in the business of looking for good economic opportunities. Whether for themselves or representing the interests of others, the primary focus of any developer is to maximize return on investment dollars. Often this focus seems to pit developers against the interests of preservation. The best investment opportunities are typically found in "hot" locations, and these locations may include downtown. Small older buildings in these prime locations often are viewed by developers as underutilized and are not considered the "highest and best use" for that property. In the view of developers, historic structures can be seen as standing in the way of progress.

However, when developers are looking for investment opportunities, one of their biggest concerns is the cost involved from "unknowns." From their perspective, a project may take years to be realized, and during that time interest rates could change, some investors may back out, and the market cycle might take a distinct change in direction. Developers spend considerable amounts of money, and run many risks, during this period of "up-front" investment before the prospects for a project can be assured.

Preservationists can best work with developers by helping elected officials define the rules of the development game before proposals are on the table. It is important to establish a public list of structures and historic districts determined to be in need of protection, along with a well-thought-out ordinance that clearly defines what development will and will not be permitted. Developers tend to be cooperative when the city and its agencies have established clear community goals and policies that make the outcome of development proposals predictable, and where opposition from special-interest groups and residents is minimal. Generally, only after developers invest a considerable amount of money in a project and then see opposition from preservationists developing as a belated response do they dig in for battle to protect their initial investment.

However, developers can be tough-minded, and preservationists may need to take a cynical, hard stance to influence them. Writer Arthur Frommer displayed that cynicism when he spoke many years ago to preservationists in Chicago:

> Adopt a more confrontational approach to the real estate developers; subordinate your normal tendency to gentility: it will not work. The developers are motivated by that most powerful of urges—short-term financial gain—a drive far stronger in most instances than the principled motives of the public advocating preservation. They will always find reasons for demolition where the dollar is at stake. They will run roughshod over your most urgent pleas.[15]

If a community has well-established historic ordinances and design review procedures, developers typically are willing to abide by them and design their project accordingly. They are willing to accommodate a community's plans and goals and look for investment opportunities within that framework. It can be a win–win situation for a community if it can both encourage investment and protect its resources at the same time. Wise community leaders can accomplish this goal and put these tools in place.

Architects

Architects generally take a broader view than developers. There are two reasons architects are generally more sympathetic to existing context and historic districts. First, they have been taught that good design should include provision for

Architects working.

considering larger community interests. An architect services his or her client as
well as a community and its interests. Second, architects' training has included
study of historic buildings and styles, and as a result they may have a greater
appreciation for historical context.

However, architects are paid by their clients, and their primary role is as an
agent for their clients' interests. There is both a financial and emotional investment in a project proposal they have created, and if design changes become necessary because of local opposition, they will need to spend additional time and
resources to redesign it. To avoid such pitfalls, it is important for preservation
interests to review project proposals as early in the design process as possible. If a
historic district commission review is one of the last steps in the development
process, it may be too late to insist on substantive changes. Review and comment
at an early stage is an excellent way to minimize conflict. It is also an excellent
idea to provide printed guidelines describing appropriate design in a historic context. These may suggest how to preserve significant historic elements when
adding to or adapting an older building, and should also give examples of how

new design can be compatible through the use of proper scale, proportion, set-back, materials, etc.

Residents

Residents are primarily concerned about quality-of-life issues, especially the impact of changes on their own residential areas. Although residents have no direct role in the decision-making process, their input can be very effective in two ways. First, they can express their opinions and emotions at the public hearings that are required for all large projects. Second, they have the power to elect officials to local government who respect their opinions and respond to their concerns. It is essential for preservationists to continually educate the public about the values of their historic heritage and the role of historic districts in preserving community character.

URBAN GROWTH BOUNDARIES AND RURAL PRESERVATION

One way to preserve the character of both urban and rural areas is to contain urban sprawl. The concern with encroaching sprawl found at the edges of most American cities has led some communities and states to adopt the concept of urban growth boundaries. In Oregon, growth boundaries define the limits of urban area growth and allow only low-density land uses beyond those established boundaries. The method accomplishes three goals: it contains the cost of infrastructure, it protects the environment, and it helps prevent piecemeal destruction of the rural landscape.

Historic preservation has focused primarily on cities and their historic landmark buildings and districts. Recently, increasing attention has been paid to protecting our rural heritage, including hamlets, individual sites, and their structures. Historic districts in rural areas follow the same regulatory process, but often include vernacular structures clustered throughout the landscape and more environmental features. Thus there is a need for a systematic process to identify and protect meaningful and valued landscapes, with provisions appropriate to the rural situation. Rural residents often take a laissez-faire attitude toward such local government control, making the establishment and protection of rural districts more difficult and challenging, but also more needed.

In recent years there has been a special interest in the conservation and protection of agricultural land. Under current market conditions, agricultural land is often worth much more to its owners when sold for suburban development than when kept and farmed. It is difficult to expect a farmer to ignore this economic reality. As a result, large areas of prime agricultural farmland—especially farmland close to urban centers—are lost each year to speculative development. Communities now recognize that such a changeover in land use not only takes farmland out of agricultural use, but also leads to both sprawl of urbanized areas and degeneration of city centers and the urban core. Over the years, a variety of programs have been tried to protect rural areas. Many communities have attempted to deal with the problem of sprawl through a land use regulations approach. When farmland is zoned for agricultural conservation, it cannot be sold for more intense development. This also reassures farmers that they will not be subject to nuisance suits from irate suburban homeowners who move in next to a farm and then complain about the noise and smell of farm operations. In New York State, over three hundred conservation districts have been formed, controlling approximately six million acres, or well over one-third of the state's farmland.

Suburban fringe development.

PRESERVATION AND TRANSPORTATION

During the decades of the 1960s through the 1980s, many historic buildings fell to the powerful pressures of "progress." There were no more heavy-handed aggressors than the bulldozers of the country's many highway programs. The rich historic fabric of downtowns and in-town neighborhoods were destroyed in an attempt to make the city center accessible to the new and dominant force of the suburban commuter. As early as 1966, Pennsylvaina Senator Joseph S. Clark said, "It is time that Congress took a look at the highway program, because it is presently being operated by barbarians, and we ought to have some civilized understanding of just what we do to spots of historic interest and great beauty by the building of eight-lane highways through the middle of our cities."[16]

This approach of running roughshod over historic neighborhoods and structures changed significantly with the 1991 passage of a landmark bill, the Intermodal Surface Transportation Efficiency Act (ISTEA; pronounced "iced tea") and currently the SAFETEA-LU bill of 2005. These bills have recognized that the Transportation Fund, controlled by the U.S. Department of Transportation, has a huge reservoir of money collected from user taxes, primarily the gas tax. Since the 1950s, this money had been used to pay for construction of the interstate highway system. But the original network of new highways was completed in the 1990s, and there was pressure to make some portion of these funds available for uses other than repairs and improvements. The new transportation bills included a provision that 10 percent of available funds would go toward the "Transportation Enhancements" program. This reservoir of funding would be made available for other types of transportation-related projects. Historic preservationists have seen this as an opportunity to redress some of the damage done during the decades of unstoppable construction, and they have successfully requested significant funding for the restoration and preservation of historic sites and structures linked to transportation. Since the first act in 1991, the Transportation Enhancements Fund has provided substantial support for the restoration and rehabilitation of historic properties across the country.

SUMMARY

The broad field of historic preservation incorporates many aspects of community and regional planning. Preservation is not an exclusive, but an inclusive, activity, and it can be seen from many perspectives. The National Trust for Historic Preservation has referred to the role of preservation simply as a responsibility to preserve our heritage and "protect the irreplaceable." It is for all of us to continue to explore the relevance of its role in planning our communities, and to become more aware of the importance of historic preservation in our everyday lives.

Chapter Ten

SUSTAINABILITY AND PARTNERING WITH THE ENVIRONMENTAL COMMUNITY

———◆———

PRESERVATION AND SUSTAINABILITY

"The earth is not given to us by our parents, it is lent to us by our children."[1]

Our culture is drunk on the new and now. This intoxication clouds our judgment, causing us to profoundly undervalue the legacy of our forebears. Clearly, preservation itself is a calculated reaction to our culture's insensitivity to the past and to the cultural vandalism that it has perpetrated in the name of progress. Preservationists recognize truth in this observation.

Beyond regretting these blows to history's legacy, our culture equally underappreciates the significance of our actions today on the future—not a distant future, but our children's. As preservation teaches us all to better value the past, it also helps us to fully awaken to our responsibilities to the future. This is the unbreakable bond between preservation and sustainability.

To keep pace with the rapidly evolving trends in sustainable design, preservationists need to be informed about sustainable technologies and their effect on historic resources, as these may well be keys to the future of many historic structures. It's like throwing the baby out with the bathwater to demolish a viable historic building and replace it with something totally new. Although the new structure may be outfitted extravagantly with new "green" technologies, the energy required to demolish the old building, the added waste stream in our landfills, and the energy required to obtain materials and erect the replacement structure often result in a huge net addition in energy consumption. Retrofitting a building with energy-efficient components and installing energy-efficient system upgrades are realistic solutions that can offset traditional models of energy use. In the future, "significance" deliberations may consider energy efficiency based on a structure's embodied energy index as a primary criterion, above general architectural and historic significance.

"The Greenest Building Is . . . One That Is Already Built"[2]

Recently the national discussion about the future of our cities, perhaps our civilization, changed from a debate over *whether* human impacts on the environment are leading to potentially severe problems to one focused on *what we can do* to diminish and even reverse those impacts. Today, preventing climate change is the rallying call for millions, not just traditional environmental activists.

However, this environmentally conscious approach still faces problems. Largely, the effort known as the "green building movement" remains blind to its most troubling truth: We cannot build our way to sustainability. Even if, with the wave of a green wand, every building constructed from this day hence has a

Redevelopment of Lowertown district, St. Paul, Minnesota.

vegetative roof, is powered only with renewable energy sources, and is built entirely of environmentally appropriate materials, sustainability would still be far from fully realized. Seeking salvation through green building fails to account for the overwhelming vastness of the existing building stock. *The accumulated building stock is the elephant in the room.* Ignoring it, we risk being trampled by it. We cannot *build* our way to sustainability; we must *conserve* our way to it.

Consider the numbers. The U.S. Department of Energy maintains a database of America's nonresidential buildings, its *Commercial Building Energy Consumption Survey.*[3] Its latest update indicated that there are some 65 billion square feet of nonresidential buildings in the United States. An economic projection by *Architect* magazine[4] estimates up to 28 billion square feet of new construction by 2030, an increase of 40 percent. The report also notes that during the same period, more than 54 billion square feet of nonresidential building stock, about 84 percent of it, will undergo substantial modification.

Picture it this way: Four out of every five existing buildings will be renovated over the next generation while two new buildings are added. Can sustainability be achieved if our green vision extends only to new buildings, ignoring the enormous challenges of existing buildings and communities? It is up to the preservation community to call attention to this issue.

Sustaining the Existing Building Stock

About 6 percent of the existing building stock was constructed before 1920. This small slice contains America's best-loved historic buildings. From a green design viewpoint, this segment also includes those structures built before the introduction of climate-control and lighting systems powered with fossil fuels. There is a wealth of traditional, vernacular, and indigenous structures that deserve close study by preservationists and green building professionals alike. Another 11 percent of the nonresidential building stock consists of twentieth-century buildings constructed up to the end of World War II. Building technology began to change rapidly during this period, turning away from traditional construction materials and methods and toward complex mechanical and electrical systems characterized by electric heat, central air conditioning and larger kitchens and bathrooms with many more modern amenities.

The buildings that make up these two older segments of the building stock garner by far the most attention from preservationists. Over the past four decades, tried-and-true conservation treatments have been developed that employ remarkably efficient methods to sustain these traditional structures. Preservationists are justified in heralding these achievements as sustainable in their own right. Indeed, a much more methodical effort is needed to measure, document, and report the effectiveness of preservation as a green building strategy based on the work accomplished with these core elements of the historic building stock.

However, it must also be acknowledged that the buildings preservationists most frequently address represent a very small percentage of the entire stock. Preservation will become more relevant to sustainability by expanding the scope of the buildings conserved. This expanded role should be paralleled by a shift in priorities among preservationists toward neighborhood revitalization models, where ordinary buildings are embraced for their contribution to a larger context.

The Modern-era Building Stock

Given the numbers, preservation will have to address a much larger building stock when modern-era buildings become more fully the stuff of preservation. The buildings from the 1950s through the 1980s constitute about 55 percent of the existing nonresidential building stock in the United States, a whopping 36 billion square feet. In part, the postwar building boom was made possible by new design attitudes, ones that emphasized new building forms and the application of new technology over traditional building types and craft.

Post-war architecture is markedly different aesthetically from its traditional predecessors and generally performs very differently as well. Both preservation and green building advocates readily agree that post-war buildings present greater challenges to both disciplines. Preservation professionals have begun to wrestle with the problems of post-war structures, including their construction materials and assemblies that often lack durability and their absolute reliance on equipment that consumes fossil fuels. This large and problematic segment of the building stock is going to require new thinking about both preservation and green building. In practical terms, the quantity of the post-war building stock dictates the need to find ways to use these buildings far into the future. Their (sometimes) lack of quality requires finding efficient yet effective ways to transform them, elevating their performance to sustainable levels.

By accepting the need to transform post-war buildings, preservation will need to be transformed as well. Preservationists have been too quick to embrace

Modern-era building, Columbus, Indiana.

historic exemptions, most relevantly, from standards such as the National Energy Code. There are alternatives to historic exemptions. Achieving reasonable accommodation and proposing alternative compliance methods are two. For both preservation and green building professionals, it is absolutely critical to study in detail and truly appreciate the characteristics that define the existing building stock. The preservation community needs to invest more resources in this endeavor.

What Is Sustainable, Really?

If preservation is going to make a valuable contribution to sustaining our communities, then preservationists need a deeper understanding of what constitutes sustainability. In today's "green marketplace," where green claims are made about virtually every product and service, clarification is required. What makes clarity most elusive is that our perspective on sustainability is evolving so rapidly.

"The greenest building is . . . one that is already built" is a credo that takes into account the massive investment of materials and energy in existing buildings (embodied energy). It is both obvious and profound that extending the useful service life of the building stock is common sense, good business, and sound resource management. A twenty-year guarantee for a building component, such as a roof, should not mean that this component is guaranteed to need replacement in twenty years. To fully capture the value of the existing building stock requires merging two disciplines: historic preservation and green building. It requires an understanding of how to respect and renew what is already here and a vision for where and how to transform the legacy of the past into the promise of tomorrow.

Building Life Cycles

As buildings are conserved, which treatments are undertaken is often determined by careful, even exhaustive, assessment of the conditions of each material and element. Buildings are complex assemblies. Conservators pick apart each assembly into its components and repair or replace what needs to be conserved. Following this process gives preservationists a very clear view of the life cycles of buildings.

But sometimes this view is confounded by the commercial notion that buildings have useful life spans that are, however, subject to the tax depreciation tables established for investments in many buildings. This can give the impression that a building's usefulness is no longer valued when it reaches the end of its depreciable life. Building owners have been known to walk away from older structures rather than reinvest the necessary capital to revitalize them. In one such case in Toledo, Ohio, a parking lot developer even offered to pay the cost to demolish an early (1895) reinforced concrete office building and split the monthly proceeds with the landowner. Fortunately, this scenario did not materialize, and this important building in the downtown was saved. The original owners had lost sight of the building's true life cycle and of its potential usefulness as a viable commercial venture.

Life-cycle analysis (LCA) and life-cycle cost analysis (LCCA) are considered fundamental tools of green building. There are quite a number of well-developed LCA protocols for rating the cradle-to-grave performance and environmental impacts of construction materials and products.[5] However, there are considerable obstacles to applying LCA to entire building projects. In short, the number of variables is simply overwhelming.

The process begins with sorting building elements into four categories: structure, building envelope, interior elements, and systems. These categories shape a workable list that differentiates building components according to their life cycle.

Preservation teaches firsthand the practical limits of durability. Structural elements can, and really should, be constructed to last for a very, very long time. By code and for safety reasons, structural elements must be constructed for survivability, that is, the ability to survive fires, earthquakes, and storms. In most cases, when survivability is achieved, almost unlimited durability is achieved at the same time.

On the other hand, building envelope elements are exposed to weathering. Periodic renewal is an unavoidable reality, ranging from simple routine maintenance, such as painting, to more substantial reconditioning and selective replacement. It is an absolute mystery to preservationists why so many "high-performance" windows are designed without any consideration for their renewal. Such systems are sold as maintenance-free. In fact, they cannot be repaired.[6] For example, today's glazing systems are complex, multicomponent assemblies. Although their thermal and solar heat-gain performance characteristics may be admirable, window assemblies made out of materials that last for hundreds of years (aluminum, glass) are doomed to early retirement due to "differential durability" problems—for example, edge seals that fail in a couple of decades.

Energy Performance

Preservationists must accept the need to improve the energy performance of the existing building stock. The fact that the electrical power that runs our buildings contributes substantially to global warming and climate change should not be ignored. Seeking exemption from this requirement does nothing more than marginalize preservation. Far too many preservationists bristle at the mention of using renewable energy at historic sites. Images of solar collectors that are promoted as looking exactly like a slate roof or in-ground geothermal heating/cooling systems immediately come to mind. But preservationists should understand more than most that good solutions come from well-integrated design, since their mandate is to protect the aesthetics inherent in historic buildings.

Over the past twenty years, green building practitioners have developed technologies that make changing the energy performance of existing structures achievable. Many preservationists are adopting them today. Energy modeling is the most powerful one. Energy models are computer-based simulation tools that predict the energy performance of a building. The characteristics of the building are entered, including climate data, building orientation and form, roofing, wall materials, and window sizes and types. The performance characteristics of all energy-consuming systems are input, including mechanical systems, lighting, and plug loads. Finally, operational and interior environmental settings are added into the mix. The program predicts energy use around the clock and year. Energy simulations can be calibrated to provide amazing accuracy. Many scenarios can be simulated so that tradeoffs between building alterations and system design can be tested.

LEADERSHIP IN ENERGY AND ENVIRONMENTAL DESIGN

The American system of evaluating a building's energy performance is based on the Leadership in Energy and Environmental Design (LEED) system developed by the U.S. Green Building Council. LEED rating systems are managed through a consensus-based process led by volunteer committees composed of a diverse group of practitioners and experts representing a cross-section of the building and construction industry. This system is constantly evolving to meet the demand for an objective tool to accurately measure better building performance.

The number and complexity of LEED systems is daunting, but simply put, the primary options are LEED-NC for New Construction and Major Renovations, or LEED-EB for Existing Buildings: Operations and Maintenance. Although LEED-EB suggests applicability to existing buildings, in actuality this system is more suited to addressing ongoing operations and maintenance issues, such as whole-building cleaning and maintenance, including chemical use; ongoing indoor air quality; energy efficiency; water efficiency; recycling programs and facilities; exterior maintenance programs; and systems upgrades to meet green building energy, water, indoor air quality, and lighting performance standards.

Comprehensive rehabilitation projects will benefit from using LEED-NC, as most work will fit within the six LEED credit categories. Basically, it is important to understand that LEED is a point-based system whereby projects earn LEED points by satisfying specific green building criteria. Within each of the six LEED credit categories, projects must satisfy particular prerequisites to earn points. The six categories include sustainable sites, water efficiency, energy and atmosphere, materials and resources, indoor environmental quality, and innovation in design. The number of points a project earns determines the level of LEED certification the project receives. LEED certification is available in four progressive levels: Certified, Silver, Gold, and Platinum.

Gerding Theater,
Portland, Oregon.
Courtesy of Brian Libby.

Case Study: Gerding Theater at the Armory, Portland, Oregon

Constructed in 1891, the City of Portland's old armory is listed on the National Register of Historic Places. The Romanesque Revival style building, which features narrow gun-sight windows and a 100-foot by 200-foot clear space spanned by arching Douglas fir trusses, was originally constructed to house local units of the Oregon National Guard.

Now occupied by the Portland Center Stage theater company, the Gerding Theater comprehensive renovation project represents combined goals to preserve this historic building and its urban context for the greater Portland community, and to achieve a LEED-NC Platinum rating for leadership in energy efficient and environmental design. The Gerding Theater is the first theater in the United States and the first building on the National Register to achieve a LEED Platinum rating. It is 29 percent more energy-efficient than code requires, it keeps and uses all its stormwater (for toilets), and there are many types of innovative mechanical systems. Skylights throughout the facility fill this fortress with natural light.

Many in the preservation industry hope that in the very near future, LEED and other systems of building evaluation will more equitably consider historic significance, embodied energy of existing resources, and cultural heritage on equal footing and with similar merit and acceptance as for new construction. In development is the new LEED-ND for neighborhood design. This is the first LEED system to specifically offer credit for the reuse of historic buildings, in addition to points for general building reuse and recycled content of materials. Furthermore, the stated intent to preserve designated historic structures and to require that work be performed in compliance with Federal Rehabilitation Standards is moving the green-sustainability movement in the right direction with respect to preserving historic buildings. This language, and the potential of LEED credits, should next be incorporated into the remaining LEED rating systems.

Case Study: IHM Motherhouse, Monroe, Michigan

An order of Catholic nuns, Sisters, Servants of the Immaculate Heart of Mary (IHM), made a pioneering decision to rehabilitate their compound as a "green" residence and offices for the two hundred nuns.[7] Their worldwide headquarters in Monroe, Michigan, consists of a 280-acre parcel with two massive Art Deco style structures (376,000 square feet each) serving as the motherhouse, and an adjacent Tudor Revival style former elementary school. In 2000, the sisters decided they had a "moral mandate" to reuse their existing facilities in an earth-friendly manner. Begun in 2001 and completed in 2003, the work on the complex has become a national model for redeveloping large, underutilized historic structures based on the tenets of sustainable development.

The sisters described their work thus: "Over the next two years, we replaced outdated and overburdened plumbing and electrical systems, reconfigured living space, and made site improvements that preserve our beautiful historic buildings, enhance the comfort of residents and ensure our capacity for future service. . . . In planning the renovation, we were mindful of the need to use our precious

Aerial photo of IHM complex, Monroe, Michigan.

resources wisely and reverently. We chose to recycle and retain original furnishings wherever possible and to review the environmental impact of new products and materials before making purchase decisions. Similarly, we chose to install environmentally friendly electrical, plumbing and heating systems."

The huge motherhouse was revitalized as the sisters' primary offices and retirement community, while the former elementary school was reused as a senior housing facility known as Norman Towers. The work included installation of a gray-water recycling system, exclusive use of high-efficiency and fluorescent lighting combined with the expanded use of natural lighting, reuse of approximately eight hundred wood windows and five hundred cherry doors, utilization of marble bath stall partitions as window sills and countertops, recycling of over 45,000 square feet of carpeting, as well as toilet fixtures, wiring, ductwork, radiators, and cabinets, and use of over half of the removed plaster for paving projects. "Green" products such as drywall made from recycled paper and recycled plastic for decks and verandas were used throughout the massive project.

Quantitatively, it is estimated that this rehabilitation has resulted in the recycling of over 184,000 pounds of paper; the saving of enough electricity to power 189 homes for a month; the reduction of overall emission of air pollution in a

Norman Towers.

proportion equal to taking 205 cars off the road for one day; reducing by 30 percent the use of fresh water and by 55 percent of overall water consumption; and the diversion of over 7,000 gallons per day of water to a wetland constructed for the purpose of filtering the gray water.

The IHM sisters' commitment toward environmentally responsible, sustainable design for its motherhouse and main campus has become "a model of development for the 21st century."[8] This work has earned them numerous accolades, including recognition by the U.S. Environmental Protection Agency with three "Energy Star" awards in 2007; the awarding of LEED certification by the U.S. Green Building Council in 2006; and being selected by the national American Institute of Architects Committee on the Environment as one of its Top 10 Green Projects in the country for 2006.

Special Case Study: New Orleans after Katrina

When does traumatic environmental devastation require a re-evaluation of historic value within our communities? Being in the path of a tornado or hurricane

Photo of Katrina devastation, New Orleans. Courtesy of National Oceanographic and Atmospheric Administration.

or deluged by a tsunami erases all sense of place and all traces of pre-existing conditions. Reconstruction would be the only option to reestablish the previous community. However, environmental destruction that is not complete—that leaves behind elements that survive—raises a larger and more difficult question of what to save and what to rebuild. Hurricane Katrina was that kind of seminal event, with no clear-cut answers.

New Orleans has, or had, twenty districts on the National Register of Historic Places, covering half the city, prior to the horrendous destruction caused by Katrina in 2005. It had the highest concentration of historic structures in the nation—more than 33,000 houses and commercial and public buildings. Many of these structures were located in the French Quarter and the Garden District sectors of the city. At the highest elevations, they escaped much of the flooding that covered 80 percent of the city. Other lesser-known historic areas of New

Orleans were almost completely destroyed. In the Holy Cross area, a neighborhood near the Mississippi River, mud and debris covered nearly every structure.

In the post-Katrina recovery period that will last for decades, the question is what to do about the historic fabric of the city, both what was lost and what remains. Many people feel that in the face of such widespread damage, sites should be completely cleared to allow efficient rebuilding. Preservationists fear that even more will be lost in the fervor to build new—an approach that is politically popular among the thousands of displaced residents. Patricia Gay, executive director of the Preservation Resource Center of New Orleans, explained: "Bulldozing might be expedient, but we're talking about people's homes and communities, corner stores, diners, and churches. We're talking in many cases about houses that have stood over one hundred years and neighborhoods that have been home to five or six generations. And we're talking about what makes our city different from every place else, and what makes visitors want to come here: in other words, our livelihood."[9]

"The goal of recovery should be to allow residents to come back home to healthy, vibrant, livable places that retain the character that makes them unique," said Richard Moe, president of the National Trust for Historic Preservation. "You can't do that by calling in the bulldozers and creating vacant lots where neighborhoods used to be. Obviously, some historic buildings—perhaps a great many of them—will necessarily be lost, but we shouldn't lose any unnecessarily."[10] Experts contend that the majority of these structures can be saved. It will take an enlightened policy at local, state, and federal levels to make appropriate decisions on what to do in New Orleans. Preservationists will need to take a much broader perspective than with most historic districts.

PARTNERSHIPS

The idea of partnering with like-minded organizations, agencies, and individuals to further the preservation cause is not a new one. Its roots are found deep in the preservation movement. Even the impetus to develop the original legislation to enact the Historic Preservation Act of 1966 was led by one of the movement's most distinguished partners, the U.S. Conference of Mayors. This effort was detailed in the seminal work, *With Heritage So Rich*, originally published by the conference's "Special Committee on Historic Preservation" in 1966.[11]

The National Trust for Historic Preservation took a bold step toward fostering partnerships when it severed its direct funding ties to the federal government in 1993, shortly after the arrival of its new president, Richard Moe. This shift amplified the need to look very broadly for new sources of funding for the organization. Since that time, the National Trust has been seen as a model of collaboration, having formed alliances with such distinct partners as private corporations and foundations; community development corporations; cities and townships; land-based organizations; architecture and landscape architecture interests; federal, state, and local agencies; and many more. A "Corporate Partner Program," for example, has included numerous business sponsors as varied as Lowe's, HGTV, and Christie's Auction House. Such partnerships are an outgrowth of this expanded approach to financing historic preservation efforts.

The list of preservation partners is long and diverse, and probably no allied area of interest has been left "unpartnered." Neighborhood organizations, park districts, departments of transportation, historical societies, economic development corporations, humanities and arts agencies, and a host of related government and quasi-government offices have made excellent preservation partners. Environmental and land-based organizations such as the Trust for Public Land, Scenic America, and the many land conservancies throughout the nation also have partnered with preservation organizations. Other groups, such as the Junior League, the Colonial Dames, and the Questers, have partnered quietly with local preservation groups on historic preservation projects for decades. Granting agencies and foundations repeatedly reveal a predilection for partnership proposals, and thus many applicants who may have seemed strange bedfellows at one time now readily coexist as project partners.

Partnering with the Environmental and Conservation Communities

The protracted estrangement of the historic preservation and natural conservation movements is provocative, complicated, and even frustrating. It wasn't so long ago that the preservation of historic sites and the conservation of unique natural areas were thought of as siblings of the larger family of interests—the family of American "antiquity" and natural treasures. Painters, writers, poets, politicians, and musicians celebrated the unique synergy between natural and cultural heritage. Personalities such as environmentalist John Muir, geographer Carl Sauer, writer Rachel Carson, anthropologist Margaret Mead, urban philosopher Jane

Jacobs, poet/writer John Burroughs, and even President Theodore Roosevelt recognized the interconnectedness between preservation of historic structures and the conservation of nature. In a 1916 speech, Roosevelt remarked: "Defenders of the short-sighted . . . in their greed and selfishness will, if permitted, rob our country of half its charm by their reckless extermination of all useful and beautiful wild things. . . . Our duty to the whole, including the unborn generations, bids us restrain an unprincipled present-day minority from wasting the heritage of these unborn generations."[12]

The naming of Yellowstone and Fort Mackinac as the first national parks in the 1870s was part of a burgeoning national effort to recognize the natural *and*

Geyser, Yellowstone Park.

cultural significance of uniquely American places. This recognition eventually blossomed into the nation's first national historic preservation law, passed during the tenure of President Theodore Roosevelt, who became a moving force behind passage of the Antiquities Act of 1906. The act gave the president the proprietary power to protect sites that had archeological, historical, and/or scientific importance. It has been used by nearly every president since its passage.

Even after establishment of the National Park Service in 1916, however, the gap between the environmental and historic preservation movements widened. Early state and local conservation efforts, such as the establishment of the Trustees of Public Reservations in Massachusetts in 1891 (which also served as a template, of sorts, for the organizational framework of the National Trust for Historic Preservation), the Adirondack Forest Preserve in 1895, and the Western Pennsylvania Conservancy in 1932, were focused on protecting important natural and cultural landscapes. Historic places were incorporated into these efforts, though often by default, as historic preservation was not generally the primary objective. The primary focus of the Western Pennsylvania Conservancy, for example, is undeveloped land holdings, but their properties also include one of the nation's most important architectural treasures, Frank Lloyd Wright's landmark residence for the Kaufmann family, Fallingwater. Many other efforts addressed both the cultural and natural landscape as intertwined entities, including the creation of the National Park Service itself in 1916, with its host of Native American and military-related sites, as well as numerous natural landmarks. Organizations such as the legendary Mount Vernon Ladies' Association of the Union (1859), the St. Augustine Historical Society (1883), and the Daughters of the Republic of Texas (1892) early on recognized the importance of preserving both the natural and built environments as valued elements of "place." The spectacular views of and from Mount Vernon and the Potomac River were acknowledged as major features of the property's heritage very early in the effort to save the Washington's home.

Interest in connecting natural and historic landscapes is not a new idea. Indeed, it can be traced to 1865, in famed landscape architect Frederick Law Olmsted's designs for a linear parkway/greenway system for Berkeley, California. Corridor parks and greenbelts gained greater popularity before 1900. Boston's famed "emerald necklace" of connected parks that encircled the city by the late 1880s, and the interconnected Minneapolis–St. Paul metropolitan park system completed in 1895, are early examples.

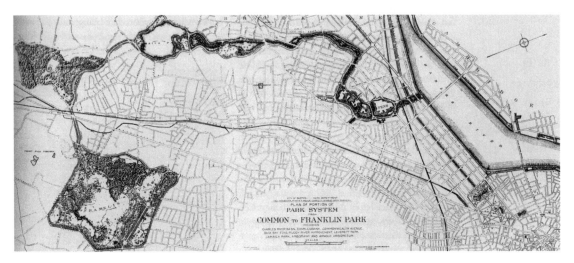

Boston's "Emerald Necklace" map.

Preservationists benefited by working with environmentalists and transportation planners on preserving natural and cultural landscapes during the construction of a number of significant parkway projects. Public interest in parkways blossomed after 1900, with projects such as the Bronx River Parkway, first authorized in 1906 and begun in 1913; the famed Blue Ridge Parkway, conceived as early as 1909, though not constructed until the mid-1930s; and the heavily landscaped Merritt Parkway, now listed on the National Register of Historic Places, which was developed as a model urban arterial roadway in the 1930s to facilitate travel between New York City and southern Connecticut. Championed by Connecticut Senator Schuyler Merritt, whose name it bears, the congressman noted at the 1934 groundbreaking, "This great highway is not being constructed primarily for rapid transit but for pleasant transit."[13]

Evidence of other early cultural parkways abounds, including the 40-Mile Loop in Portland, Oregon, originated by the Olmsted firm in 1903; the Natchez Trace that followed an ancient trail in Alabama, Mississippi, and Tennessee and was developed as a recreational parkway in the mid-1930s; and Detroit's Hines Parkway and Cleveland's Rockefeller Park/Parkway and Cultural Gardens, both from the 1920s. Even whole communities were impacted, as "greenbelt" or "garden" towns sprang up throughout England and America at the turn of the century, largely through the influence of celebrated English planner Ebenezer Howard. The new town version of the greenbelt idea was adopted virtually intact, however, in the New Deal greenbelt towns of the 1930s. In the same decade, the Civilian Conservation Corps (CCC) was actively engaged in implementing a variety of greenway designs throughout the nation through canal restorations, park construction, and civic beautification projects.

Parkways that were originally created as recreational corridors for walking, bicycling, or carriage riding were radically altered after the introduction of the automobile. Interest in recreational driving on landscaped or naturalistic roadways soared following the ready availability of automobiles. "Although Henry Ford succeeded beyond his wildest dreams in turning the automobile from a purely recreational vehicle into a necessity, 'driving for pleasure' . . . is still near the top of the list of all outdoor recreational activities."[14]

There also are numerous examples of groups interested in the preservation of long-extant historic traces, trails, and roads. Some led pioneers through the wilderness, including the Oregon Trail, Zane's Trace, the California Mission Trail (part of El Camino Real), and the Natchez Trace. Their later commercial and recreational counterparts, such as the National Road, the Blue Ridge Parkway, the Columbia River Highway, or Route 66, were part of a movement to establish safe and scenic roads across the nation. Famous routes, like the Appalachian Trail or the Shenandoah Parkway, got their start in the 1930s, while newer routes, such as the North Country National Scenic Trail, eventually will link seven states in the northern portion of the United States via a 4,600-mile-long hiking trail connecting New York to North Dakota, with historic sites all along its length. In some cases, the trail makes broad diversions to take advantage of historic and natural features, as in the case of the detour into the historic Maumee Valley in northern Ohio. Another notable effort to connect natural with cultural sites can be found among the many Rails-to-Trails organizations in the last quarter of the twentieth century. Utilizing abandoned railroad rights-of-way, recreational agencies have spent millions of public and private dollars on the conversion of these corridors into trails and bikeways; in some cases they even serve a secondary purpose as the location of buried utilities, most notably for the positioning of fiber-optic cables along these reclaimed transportation routes. Estimating that there are over one hundred thousand miles of such trails nationwide, the Rails-to-Trails Conservancy keeps track of the over one thousand different rail–trail pathways that criss-cross the country. The appeal for historic preservationists is that many of these rail–trail corridors pass directly through, or border, significant historic sites, incorporating historic structures as part of the route.

Scenic Youghiogheny River, Fayette County, Pennsylvania.

The concept of the interconnectedness of natural and cultural resources is increasingly being understood and embraced. Many states, as well as the federal government, administer scenic river and byway programs that commonly highlight the historic as well as the natural resources of river corridors and picturesque roads and highways. The Great Lakes Circle Tour, a cooperative venture between the United States and Canada, extols the wonders of the scenic, natural, and cultural heritage of the Great Lakes basin. Each state/province has produced brochures, Web sites, and guidebooks that emphasize their distinctive natural and historic treasures as visitors circumnavigate the seven-thousand-mile trek around the five Great Lakes. Created under President Clinton in 1997, the American Heritage Rivers project is coordinated by the U.S. Environmental Protection Agency. Its objectives specifically call for activities directly linked with historic preservation. The American Heritage Rivers initiative has three objectives: natural resource and environmental protection, economic revitalization, and historic and cultural preservation. The program covers some of the most well-known rivers in the nation, including all or portions of the Detroit, Hudson, Mississippi, New, Potomac, Rio Grande, and Willamette rivers.

TRUST FOR PUBLIC LAND

The Trust for Public Land (TPL) is a national, nonprofit land conservation organization founded in 1972. It has grown from a small group of people concerned with preserving the Marin headlands just north of San Francisco to an organization with more than twenty-four offices across the mainland. TPL and local groups work with private and corporate landowners, community groups, cities and towns, and public agencies at the state and federal levels to conserve land for people, including preserving historic landmarks and landscapes.

TPL supports conservation efforts in a number of important ways. For one, it provides interim site protection when necessary and can take swift action to take desirable land off the market until buyers can be found for public purchase. In addition, it assists with real estate transactions and financing, and will, when necessary, conduct independent negotiations with landowners. TPL can bridge financing through revolving funds, loans, and lease–purchase agreements. It also provides planning assistance, helps identify opportunities for parks and land protection, and gives information and technical support on public finance campaigns. Working with local groups, TPL can offer technical assistance to community organizations and provide ongoing support to local land trusts.

Case Study: Witch Hollow Farm

One project well illustrates the work of the TPL. Witch Hollow Farm is a historic homestead built about 1700 in West Boxford, Massachusetts. The house is steeped in local history and received its name sometime in the eighteenth century from local rumors that witches had been seen congregating in the hollow behind the house and nearby pond. The deep meadow grass surrounding the homestead provides a fine habitat for wildlife. The town of West Boxford owned the property under a Conservation Commission.

By the 1990s this area of northern Massachusetts had become very desirable for upscale homes. In 1996, when the homestead and the remaining 22 acres of

Boxford House at Witch Hollow Farm, West Boxford, Massachusetts.

farmland were threatened with purchase by developers offering top dollar to put up million-dollar-plus homes, the town had little ability to protect the farmstead. As a last resort, they approached TPL with a request to purchase the property and hold it off the market. TPL acquired the farm, sold the house and barn with a covenant to protect the buildings to a private buyer, and transferred 17 acres of agricultural fields to the town for permanent conservation with an easement. Today, thanks to intervention from TPL, both Boxford House and Witch Hollow Farm retain their historic integrity and are protected against the pressures of inappropriate development.

Chapter Eleven

HERITAGE TOURISM, CULTURAL LANDSCAPES, AND HERITAGE AREAS

——◆——

There is an important link between preservation and tourism that is sustained by three major reasons people become tourists: for rest and recreation, to view great natural sights, and because of an interest in achievements of the past. Historic preservation can serve as an important form of tourism that brings economic benefits to a community. Tourism advocates throughout the world recognize that history pays because it attracts people and income from tourists and helps fund further preservation efforts. Local officials concerned about drawbacks of historic designation need not fear. As noted travel publisher Arthur Frommer puts it, "There is no evidence, not a single indication, of any city that has declined commercially from historic preservation policies."

HERITAGE INTERPRETATION

Heritage interpretation is a term increasingly used to represent a new approach to preservation that encourages travelers to appreciate heritage sites and local cultures in new and richer ways. It is analogous to the concept of ecotourism (environmentally sustainable ecological tourism) within the tourist industry.

Frommer describes the need to counter the typical touring format with this multidimensional approach: "After 30 years of writing standard guidebooks, I began to see that most of the vacation journeys undertaken by Americans were trivial and bland, devoid of important content, cheaply commercial, and unworthy of our better instincts and ideals. . . . Those travels, for most Americans, consist almost entirely of 'sight-seeing'—an activity as vapid as the words imply. We rove the world, in most cases, to look at lifeless physical structures of the sort already familiar from a thousand picture books and films. We gaze at the Eiffel Tower or the Golden Gate Bridge, enjoy a brief thrill of recognition, return home, and think we have traveled."[1]

Heritage interpretation draws together formerly separated activities: historic preservation, tourism, "living history" presentations, and the "edutainment" and "experience" industries. It interprets local culture and history, often in a living history (first- or third-person interpretation) setting, and makes it accessible to the public by providing heritage-based interpretative experiences for visitors and tourists. The growth in this approach to tourism is an indicator that people have a sincere interest in understanding the culture of places rather than the superficiality inherent in the more traditional "sight-seeing" tourism experiences of the past.

Some examples of these activities include:

- On the Amtrak train between Gallup and Albuquerque, New Mexico, a Navajo interprets Native American culture, religion, history, and geology to passengers as they pass through this magical landscape.
- In Fort Myers, Florida, at the former winter home of Thomas Edison, a "surprise hitchhiker" meets and boards motor coach tours. The hitchhiker is a living portrayal of Thomas Edison, presented by a local amateur actor.
- In Lucas County, Ohio, visitors are welcomed aboard a recreated c. 1840 canal boat by period-appropriate (in clothing and dialogue) "canawlers" for a journey on a restored portion of the original Miami & Erie Canal.
- In Sylvania, Ohio, visitors are immersed in an Underground Railroad experience where costumed, lantern-toting "conductors" lead participants to an authentic "safe house" along the escape route in the very ravine where slaves once sought their freedom.[2]

In the best presentations of cultural heritage, local cultures play an active role in determining what activities are appropriate; they have either outright control of the programs or an equal voice in their planning. The use of heritage should be

Thomas Edison home, Fort Myers, Florida.

a conservation tool; it should not exploit or demean residents. Indigenous participants can serve as the custodians of their culture, presenting authentic "heritage experiences" to guests and training their youth to continue these interpretive programs in the future.

One outgrowth of heritage interpretation is the recognition that the natural and cultural stories of a community should be interpreted not only for visitors but also for local residents, who often have little knowledge of their own heritage. In communities such as Rochester, New York, and Honolulu, Hawaii, community interpretation plans are used as tools for heightening a community's awareness of its own local resources. Such cultural storytelling is a process "as old as time, and is just as much the province of emotionally-invested and knowledgeable local residents as it is the province of trained professionals."[3]

Street Exhibit,
Ann Arbor, Michigan.

Case Study: Historical Street Exhibits Program

The Downtown Ann Arbor Historical Street Exhibits Program is the first of its kind in the nation. Through uniquely designed transparent glass frames, images of the past are superimposed on the existing streetscape and viewed as a living part of the present. By juxtaposing historical images upon the architecture of the current streetscape, the relevance of the past to preservation and adaptive use is immediately apparent. The exhibits at sixteen different sites provide the public with an easily accessible history of the growth and development of the town and its architecture, and also serve as an educational resource for public schools. The exhibits comprise a historical walking tour of downtown Ann Arbor, and are used to educate both residents and visitors on the community's history. Because it brings local history to the sidewalk, rather than in books, the project has been referred to amusingly as "guerrilla history."

The Downtown Ann Arbor Historical Street Exhibits Program began at the grass-roots level. Local residents developed the idea as a way to present to the public images of historic architecture that no longer existed. The Ann Arbor Historic District Commission became the official project sponsor. The actual design concept emerged from an intense one-day design charrette, a session that included the participation of twenty volunteer architects and design professionals. In addition, a group of seven local historians worked on the historical photos and text making up the exhibits. The project has taken years to come to full fruition, relying totally on volunteer participation, but represents a successful and unique way to present local history and historic architecture to the general public.

LANDSCAPE PRESERVATION

Historic landscapes present one of the most intriguing and difficult types of preservation. Buildings remain relatively static in their form, whereas natural elements like trees and shrubs change with each growing season. Significant historic gardens, such as the Washington garden around Mount Vernon and, on a bigger scale, Central Park in New York City, should be preserved largely in their original states. But this is a process of continual research, renewal, and replanting. The protection of scenic features such as Niagara Falls and historic battlefields like Gettysburg involves a different set of concerns and problems from those found with landmark buildings.

Perhaps the most common, though difficult, type of landscape preservation project is the reconstruction of historic gardens. Although gardens are often referred to in writings, seldom are accurate drawings or other documentation available. Other than for palatial structures, the tradition of recording garden plans does not generally exist; gardens were most often in the care of gardeners or caretakers, who transferred their knowledge through oral apprenticeship traditions rather than on paper.

One of the greatest legacies of historic landscapes is that of the seminal landscape architect, Frederick Law Olmsted. Among the significant projects with which he was involved were the Chicago Columbian Exposition of 1893, the "emerald necklace" parks of Boston mentioned above, Detroit's thousand-acre Belle Isle, and the most well known, Manhattan's Central Park. As beautiful as these landscape designs were, and as important as they have been to city planning, they are increasingly threatened by an American lifestyle that is not compatible with the sense of purpose Olmsted gave them. Olmsted wrote, "We want a ground to which people may easily go after their day's work is done, and where they may stroll for hours, seeing, hearing, and feeling nothing of the bustle and jar of the streets, where they shall, in effect, find the city put far away from them."[4] Preservationists recognize that preserving the physical park is not sufficient, for such a property's true significance lies in how it is used and respected as a community amenity.

CULTURAL LANDSCAPES

What exactly is a cultural landscape? According to noted geographer Carl Sauer, who proposed this definition in 1927, a cultural landscape[5] is composed of "the forms superimposed on physical landscape by the activities of man."[6] In the broadest sense, the entire nation is a cultural landscape, a natural landscape impacted by deliberate human activity. Normally, however, we tend to think of cultural landscapes in more local or regional terms. For example, geographers often study areas of ethnicity to understand settlement patterns, folkways, and even building types. The concept of cultural landscape has great importance for preservationists and historians who may be conducting a comprehensive historic survey of an area or neighborhood and working to develop a statement of historic context.

Evidence of human activity plays a key role in formulating boundaries for Cultural Landscapes and Heritage Corridors and Areas. There are two primary methods of establishing the boundaries of cultural landscapes: cultural and political. The most comprehensive is the *cultural approach*, which considers the extent of a cultural phenomenon. If an area developed as the result of a Native American or pioneer trail or was influenced by a canal, railroad, or the existence of great stands of forests or deposits of underground minerals, then a cultural boundary could be determined that includes all those areas/communities that identify with that cultural event. The *political approach* defines an area that has been influenced by specific political phenomenon, such as legal boundaries or subdivisions (e.g., townships, towns, counties, states).

Example of a "cultural landscape," Fayette State Park historic townsite (iron smelting site), Garden, Michigan.

Historic sites or landscapes are considered cultural landscapes when they are defined as significant for their association with a historic event, activity, or person, and may include battlefields, historic campgrounds, trails, and farms, but also historic scenes,[7] designed landscapes,[8] vernacular landscapes,[9] and ethnographic landscapes.[10] Harder to define than historic buildings, or even groups of buildings in historic districts, cultural landscapes include larger areas of interest where details of the human story or the impact of cultural settlement are evident. Often it is the concept of place, or personal experiences with an actual place, that create very real and palpable associations larger than life—certainly larger than the visual panorama of existing materials and landforms.

MARITIME LANDSCAPES

An allied and growing movement in the field of preservation, especially in coastal areas, is maritime preservation. Like landscape preservation, maritime landscapes often involve large-scale and challenging efforts. The great loss of the country's maritime heritage and its need for attention has been recognized only relatively

Cape Hatteras lighthouse, Hatteras Island, North Carolina.

recently. To encourage these efforts, the National Trust for Historic Preservation and many state and regional preservation organizations established offices and departments to handle maritime preservation issues. These offices can provide technical assistance to groups and individuals involved in such efforts as the preservation, restoration, and reuse of lighthouses and other maritime structures as well as the designation and protection of historic ships and even undersea ship-wrecks and preserves. Maritime preservation also includes efforts to preserve entire waterfront districts, which often have opposing threats—both abandon-ment and development pressures. On another level, the need to preserve some of the older maritime skills, from knot tying and scrimshawing to sailing techniques and wooden boat building, is also recognized as an important aspect of maritime preservation.

Cape Hatteras Lighthouse, located on North Carolina's Outer Banks, is the tallest brick lighthouse in the United States. When originally constructed in

1870, it was 1,500 feet from the shore. Soil erosion along the Atlantic Coast had brought the ocean very close to the lighthouse, and the structure was in imminent danger. The National Park Service studied the case and had to weigh their mandate of preserving historical structures with that of preserving natural processes along the Atlantic seaboard. The three main options considered were: (1) stabilizing the beach in front of the lighthouse with the construction of concrete groins; (2) constructing a seawall; and (3) relocation of the lighthouse farther inland. A report from the Ad Hoc Committee of the Faculty of North Carolina State University concluded that moving the lighthouse was the only choice that was "technically feasible and consistent with both current knowledge of the shoreline and with existing public policy."[11] During the summer of 1999, the lighthouse was painstakingly moved a half mile inland from the encroaching ocean as part of a $12 million restoration project.

HERITAGE CORRIDOR AND AREA CONCEPTS

An important illustration of how historic preservationists have established closer working relationships with environmental, business, conservation, and recreation groups, both across the country and internationally, is found in the recent development of Heritage Corridors and Heritage Areas. Conceived in the early 1980s, these federally or state-designated entities combine distinctive natural, cultural, recreational, commercial, agricultural, scenic, and urban resources to tell the story of a particular region through a unified approach focused on heritage tourism as a generator of economic development. Not to be confused with National Parks or Recreation Areas, these selected areas do not involve land purchases by the federal government. Rather, partnerships are formed with existing entities that already own or control sites within the designated area. Organizations from hiking clubs to garden clubs to camera clubs to Chambers of Commerce to natural resource groups to historical societies and preservation groups have banded together to preserve and interpret the unique places that give a location its own distinctive character. As a consequence of these partnerships, allied organizations such as the American Heritage Rivers program, the Trust for Public Land, and Scenic America, and regional/local organizations such as land conservancies, park districts, and land use development agencies are now playing important roles in the preservation of historic sites. The United States Congress provides monetary support and technical services for a ten-year renewable period through the National Park Service's Rivers, Trails, and Conservation Assistance Program.

The expansion of the historic preservation movement to include larger areas of interest, such as cultural landscapes, Heritage Corridors, and Heritage Areas, is partly a reflection of the increasing importance of understanding the historic context of places. The development of the nation's first heritage corridor in the early 1980s served as a harbinger of this shift in the preservation paradigm. The phrase "Heritage Corridor" was devised to delineate cohesive linear landscapes that, along with their associated resources, followed elongated cultural corridors such as railroads, canals, rivers, roadways, and similar extended landscapes. Use of the term Heritage Corridor actually antedates widespread recognition and use of the phrase "Heritage Area," which has evolved as the preferred way to describe cohesive cultural areas that are both corridor-based as well as those not linear in nature. The definition of a National Heritage Area was provided within the original congressional legislation: "A place where natural, cultural, historic, and scenic resources combine to form patterns of human activity shaped by geography, history, and other human and environmental circumstances. . . . These patterns make them representative of the national experience through the physical features that remain and the traditions that have evolved in them. Continued use of National Heritage Areas by people whose traditions helped to shape the landscapes enhances their significance."[12]

The Lowell National Historical Park in Massachusetts,[13] previously discussed in Chapter 6, is an early example of this type of partnership collaboration within the National Park Service, although it predates the establishment of the Heritage Area management model. The Lowell example is important because it is seen as a model within the National Park Service and by many involved in the Heritage Area movement. Though it is federally owned and managed, the emphasis is on cooperation among the various public agencies and private organizations that maintain a physical connection with the historic park. Also, the thematic approach is perhaps clearer and easier to understand at Lowell, a fundamentally industrial location where economic history and industrial themes play a principal role in the overall interpretation. In short, Lowell helped pave the way for the current steering of the preservation movement toward preserving the larger cultural landscape and the subsequent Heritage Corridor and Heritage Area designations.

By 2007 there were thirty-seven federally designated National Heritage Areas and Corridors, with the majority located east of the Mississippi River. Pennsylvania leads the listing with six such designations. Places with dominant industrial, agricultural, and/or cultural linkages are common, including the Illinois & Michigan Canal National Heritage Corridor (1984), the Southwestern Pennsylvania Industrial Heritage Route (1988), the Ohio & Erie National Heritage Corridor (1996), the Yuma Crossing National Heritage Area (2000), and the Gullah/Geechee Cultural Heritage Corridor (2006). Each was the result of direct involvement by the National Park Service, either voluntarily or at the behest of a U.S. congressional member, and involved cooperative ventures among the public sector and private enterprise. Each of these heritage areas is designated as a National Park by the National Park Service, though several are discontinuous. In addition, "technical assistance" is provided by several arms of the National Park Service. This arrangement has resulted in both internal and external competition for these funds, which are aimed at park management plans—the form and style of which are, however, vastly different.

Case Study: The Illinois & Michigan National Heritage Corridor

Not surprisingly, preservation of larger areas in such an integrated form has increasingly attracted the attention of preservationists, especially in response to the growing importance being placed on the concept of historic context. Though not the first integrated preservation effort, the Illinois & Michigan (I&M) Canal National Heritage Corridor is important because it was the nation's first officially designated Heritage Corridor. It set a standard for other corridors to follow. Charles Little, in *Greenways for America*, specifically commented on the significance of the I&M model and its revolutionary approach to designation and management: "The new approach that . . . the National Park Service, state and local officials, and business leaders came up with was to make the corridor a national park without having the park service own any of the land. It would be a national heritage corridor instead, locally administered, the first of its kind. Moreover, unlike most parks, this one had an economic as well as a preservation objective: to improve the climate, throughout the length of the corridor, for economic growth and development.[14]

The I&M Canal National Heritage Corridor is the result of a complex mix of politics, citizen action, and a desire to understand and appreciate individual and collective "sense of place." The corridor stretches 120 miles along either side of the former I&M Navigation Canal. Extending from Chicago southwesterly to LaSalle/Peru, Illinois, it encompasses some 450 square miles of land.

Historic photo of I&M Canal at Lockport, Illinois. Courtesy of Jerry Adelmann.

In 1848, the Illinois & Michigan Navigation Canal opened, connecting the Great Lakes to the Mississippi River watershed via the Illinois, Chicago, and DesPlaines Rivers. The canal flourished for several decades, but then began a slow decline that culminated in its eventual abandonment due to the success of the railroads. The existence of this canal, however, played a pivotal role in the establishment of Chicago as a major midwestern metropolitan area, therefore directly impacting the economic development of the nation. The I&M canal itself lay fallow for most of the twentieth century until citizen groups, reacting to the proposed sale of canal lands by the state in the 1960s, ignited interest in preserving the once-active commercial corridor, not as a canal but as a park and linear trail system.

The I&M Canal National Heritage Corridor was, in fact, the culmination of interest in preserving portions of the former industrial corridor that included the restorative Civilian Conservation Corps projects of the 1930s and the intercession of the Openlands Project in the 1960s. The Openlands Project was formed in 1963 to encourage and accelerate the preservation of open space in northeastern Illinois, and the I&M became its *cause célèbre*. Assuming a leadership role in preserving the I&M canal, Openlands initiated a drive to establish the canal as a linear historical park and recreational trail. Their successful efforts culminated in 1974 with the opening of the first fragment of what would become the I&M National Heritage Corridor, a 60-mile hiking trail along the canal towpath extending from Joliet to LaSalle/Peru, Illinois. The Canal Corridor Association assumed management of the corridor in 1988 under the direction of Gerald Adelmann.

Another factor that distinguished the I&M Canal National Heritage Corridor from other park-oriented corridors and greenways was its strong emphasis on "heritage," a term so definitive that it became a component of the formal name for this new genre of national park. Of course, heritage interpretation long has been a component of National Park Service planning and preservation activities, but this particular designation and resultant management plan, with its myriad of partners and funding sources, was unique within the park service.

Perhaps the most significant aspect of the I&M Canal National Heritage Corridor is that it represents a fundamental departure from traditional National Park Service designation. Unlike most other National Parks, the I&M is neither federally owned nor managed exclusively by the National Park Service, but retains local autonomy and ownership. To many, this hybrid model signaled a new era in park development and management. Coupled with an emphasis on decentralized statutory and decision-making authority initiated by 1980 amendments to the 1966 Historic Preservation Act, the National Park Service and other federal bureaucrats adopted new policies, downloading many responsibilities to second- and third-tier agencies. Consequently, National Park Service preservation programs have been characterized by efforts to decentralize authority from National Park Service to other members of the preservation community, especially from the federal level to state and local participants. It is within this evolution of preservation ideology that the Heritage Corridor/Area concept emerged. As noted, since 1984, several dozen new areas have been added to the ranks of nationally designated Heritage Areas. Some were designated before broad local support developed, but they had strong support on Capitol Hill and came into existence at the behest of individual congressional representatives—a political scenario that has been the hallmark of more than a few of these designations.

The overarching importance of this type of designation lies in its recognition of the larger landscape as a part of an interconnected cultural and environmental system and the subsequent attempt by the National Park Service and its local partners to foster homogeneous management of that system as a natural and cultural entity. In most Heritage Areas, the reliance on a public–private partnership to effect that management is vital to individual success as well as to the sustainability of the Heritage Area itself.

Heritage Areas

Diverse interest in the concept of Heritage Areas emerged following the designation in 1988 of the nation's first official Heritage Area (as opposed to *corridor*), known as America's Industrial Heritage Project (AIHP). Located in southwestern Pennsylvania, the designation included nine counties where, supporters argued, the American industrial revolution was born. "Iron ore, coal, gas, and stone, abundant in southwestern Pennsylvania, fueled the successes and tragedies that accompanied the industrialization of America."[15] Driven by a 1985 congressional study conducted by the National Park Service, "Reconnaissance Survey of Western Pennsylvania Roads and Sites," the Heritage Area concept was given credence through the study's recommendations. The study proposed federal recognition of the region's significant cultural and natural resources related to coal mining, iron and steelmaking, transportation, and related industrial themes, and promotion of a greater appreciation of their importance to the nation's past and present. The recognition of this diverse and dispersed landscape as a cultural entity was a political and cultural phenomenon that has been recognized for its ability to effect disparate partnerships, including 999 municipalities within 8,000 square miles, and for its aggressive application of the Heritage Area concept to achieve widespread, large-scale preservation, to promote tourism, and to encourage economic activity.

The economic aspect, particularly in the I&M and AIHP ventures, has been critical in the justification of their benefits to Congress in order to obtain federal designation and funding. The success and cost of this form of federal recognition had, until recently, a chilling effect on Congress, which for some time declined to designate new Heritage Corridors or Heritage Areas until clarification of need, national significance, and long-term expense could be assessed. Despite the potential for the advancement of arguments that this type of designation is a grand ruse designed to relieve the National Park Service of its public responsibilities in developing new parks, or that it is a device of commercial interests for private gain, no such contentions have been forthcoming, and designations continue.

Interest in establishing Heritage Corridors and Heritage Areas has grown significantly in the decades since the creation of the I&M Canal National Heritage Corridor. A nonprofit organization, the Alliance of National Heritage Areas, was founded in 1997 as a means for nationally designated Heritage Corridors and Areas to communicate, educate, and promote themselves via a national agenda and conferences.

NOTES

CHAPTER ONE

1. Clem Labine, "Preservationists Are Un-American," *Historic Preservation* (March 1979), 18.
2. John W. Lawrence, Dean of the School of Architecture, Tulane University, April 24, 1970.
3. Adele Chatfield-Taylor, "From Ruskin to Rouse," in *Historic Preservation: Forging a Discipline*, ed. Beth Sullebarger (New York: Preservation Alumni, 1985), 27–28.
4. Robin E. Datel, "Southern Regionalism and Historic Preservation in Charleston, South Carolina," *Journal of Historical Geography* 16 (1990): 197–215.
5. Eugène Emanuel Viollet-le-Duc, *Dictionnaire raisonné,* 1854–1868.
6. Norman Williams Jr., Edmund H. Kellogg, and Frank B. Gilbert, *Readings in Historic Preservation* (New Brunswick, NJ: Center for Urban Policy Research, 1983), 16.
7. John Ruskin, "The Lamp of Memory," *The Seven Lamps of Architecture* (London: Hazell, Watson, and Viney: 1891), 353, 339.
8. Adele Chatfield-Taylor, "From Ruskin to Rouse," 30.
9. Ruskin, "The Lamp of Memory," 185.
10. David Lowenthal, "A Global Perspective on American Heritage," in *Past Meets Future: Saving America's Historic Environments,* ed. Antoinette J. Lee (Washington, D.C.: Preservation Press, 1992), 162.

CHAPTER TWO

1. Ann Pamela Cunningham. Farewell address recorded in minutes of the Mount Vernon Ladies' Association of the Union, June 1874, 5.
2. George Humphrey Yetter, *Williamsburg Before and After: The Rebirth of Virginia's Colonial Capital* (Williamsburg, Virginia: The Colonial Williamsburg Foundation, 1996), 51.
3. Norman Williams Jr., Edmund H. Kellogg, and Frank B Gilbert, eds., *Readings in Historic Preservation: Why? What? How?* (New Brunswick, NJ: Center for Urban Policy Research, 1983), 40.
4. Robin E. Datel, "Southern Regionalism and Historic Preservation in Charleston, South Carolina," *Journal of Historical Geography* 16 (1990): 197–215.

5. From the HABS Web site, www.cr.nps.gov/habshaer/habs/habshist.htm, May 1999.

6. William J. Murtagh, *Keeping Time: The History and Theory of Preservation in America* (New York: Sterling, 1990), 47.

7. Jane Jacobs. *The Death and Life of Great American Cities* (New York: Random House, 1961).

8. Albert Rains and Laurance G. Henderson, *With Heritage So Rich,* rev. ed. (United States Conference of Mayors. Washington, D.C.: Preservation Press, 1983), 208.

9. Correspondence with National Trust for Historic Preservation, 2008.

10. *Report to the President and Congress of the United States* (Washington, D.C.: Advisory Council on Historic Preservation, 1990), 70.

11. Antoinette J. Lee, *Past Meets Future: Saving America's Historic Environments* (Washington, D.C.: Preservation Press, 1992), 74.

12. Antoinette J. Lee, *Past Meets Future,* 16.

13. 44th National Preservation Conference, sponsored by the National Trust for Historic Preservation. Charleston, South Carolina, 1990.

CHAPTER THREE

1. Rexford Newcomb, *Architecture of the Old Northwest Territory* (Chicago: University of Chicago Press, 1950), 115.

2. John Maass, *The Gingerbread Age* (New York: Bramhall House, 1957), 32–33.

3. Bertram Grosvenor Goodhue, *The Craftsman,* 1916.

4. James C. Massey and Shirley Maxwell, "Pre-Cut Houses," *Old House Journal* (November–December 1990): 41.

5. Henry-Russell Hitchcock and Philip Johnson, *The International Style: Architecture Since 1922* (New York: W.W. Norton, 1932).

6. Robert Venturi, *Complexity and Contradiction in Architecture,* 2nd ed., (New York: Museum of Modern Art, 1966), 22–23.

7. See page 140 for a sketch of this building.

8. Sometimes referred to as computer-aided design and drafting (CADD).

9. Brent Brolin, *Architecture in Context* (New York: Van Nostrand Reinhold, 1980), 7.

10. William Faulkner. *Requiem for a Nun,* 1st ed., (New York: Routledge, 1987). From *Faulkner Manuscripts,* 1951.

11. Kurt Anderson, "Spiffing Up the Urban Heritage," *Time* (November 23, 1987): 76.

12. *The Secretary of the Interior's Standards for Rehabilitation and Guidelines for Rehabilitating Historic Buildings,* rev. ed. (Washington, D.C.: U.S. Department of the Interior, National Park Service, Heritage Preservation Services, 1995), Standard No. 9.

13. See chapter 7 for descriptions and examples of the four approaches to treatment.

14. Quoted in "The Future of Preservation," *Architecture* (February 1998): 80.

15. Michael A. Tomlan. "Preservation Practice Comes of Age," 75. From Antoinette J. Lee, ed., *Past Meets Future: Saving America's Historic Environments.* (Washington, D.C.: Preservation Press, 1992).

CHAPTER FOUR

1. *Berman v. Parker,* 348 U.S. 26, 33 (1954).

2. Justice William Douglas in *Berman v. Parker* decision.

3. *Figarsky v. Historic District Commission,* 171 Conn. 198, 368 A.2d 163 (1976).

4. *Maher v. City of New Orleans,* 371 F. Supp. 653, 663 (E.D. La. 1974).

5. *Maher v. City of New Orleans* decision.

6. *Penn Central Transportation Company v. City of New York,* 438 U.S. 104, 98 S.Ct. 2646 (1978).

7. Charles M. Haar and Michael Allan Wolk, *Land Use Planning: A Casebook on the Use, Misuse, and Reuse of Urban Land,* 4th ed. (Boston: Little, Brown, 1989), 543.

8. *Penn Central Transportation Company* v. *City of New York,* Appeal from the Court of Appeals of New York, No. 77–444, 42 N.Y. 2d 324, 366 N.E. 2d 324, affirmed.

9. *Penn Central Transportation Company* v. *City of New York,* Appeal from the Court of Appeals of New York, No. 77–444, 42 N.Y. 2d 324, 366 N.E. 2d 324, affirmed.

10. See Charles M. Haar and Jerold S. Kayden, *Landmark Justice: The Influence of William J. Brennan on America's Communities* (Washington, D.C.: The Preservation Press, 1989), 154–68.

11. This was shown in *Society for Ethical Culture* v. *Spatt,* 416 N.Y.S. 2d, affirmed, 415 N.E. 2d 922 (N.Y. 1980), which upheld the designation of a meeting house structure.

12. Jane Brown Gillette, "Judgment Day," *Historic Preservation* (September–October 1991): 57. Note: The case was resolved in 1991 when the U.S. Supreme Court refused to review the decision of the U.S. Court of Appeals for the 2nd Circuit.

13. Jane Brown Gillette, "Judgment Day," 57.

14. Jane Brown Gillette, "Judgment Day," 60.

15. Amy Worden, "Court Denies St. Bart's Plea," *Preservation News* (February 1990): 22.

16. Amy Worden, "Court Denies St. Bart's Plea," 22.

17. Kim Kelster, "Supreme Court Rules for Preservation," *Preservation News* (April 1991): 2.

18. Brent Brolin, *The Battle of St. Bart's: A Tale of the Material and the Spiritual* (New York: William Morrow & Co., 1988), 194.

19. *Kelo vs. City of New London,* 545 U.S. 469 (2005).

CHAPTER FIVE

1. *National Register Criteria for Evaluation* (Washington, D.C.: U.S. Department of the Interior), from www.nps.gov/history/nr/listing.htm (2008).

2. From National Park Service publication, 1991c: 44–5.

3. www.galinsky.com/buildings/getty/index.htm, September 2007.

4. The Henry Ford Museum has a 1946 diner, a 1941 Texaco gas station, and a 1960 Holiday Inn room in its collection, but displaying historic buildings in a museum is less desirable than preserving them at their original site.

5. See the Web site www.mission66.com/cyclorama for information on this effort.

6. From a Department of the Interior news release, 26 March 2006.

7. See the National Historic Landmarks Program Web Site, www.nps.gov/history/nhl.

8. From the Web site ecfr.gpoaccess.gov (Title 36: Parks, Forests and Public Properties) February 2006.

CHAPTER SIX

1. Roberta Brandes Gratz, *The Living City* (New York: Simon and Schuster, 1989), 287.

2. David Hamer, *History in Urban Places* (Columbus: Ohio State University Press, 1998), 95.

3. A full history of the neighborhood can be found at www.livebaltimore.com/nb/list/setonhll/history.

4. See Russell Wright, *A Guide to Delineating Edges of Historic Districts* (Washington, D.C.: Preservation Press, 1976).

5. Kevin Lynch, *The Image of the City* (Cambridge, Massachusetts: MIT Press, 1960).

6. Norman Tyler, "An Evaluation of The Health of the Downtowns In Eight Michigan Cities." (University of Michigan Dissertation, 1987).

7. *Maher v. City of New Orleans,* 516 F2d 1051.

8. *Texas Antiquities Commission v. Dallas County Community College District,* 554 S.W. 2d

924 (Texas 1977), and *Historic Green Springs, Inc. v. Bergland*, 497 F. Supp. 839 (E.D. Va. 1980).

9. Alaska Statutes 29–55–010 through 29–55–020. From www.ncsl.org/programs/arts/gethistrec.cfm?record=822.

10. Arkansas code annotated 214–172–201 through 214–172–212. From www.ncsl.org/programs/arts/gethistrec.cfm?record=1030.

11. District of Columbia code 5–1001 through 5–1015. From www.ncsl.org/programs/arts/gethistrec.cfm?record=786.

12. Indiana Statutes Annotated 36–7–11.2–1 through 36–7–11.2–67. From www.ncsl.org/programs/arts/gethistrec.cfm?record=1361.

13. *Virginia Historic Landmarks Commission v. Board of Supervisors of Louisa County*, 21 Va. 468, 230 S.E. 2d229 (1976).

14. Based on information from Connie Malone, *United States Preservation Commission Identification Project* (August 1994), National Alliance of Preservation Commissions.

15. See *Robert's Rules of Order Newly Revised In Brief*, Robert M. Henry III, William J. Evans, Daniel H. Honemann, Thamas J. Balch, Henry M. Robert (Cambridge, Massachusetts: De Capo Press, 2004). The rules can also be found online at www.rulesonline.com.

16. Christopher Duerksen, *A Handbook of Historic Preservation Law* (Washington, D.C.: Conservation Foundation, 1983), 70.

CHAPTER SEVEN

1. "The Secretary of the Interior's Standards for the Treatment of Historic Properties," (U.S. Department of the Interior, National Park Service, 1992.)

2. National Historic Landmark Program Web site, from tps.cr.nps.gov/nhl/detail.cfm?ResourceId=1044&ResourceType=Building.

3. Research completed in 1990 by Ilene Tyler and Frank Welsh is referenced in this 2001 article, showing the ongoing use of conservation data: Norman Weiss, Pamela Jerome, Stephen Gottlieb, "Fallingwater Part 1: Materials-Conservation Efforts at Frank Lloyd Wright's Masterpiece," *APT Bulletin* 32, no. 4 (2001): 44–55.

4. John Reps, *Views and Viewmakers* (Columbia, MO: University of Missouri Press, 1984). John Reps, *Birds Eye Views* (New York: Princeton Architectural Press, 1998).

5. Historic Structures Report, Milwaukee City Hall Historic Building Restoration, Milwaukee, Wisconsin. Quinn Evans Architects, 2004. "Appendix A: Clock Tower Report: Developmental History and Recommendations."

6. Refer to chapter 11 for definitions of the types of historic sites variously called cultural landscapes.

7. National Park Service, Office of Policy: NPS-28, *Cultural Resource Management*, 1998.

8. Charles A. Birnbaum, *Preservation Brief 36: Protecting Cultural Landscapes: Planning, Treatment, and Management of Historic Landscapes*. National Park Service, Technical Preservation Services.

9. Ilene R. Tyler, "Replicating the John J. Earley Concrete Mix to Restore the Nashville Parthenon," *APT Bulletin* 35, no. 2–3 (2004).

CHAPTER EIGHT

1. Donovan D. Rypkema, *The Economics of Historic Preservation: A Community Leader's Guide*. (Washington, D.C.: National Trust for Historic Preservation, 2005).

2. Donovan Rypkema presentation to National Audubon Society of New York's conference on smart growth (abridged), March 3, 1999.

3. Randall Mason, "Economics and Historic Preservation: A Guide and Review of the Literature" (2005). The Bookings Institution Metropolitan Policy Program.

4. Reported by Ken Bernstein, director of preservation issues for the Los Angeles Conservancy.

5. Thomas D. Bever, "Economic Benefits of Historic Preservation," in *Readings in Historic Preservation: Why? What? How?*, ed. Norman Williams, Jr., Edmund H. Kellogg, and Frank B. Gilbert (New Brunswick, N.J.: Center for Urban Policy Research, 1983), 81.

6. Thomas D. Bever, "Economic Benefits of Historic Preservation," 79.

7. Thomas D. Bever, "Economic Benefits of Historic Preservation," 80.

8. See chapter 10 for a discussion of Leadership in Energy and Environmental Design (LEED).

9. Every effort has been made to present current information. However, the Internal Revenue Code is complex and changes frequently. Furthermore, the provisions of the tax code regarding at-risk rules, passive activity limitation, and alternative minimum tax can affect a taxpayer's ability to use these tax credits. Interested applicants are strongly advised to consult an accountant, tax attorney, or other professional tax advisor, legal counsel, or the Internal Revenue Service for help in determining whether these incentives pertain to their own situations.

10. See National Trust for Historic Preservation and Land Trust Exchange, *Appraising Easements: Guidelines for Valuation of Historic Preservation and Land Conservation Easements* (Washington, D.C.: National Trust for Historic Preservation, 1984).

11. Thomas Coughlin, *Easements and Other Legal Techniques to Protect Historic Houses in Private Ownership* (Washington, D.C.: Historic House Association of America, 1981).

12. GAO study on abuses of tax incentives and appraisals.

13. Donna Ann Harris, "Philadelphia's Preservation Incentive," *Historic Preservation Forum* (Washington, D.C.: National Trust for Historic Preservation, September–October 1992), 10.

14. Prepared by John M. Sanger Associates, Inc., for the Foundation for San Francisco's Architectural Heritage.

15. Tax Reform Act of 1976 (P.L. 94–455).

16. Revenue Act of 1978 (P.L. 95–600).

17. Robert E. Stipe and Antoinette J. Lee, *The American Mosaic*, 24.

18. Kim Keister and Arnold Berke, "If Not Now, When?" *Historic Preservation News* (December 1993–January 1994), 22.

19. Nellie Longsworth, comments at a symposium sponsored by *Progressive Architecture* and the AIA, "What Price Success," quoted in *Progressive Architecture* (August 1985), 110.

20. Economic Recovery Tax Act of 1981 (P.L. 97–34).

21. Thomas J. Colin, "A Historic Anniversary," *Historic Preservation* (May–June 1986).

22. See *Preserving America's Heritage: The Rehabilitation Investment Tax Credit.* (Touche Ross & Company and the Ohio Historic Preservation Office, 1987).

CHAPTER NINE

1. Richard Roddewig and Bradford White, *Preparing a Historic Preservation Plan*. Planning Advisory Service Report 450 (Chicago: American Planning Association, 1994).

2. Robert M. Ward and Norman Tyler, "Integrating Historic Preservation Plans with Comprehensive Plans," *Planning* (October 2005).

3. A few E-mails were "undelivered," and the balance did not reply. The surveys indicated that some states do not have state planning legislation, and their responses were not recorded in the study database.

4. Pennsylvania Municipalities Planning Code Act of 1968, P.L. 805, No. 247 as reenacted and amended.

5. Robert E. Stipe, "What Is a Local Preservation Plan?" *The Alliance Review* (Fall 1989), National Alliance of Preservation Commission.

6. Eric Damian Kelly and Barbara Becker. *Community Planning: An Introduction to the Comprehensive Plan* (Washington, D.C.: Island Press, 2000).

7. Norman Tyler. "The Evaluation of Downtown Health in Sixteen Michigan Cities." (Michigan State University Dissertation, 1998).

8. Norman Tyler, "An Evaluation of the Health of the Downtowns in Eight Michigan Cities." (University of Michigan Dissertation, 1987), and "The Evaluation of Downtown Health in Sixteen Michigan Cities." (Michigan State University Dissertation, 1998).

9. Information from www.mainst.org/about/approach.htm, May 1999.

10. Information from www.mainst.org/about/approach.htm, May 1999.

11. B. Joseph Pine II and James H. Gilmore, *The Experience Economy* (Boston: Harvard Business School Press), x.

12. Donovan Rypkema, speech on sustainability, National Trust for Historic Preservation, Portland, Oregon.

13. Survey conducted by Ilene R. Tyler, member of League of Historic American Theaters (LHAT), for presentation of "Downtown Revitalization: How Renovation of a Performing Arts Facility Can Improve a Community's Economic Health," at annual LHAT conference, Miami, Florida, July 23, 2003.

14. Study of Soho presented at annual conference of Association of European Schools of Planning, Leuven, Belgium, July 2003.

15. Arthur Frommer, "The Link between Tourism and Preservation." Speech delivered at the Art Institute of Chicago, November 5, 1992.

16. Quoted in J. Barry Cullingworth, *The Political Culture of Planning: American Land Use Planning In Comparative Perspective.* (New York: Routledge, 1993), 112

CHAPTER TEN

1. An African proverb.

2. Much of this section on preservation and sustainability is used with permission from the article, "The Greenest Building Is . . . One That Is Already Built" by Carl Elefante in *Forum Journal* 21, no. 4 (Summer 2007).

3. United States Department of Energy, Energy Information Administration, Commercial Building Energy Consumption Survey (CBECS), 2003 Detailed Tables, Table B1. Summary Table: Total and Means of Floorspace, Number of Workers, and Hours of Operation for Non-Mall Buildings, 2003, can be found at www.eia.doe.gov.

4. Arthur C. Nelson, "America Circa 2030: The Boom To Come," *Architect* 95, no. 11 (Hanley Wood Business Media: October 2006): 93–97.

5. Life Cycle Assessment (LCA) tools are largely targeted at products and, more specifically, the impacts associated with their manufacture and use. The U.S. Environmental Protection Agency (EPA) and National Institute of Standards and Technology (NIST) have developed the Building for Environmental and Economic Sustainability (BEES) software tools for rating environmental performance, in essence the "official" U.S. government LCA tool.

6. From Michael Jackson, FAIA, with the Illinois Historic Preservation Agency.

7. Sources: IHM Web site and "Geothermal System Helps Sisters Fulfill Spiritual, Moral Mandate," Jerry Rackley, *GeoOutlook Magazine,* 2003. See also theacuffs.com/ urbancatalystsassociates/cases/Motherhouse.pdf.

8. From IHM Web site: www.ihmsisters.org/www/sustainable_community/sustainable _renovation/sustainrenovation.asp.

9. Jeannie McPherson. "The National Trust for Historic Preservation Responds to Hurricane Katrina." *Organization of American Historians Newsletter* 33, no. 4 (November 2005). Available at www.oah.org/pubs/nl/2005nov/mcpherson.html.

10. Ibid.

11. Albert Rains and Laurance G. Henderson, *With Heritage So Rich,* rev. ed. (United States Conference of Mayors. Washington, D.C.: Preservation Press, 1983).

12. Teddy Roosevelt in a 1916 speech, "Bird Reserves at the Mouth of the Mississippi." From *A Book-Lover's Holidays in the Open.* (New York: Charles Scribner's Sons, 1920).

13. Quote from Congressman Schuyler Merritt at groundbreaking ceremony for Merritt Parkway. July 1934. "Origins of the Merritt Parkway," The Merritt Parkway Conservancy Web site, www.merrittparkway.org/pages/history.asp (September 2008).

14. Charles E. Little. *Greenways for America.* (Baltimore: The Johns Hopkins University Press 1990), 170

CHAPTER ELEVEN

1. Arthur Frommer, assisted by Pauline Frommer. *Arthur Frommer's New World of Travel, 5th ed.* (New York: Simon & Schuster McMillan Co., 1996), xiii.

2. The "living history" experiences of the last two entries are sponsored by the Toledo Area Metroparks, which are among an ever-growing number of park systems that increasingly meld the cultural and natural landscapes as part of their normal interpretive activities.

3. Gabe Cherem. "Shamans, Stories, and 'Sis-ciplines': Part I," *Interpretation Central Clearinghouse Newsletter* (July–August 1993): 1–2.

4. Jane Holtz Kay, "The Country in the City: Olmsted's Centennial Survival (barely)," *Boston Globe* (October 26, 2003).

5. Harm de Blij and Peter Muller. *Geography: Realms, Regions, and Concepts* (New York: John Wiley & Sons, Inc., 1994), 20.

6. Quote from Carl Sauer in R.D. Dikshit, *Geographical Thought: A Contextual History of Ideas.* (New Delhi: Prentice-Hall of India, 2004), 108.

7. *Historic scene* is defined as the overall appearance of cultural resources and their surroundings as they appeared in the historic period.

8. *Designed landscape* is defined as a landscape that was consciously designed or laid out by a landscape architect, master gardener, architect, or horticulturist according to design principles, or an amateur gardener working in a recognized style or tradition. The landscape may be associated with a significant person(s), trend, or event in landscape architecture, or illustrate an important development in the theory and practice of landscape architecture. Aesthetic values play a significant role in designed landscapes. Examples include parks, campuses, and estates.

9. *Vernacular landscape* is defined as a landscape that evolved through use by the people whose activities or occupancy shaped that landscape. Through social or cultural attitudes of an individual, family, or a community, the landscape reflects the physical, biological, and cultural character of those everyday lives. Function plays a significant role in vernacular landscapes. These landscapes can be a single property, such as a farm, or a collection of properties, such as a district of historic farms along a river valley. Examples include rural villages, industrial complexes, and agricultural landscapes.

10. *Ethnographic landscape* is defined as a landscape containing a variety of natural and cultural resources that associated people define as heritage resources. Examples are contemporary settlements, religious sacred sites, and massive geological structures. Small plant communities, animals, and subsistence and ceremonial grounds are often components.

11. U.S. Department of the Interior, 1994, p.1.
12. National Park Service definition of a National Heritage Area.
13. See chapter 6 for more on Lowell.
14. Charles E. Little, *Greenways for America* (Baltimore: The Johns Hopkins University Press, 1990).
15. United States Department of the Interior, National Park Service, *America's Industrial Heritage: Southwestern Pennsylvania* (Washington, D.C.: Southwestern Pennsylvania Heritage Preservation Commission, 1991).

FURTHER READING

❧

PERIODICALS

Bulletin of the Association for Preservation Technology. Association for Preservation Technology. Williamsburg, Virginia. (www.apti.org/publications)

Common Ground: Preserving our Nation's Heritage, National Park Service

Cultural Resource Management: U.S. Department of the Interior, National Park Service. Washington, D.C. (www.cr.nps.gov/crm)

Future Anterior: Journal of Historic Preservation, History, Theory and Criticism, Columbia University

Heritage News, National Park Service (e-newsletter)

Historic Preservation Forum. National Trust for Historic Preservation. Washington, D.C. (forum.nationaltrust.org)

Journal of Preservation Education and Research, National Council for Preservation Education

Journal of the Society of Architectural Historians. Society of Architectural Historians. Chicago, Illinois.

The Old House Journal. Brooklyn, New York. (www.oldhousejournal.com)

This Old House. Time Publishing Ventures, Inc. New York, New York. (www.pbs.org/wgbh/thisoldhouse/magazine/index.html)

Preservation. National Trust for Historic Preservation. Washington, D.C. (www.preservationnation.org/magazine/www.nationaltrust.org/main/magazine/magazine.htm)

Traditional Building: The Professional's Source for Historical Products. Brooklyn, New York. (www.traditional-building.com)

STYLE IDENTIFICATION REFERENCES

Baker, John Milnes. *American House Styles: A Concise Guide.* New York: W. W. Norton, 1993.

Blumenson, John J.-G. *Identifying American Architecture: A Pictorial Guide to Styles and Terms 1600–1945.* Revised ed. New York: W.W. Norton and Company, 1990.

Glassie, Henry. *Vernacular Architecture.* In *Material Culture*; Bloomington: Indiana University Press, 2000.

Hammett, Ralph W. *Architecture in the United States: A Survey of Architectural Styles Since 1776.* New York: John Wiley & Sons, 1976.

Harris, Cyrl M. *Illustrated Dictionary of Historic Architecture.* New York: Dover Publications, 1983.

Longstreth, Richard. *The Buildings of Main Street: A Guide to American Commercial Architecture.* Lanham, Maryland: AltaMira Press, 2000.

McAlester, Virginia, and Lee McAlester. *A Field Guide to American Houses.* New York: Alfred A. Knopf, 1984.

Noble, Allen G. *Wood, Brick, and Stone: The North American Settlement Landscape.* Amherst : University of Massachusetts Press, 1984.

Phillips, Steven J. *Old House Dictionary: An Illustrated Guide to American Domestic Architecture (1600 to 1940).* Lakewood, Colorado: American Source Books, 1996.

Poppeliers, John S., Allen Chambers, and Nancy B. Schwartz. *What Style Is It?: A Guide to American Architecture.* Rev. Sub. ed. Hoboken, New Jersey: John Wiley and Sons, Inc., 2003.

Rifkind, Carole. *A Field Guide to American Architecture.* New York: Random House Value Publishing, 1987.

Whiffen, Marcus, and Frederick Koeper. *American Architecture, 1607–1976.* Cambridge, Mass.: MIT Press, 1992.

GENERAL BOOKS

Advisory Council on Historic Preservation. *Annual Report to the President and the Congress of the United States.* Washington, D.C.: GPO, 1968–present.

Americans with Disabilities Act (ADA): Accessibility Guidelines for Buildings and Facilities. (www.access-board.gov/adaag/html/adaag.htm) 2002.

Arendt, Randall, Elizabeth A. Brabec, Harry L. Dodson, and Christine Reid. *Rural by Design: Maintaining Small Town Character.* Chicago: Planners Press, 1994.

Brand, Stewart. *How Buildings Learn: What Happens After They're Built.* Penguin, 1995.

Brolin, Brent. *Architecture in Context.* New York: Van Nostrand Reinhold, 1980.

Burden, Ernest. *Illustrated Dictionary of Architectural Preservation.* New York: McGraw Hill. 2004.

Burns, John A. (Editor). *Recording Historic Structure, 2nd Edition.* New York: Wiley, 2003.

Byard, Paul Spencer. *The Architecture of Additions: Design and Regulation.* New York: W. W. Norton and Company, 2005.

Curtis, John O. *Moving Historic Buildings.* U.S. Department of the Interior, Technical Preservation Services Branch. Washington, D.C.: GPO, 1979.

Department of Interior. *The Preservation of Historic Architecture: The U.S. Government's Official Guidelines for Preserving Historic Homes.* The Lyons Press, 2004. (Preservation Briefs Nos. 1-42, reprints in book form)

Duerksen, Christopher, Richard Roddewig, and Byrd Wood. *Takings Law in Plain English.* 3rd ed. Washington, D.C.: National Trust for Historic Preservation, 2002.

Earl, John. *Building Conservation Philosophy, Third Edition.* Reading, England: College of Estate Management. 2003.

Feilden, Bernard M. *Conservation of Historic Buildings, 3rd ed..* Oxford, UK: Architectural Press, 2003.

Fitch, James Marston. *American Building 1: The Historical Forces That Shaped It.* New York: Houghton Mifflin, 1972.

Fitch, James Marston. *American Building 2: The Environmental Forces That Shaped It. 2nd ed*. New York: Schocken, 1973.

Fitch, James Marston, *Historic Preservation: Curatorial Management of the Built World*. Charlottesville, Virginia: University of Virginia Press, 1990.

Greer, Nora Richter. *Architecture Transformed: New Life for Old Buildings*. Gloucester, Massachusetts: Rockport Publishers, Inc. 1998.

Grieff, Constance, ed. *Lost America: From the Atlantic to the Mississippi*. Vol. 1. Princeton, N.J.: Pyne Press, 1971.

Grieff, Constance, ed. *Lost America: From the Mississippi to the Pacific*. Vol. 2. Princeton, N.J.: Pyne Press, 1972.

Guidelines for Completing National Register of Historic Places Forms. U.S. Department of the Interior, National Park Service, Interagency Resources, 1991.

Harris, Cyril M. *Illustrated Dictionary of Historic Architecture*. New York: Dover Publications, 1983.

————. *American Architecture: An Illustrated Encyclopedia*. New York: W. W. Norton, 2002.

Hitchcock, Henry-Russell. *Architecture: Nineteenth and Twentieth Centuries*. Cumberland, Rhode Island: Yale University Press, 1989.

Hosmer, Charles B., Jr. *Presence of the Past: A History of the Preservation Movement in the United States before Williamsburg*. New York: Putnam, 1965.

Hosmer, Charles B., Jr. *Preservation Comes of Age: From Williamsburg to the National Trust, 1926–1949*. Charlottesville: University Press of Virginia, 1981.

Jacobs, Jane. *The Death and Life of Great American Cities*. New York: Random House, 1961.

Kyvig, David E. and Myron A. Marty. *Nearby History : Exploring the Past Around You*. 2nd ed. Walnut Creek, CA : AltaMira Press, 2000.

Lee, Antoinette J., Ed. *Past Meets Future: Saving America's Historic Environments*. Washington, D.C.: Preservation Press, 1992.

Lowenthal, David. *The Past is a Foreign Country*. Cambridge, England: Cambridge University Press, 1999.

Lynch, Kevin. *What Time Is This Place?* Cambridge, Mass.: MIT Press. 1976.

Murtagh, William J. *Keeping Time: The History and Theory of Preservation in America (3rd Edition)*. New York: John Wiley and Sons, Inc. 2005.

National Park Service. *Respectful Rehab: Answers to Your Questions about Old Buildings*. Technical Preservation Services, U.S. Department of the Interior, Washington, D.C.: Preservation Press, 1982.

National Trust for Historic Preservation, Tony P. Wrenn, and Elizabeth D. Mulloy. *America's Forgotten Architecture*. Washington, D.C.: National Trust for Historic Preservation, 1976.

National Trust for Historic Preservation. *Old and New Architecture: Design Relationship*. Washington, D.C.: The Preservation Press. 1980.

Noble, Allen G., ed. *To Build in a New Land : Ethnic Landscapes in North America*. Baltimore: Johns Hopkins University Press, 1992.

Page, Max. *Giving Preservation a History. Histories of Historic Preservation in the United States*. Routledge, 2003.

Pile, John. *A History of Interior Design, Second Edition*. Hoboken, New Jersey: John Wiley and Sons, Inc. 2005.

Rains, Albert, and Laurance G. Henderson. *With Heritage So Rich*. Rev. ed. United States Conference of Mayors. Washington, D.C.: Preservation Press, 1983.

Reps, John. *Bird's Eye Views: Historic Lithographs of North American Cities*. New York: Princeton Architectural Press, 1998.

————. *Views and Viewmakers of Urban America*. Columbia: University of Missouri Press, 1984.

Roddewig, Richard J. Preparing a Historic Preservation Ordinance. Chicago: American Planning Association Planning Advisory Service Report Number 374, 1983.

Ruskin, John. *The Seven Lamps of Architecture*. Mineola, Whitefish, Montana: Kessinger Publishing, 2007.

Rypkema, Donovan D. *The Economics of Historic Preservation: A Community Leader's Guide, 2nd Edition*. National Trust for Historic Preservation, 2005.

Sawin, Martica, ed. *James Marston Fitch: Selected Writings 1933–1997*. New York : W.W. Norton & Co., 2006.

Schlereth, Thomas J., ed. *Material Culture: A Research Guide*. Lawrence, Kan. : University Press of Kansas, 1985.

Schmickle, William E. *The Politics of Historic Districts: A Primer for Grassroots Preservation*. Lanham, MD: AltaMira Press, 2007.

Smith, E. Kidder. *A Pictorial History of Architecture in America*. Marshall Davidson, Ed. New York: W.W. Norton, 1976.

Stilgoe, John R. *Common Landscape of America, 1580 to 1845*. New Haven: Yale University Press, 1982.

Stipe, Edward E. *A Richer Heritage. Historic Preservation in the Twenty-First Century*. The University of North Carolina Press, 2003.

Stipe, Robert E., and Antoinette J. Lee. *The American Mosaic: Preserving a Nation's Heritage*. Detroit, Michigan: Wayne State University Press, 1997.

Stokes, Samuel N. *Saving America's Countryside: A Guide to Rural Conservation*. Baltimore: Johns Hopkins University Press, 1997.

Swanke Hayden Connell Architects. *Historic Preservation: Project Planning and Estimating*. Kingston, Massachusetts: R.S. Means Company, Inc. 2001.

Upton, Dell., ed. *America's Architectural Roots: Ethnic Groups That Built America*. New York: John Wiley, 1995.

Upton, Dell and John Michael Vlach, eds. *Common Places : Readings in American Vernacular Architecture*. Athens : University of Georgia Press, 1986.

U.S. Department of the Interior, National Park Service, Preservation Assistance Division. *The Secretary of the Interior's Standards for Rehabilitation and Guidelines for Rehabilitating Historic Buildings*. Rev. ed. Washington, D.C.: U.S. Department of the Interior, 2005.

Venturi, Robert. *Complexity and Contradiction in Architecture*. New York: Museum of Modern Art, 2002.

Weaver, Martin E. *Conserving Buildings: Guides to Techniques and Materials*. New York: John Wiley & Sons, 1997.

Williams, Norman, Jr., Edmund H. Kellogg, and Frank B. Gilbert, eds. *Readings in Historic Preservation: Why? What? How?* New Brunswick, N.J.: Center for Urban Policy Research, 1983.

Yetter, George Humphrey. *Williamsburg Before and After: The Rebirth of Virginia's Colonial Capital*. Williamsburg, Virginia: The Colonial Williamsburg Foundation, 1996.

Young, Robert A. *Historic Preservation Technology: A Primer*. New York: Wiley, 2008.

PRESERVATION RESOURCES

American Association for State and Local History

Although a multinational organization (United States and Canada), the intent of the ASLH is to promote knowledge, understanding, and activities in history at the local level. This nonprofit, educational organization relies on memberships for funding.

Contact:

American Association for State and Local History
1717 Church Street
Nashville, Tennessee 37203-2991
www.aaslh.ord/index.html

American Cultural Resources Association

The membership of ACRA, formed in 1995, is made up of interdisciplinary professionals; the largest percentage are archeologists, but other architecture and planning disciplines are represented. The organization supports a number of preservation issues.

Contact:

American Cultural Resources Association
c/o Thomas R. Wheaton, Executive Director
6150 East Ponce de Leon Avenue
Stone Mountain, Georgia 30083
www.acra-crm.org

American Institute of Architects

The AIA has 58,000 members in more than thirty local, state, and international chapters, and a national headquarters in Washington, D.C. Through its public outreach, education, and government affairs activities, the AIA provides technical bulletins to its members regarding issues of preservation.

Contact:
American Institute of Architects
1735 New York Avenue NW
Washington, D.C. 20006
www.aiaonline.com

American Institute for Conservation of Historic and Artistic Works (AIC)

AIC is the national membership organization of conservation professionals dedicated to preserving the art and historic artifacts of our cultural heritage for future generations.
Contact:
AIC
1717 K Street NW, Suite 200
Washington, DC 20036-5346
202-452-9545
202-452-9328 (fax)
info@aic-faic.org

American Planning Association

The APA is a professional organization dedicated to advancing the art and science of physical, economic, and social planning at the federal, state, and local levels. Its objectives include "encouraging planning that will contribute to public well-being by developing communities and environments that meet the needs of people and of society more effectively." The Planners Book Service makes available a variety of publications on historic preservation planning.
Contact:
American Planning Association
122 South Michigan Avenue, Suite 1600
Chicago, Illinois 60603
www.planning.org

Association for Preservation Technology International (APT)

The international APT was formed in 1968 to provide a central source and network for the preservation disciplines. It offers a forum for the exchange of information on conservation problems and techniques. It provides contact with top professionals and other international preservation organizations through its publications, courses, and an annual conference.
Contact:
Association for Preservation Technology
P.O. Box 3511
Williamsburg, Virginia 23187
www.apti.org

Campbell Center for Historic Preservation Studies

The Campbell Center is one of a number of centers for the study of preservation technology. Summer workshops and laboratories cover a variety of topics. The program is geared to those in midcareer in the fields of historic preservation, collection care, and conservation. Located in Mount Carroll, Illinois, on the site of a former seminary, the campus was purchased by the Campbell Center in 1979. Courses in preservation technology typically include Identification and Analysis of Historic Paint, Exposing Decorative Paint Schemes, Deterioration and Conservation of Wood, Workshop on Masonry Preservation, and Preservation of Historic Landscapes.

Contact:
Campbell Center for Historic Preservation Studies
P.O. Box 66
Mount Carroll, Illinois 61053
www.campbellcenter.org

C.H.I.N.

The Canadian Heritage Information Network (CHIN) is an agency within the federal Department of Canadian Heritage. CHIN provides information on Canadian museum collections, sponsors computer list-servs on topics of Canadian heritage, and gives training in collections management.
Contact:
Department of Canadian Heritage
Les Terrasses de la Chaudière
15 Eddy Street, 15-4-A
Hull, Quebec, Canada K1A OM5
www.chin.gc.ca

DOCOMOMO

This international organization was founded in 1990 to press for the documentation and conservation of the best examples of architecture from The Modern Movement. The name DOCOMOMO comes from the phrase DOcumentation and COnservation of the MOdern MOvement.
Contact:
DOCOMOMO International
Delft University of Technology, Faculty of Architecture
Berlageweg 1
2628CR Delft, The Netherlands
www.ooo.nl/docomomo/start.htm

International Council of Monuments and Sites

ICOMOS encourages preservation activities at the national and international levels through education and training, international exchange of people and information, technical assistance, documentation, and advocacy. The U.S. Committee of ICOMOS includes professionals, practitioners, supporters, and organizations committed to conservation of the world's cultural heritage. The committee publishes a monthly newsletter, has ten specialized subcommittees, and administers an electronic mailing list called usicomos.
Contact:
International Council on Monuments and Sites
401 F Street NW, Room 331
Washington, D.C. 20001
www.unesco.org/whc/ab_icomo.htm

National Alliance of Preservation Commissions

The NAPC forms a network of over 2,000 landmark and historic district commissions and boards of architectural review in the United States. It provides a forum for the exchange of views among active preservationists and gives local commissioners a national voice.

National Alliance of Preservation Commissions
P.O. Box 1605
Athens, Georgia 30603
www.arcat.com/search/profile.cfm?id=8371

National Center for Preservation Technology and Training, National Park Service

The NCPTT was created through amendments to the National Historic Preservation Act of 1966 and is supported through appropriations given to the National Park Service. Located in Natchitoches, Louisiana, the center is an interdisciplinary effort to enhance the art, craft, and science of preservation and conservation of the built environment. Its activities comprise research, training, and information management. Each year it supports these activities through Preservation Technology and Training grants. Through its Internet online service, NCPTT provides information about current research and educational opportunities.
Contact:
National Center for Preservation Technology and Training
Northwestern State University, Box 5682
Natchitoches, Louisiana 71497
www. ncptt.nps.gov

National Council for Preservation Education

The National Council is a certifying organization for preservation education programs around the country. The organization works with federal agencies to set up a program of summer internships for preservation students.
Contact:
National Council for Preservation Education
c/o Ted Ligibel (E-mail: tligibel@emich.edu)
235 Strong Hall
Historic Preservation Program
Eastern Michigan University
Ypsilanti, Michigan 48197
www.ncpe.us

National Main Street Center

The Main Street Program is administered through the National Main Street Center, established in 1980 and part of the National Trust for Historic Preservation. The center works with communities across the nation to revitalize their historic or traditional commercial areas. The center provides side services related to downtown revitalization, including training programs, technical assistance, an online business card service for professionals, a newsletter, a regular National Town Meeting conference, a certification program, and an awards program for successful revitalization efforts.
Contact:
National Main Street Center of the National Trust for Historic Preservation
1785 Massachusetts Avenue NW
Washington, D.C. 20036
www.mainst.org

National Park Service, Department of the Interior

The Heritage Preservation Services Division of the National Park Service provides federal support to preservation activities across the country. Its four general areas of activities are planning and preservation, grants and tax credits, geographic information systems (computerized mapping), and training and internships.

Contact:
Heritage Preservation Services
National Center for Cultural Resources Stewardship and Partnership Programs
National Park Service
1849 C Street NW, NC330
Washington, D.C. 20240
www2.cr.nps.gov

National Preservation Institute

The NPI is a nonprofit organization offering specialized information on education and training in preservation. It conducts seminars and workshops for sponsoring organizations, and provides technical assistance to owners of historic properties.

Contact:
National Preservation Institute
P.O. Box 1702
Alexandria, VA 22313
www.npi.org/about.html

National Trust for Historic Preservation

The National Trust for Historic Preservation was established in 1949 as the umbrella organization for preservation activities at federal, state, and local levels across the country. Although established by Congress, it has a quasipublic/private status, relying primarily on memberships and donations to cover expenses. The Trust has a wide range of activities, including stewardship of nineteen historic properties across the country. Other significant activities include sponsorship of an annual national preservation conference, publication of *Preservation* magazine, and support for its National Main Street Center.

Contact:
National Trust for Historic Preservation
1785 Massachusetts Avenue NW
Washington, D.C. 20036
www.nationaltrust.org

Partners for Sacred Places

This nondenominational, nonprofit organization was founded in 1989 to promote the preservation of historic religious properties. It provides assistance through free information and advice about property maintenance, fundraising, and professional references. It also coordinates conferences and training programs, publishes reference books on property maintenance, and generally advocates for religious properties.

Contact:
Partners for Sacred Places
1616 Walnut Street, Suite 2310
Philadelphia, Pennsylvania 19103
www.sacredplaces.org

Planning and Architecture Internet Resource Center

This Web site provides some of the best links to Web sites relating to architecture and planning and has a significant listing on historic preservation. The site is sponsored by the State University of New York at Buffalo.

www.arch.buffalo.edu/pairc

Preservation Action

Since its founding in 1974, Preservation Action has lobbied for stronger legislation at the federal, state, and local levels. The organization's goals are to elevate historic preservation as a national priority through legislative actions; monitor federal agency actions that affect the preservation of the nation's historic and cultural resources; participate directly in policy development; and create an environment for others to succeed with their preservation initiatives.

Contact:
Preservation Action
1350 Connecticut Avenue NW
Washington, D.C. 20036
www.preservenet.cornell.edu/pa.htm

Preserve/Net

Preserve/Net is an Internet site, administered by Cornell University, featuring a wealth of information on preservation across the country as well as links to other Web sites. Included at the Preserve/Net site is the Preservation Education Directory, a state-by-state listing of preservation programs at universities in the United States.

Contact:
Preserve/Net
www.preservenet.cornell.edu/preserve.html

RESTORE

This educational corporation offers the opportunity for training in state-of-the-art architectural conservation and preservation maintenance techniques. Workshop students include a cross section of architects, engineers, craftworkers, contractors, cultural resource managers, architectural conservators, preservationists, and others involved in the building industry.

Contact:
RESTORE
152 Madison Avenue, Suite 1603
New York, New York 10016

Society for American Archeology, University of Connecticut

The SAA is the largest archeological organization in the country. Begun in 1934, the Society's goal is to stimulate interest in archeology. It encourages public access to archeological sites and works to protect sites against looting and damage.

Contact:
SAA
900 Second Street, NE #12
Washington, D.C.
20002-3557
www.saa.org

Society of Architectural Historians

SAH encourages interest in architecture and architectural history and promotes the preservation of significant structures and sites. It has thousands of members throughout the United States and no membership requirements. Its primary activities are an annual conference, support for local chapters, and publication of the Journal of the Society of Architectural Historians.

Contact:
The Society of Architectural Historians
Charnley-Persky House
1365 North Astor Street
Chicago, Illinois 60610-2144
www.sah.org

Society for Commercial Archeology

Established in 1977, The Society is dedicated to preserving significant elements of the 20th century commercial landscape. Its primary focus is roadside architecture, including signs, symbols, and artifacts.

Contact:
Society for Commercial Archeology
P.O. Box 235
Geneseo, NY
14454-0235
www.sca-roadside.org

DEGREE AND CERTIFICATE PROGRAMS
IN HISTORIC PRESERVATION

DEGREE PROGRAMS IN HISTORIC PRESERVATION

In 1978, *Preservation News* listed fifteen programs in preservation at colleges and universities in the United States. Since that time the number of programs has grown to over sixty undergraduate, graduate, and certificate programs. Most are now member institutions of the National Council for Preservation Education (NCPE), founded in 1980 to certify historic preservation educational programs. These programs together enroll over 1,800 students, thought to be largest group of preservation students found anywhere in the world.

In addition to the NCPE programs listed here, a number of concentration or specialist programs can be found within the architecture, planning, and history curricula at various colleges and universities. For a complete list of NCPE member programs, see www.ncpe.us.

UNDERGRADUATE DEGREE PROGRAMS

Belmont Technical College
Building Preservation Technology
St. Clairsville, OH
www.btc.edu

College of Charleston
Department of Art History
Charleston, SC
www.cofc.edu/arthistory/hpcp_01.html

Colorado Mountain College
Historic Preservation Program
Leadville, CO
www.coloradomtn.edu/HistoricPreservation

Roger Williams University
School of Architecture, Art & Historic
Preservation
Bristol, RI
www.rwu.edu/academics/schools/saahp

Salve Regina University
Cultural and Historic Preservation Programs
Newport, RI
www.salve.edu/departments/chp/index.cfm

Savannah College of Art & Design
Historic Preservation Department
Savannah, GA
www.scad.edu/historic-preservation

S.E. Missouri State University
Historic Preservation Program
Cape Girardeau, MO
www4.semo.edu/histpres

University of Mary Washington
Department of Historic Preservation
Fredericksburg, VA
www.umw.edu/cas/historicpreservation
/default.php

Ursuline College
Historic Preservation Program
Pepper Pike, OH
www.ursuline.edu/academics

UNDERGRADUATE PROGRAMS WITH CERTIFICATES (OR EMPHASIS)

Bucks County Community College
Historic Preservation Program
Newtown, PA
www.bucks.edu/catalog/3127.html

College of the Redwoods
Historic Preservation and Restoration
Technology
Eureka, CA
www.redwoods.edu/departments
/construction

GRADUATE DEGREE PROGRAMS

Ball State University
Graduate Program in Historic Preservation
Muncie, IN
www.bsu.edu/cap

Boston University
Preservation Studies Program
Boston, MA
www.bu.edu/amnesp

Columbia University
Historic Preservation Program
New York, NY
www.arch.columbia.edu/hp

Cornell University
Graduate Program in Historic Preservation
Planning
Ithaca, NY
www.aap.cornell.edu/crp/programs

Eastern Michigan University
Historic Preservation Program
Ypsilanti, MI
www.emich.edu/public/geo/HP/HP.html

Georgia State University
Heritage Preservation Program
Atlanta, GA
www2.gsu.edu/~wwwher

Goucher College
Historic Preservation Program
Baltimore, MD
www.goucher.edu

Middle Tennessee State University
Public History/Preservation
Murfreesboro, TN
www.mtsu.edu/publichistory;
http://histpres.mtsu.edu/histpres

Northwestern State University
Heritage Resources Program
Natchitoches, LA
www.nsula.edu/heritageresources

Pratt Institute
Historic Preservation
New York, NY
www.pratt.edu/historic_preservation

Savannah College of Art & Design
Historic Preservation Department
Savannah, GA
www.scad.edu/historic-preservation

School of the Art Institute of Chicago
Historic Preservation Program
Chicago, IL
www.saic.edu/degrees_resources/gr_degrees
/mshp/index.html

Tulane University
School of Architecture
New Orleans, LA
http://tulane.edu

University of Georgia
Graduate Studies in Historic Preservation
Athens, GA
http://www.sed.uga.edu

University of Kentucky
Department of Historic Preservation
Lexington, KY
www.uky.edu/Design/historicpreservation
.html

University of Maryland
Graduate Program in Historic Preservation
College Park, MD
www.arch.umd.edu

University of Oregon
Historic Preservation Program
Eugene, OR
http://hp.uoregon.edu

University of Pennsylvania
Graduate Program in Historic Preservation
Philadelphia, PA
www.design.upenn.edu/new/hist/index.php

University of Southern California
Historic Preservation Program
Los Angeles, CA
http://arch.usc.edu

University of Texas
Historic Preservation Program
Austin, TX
http://soa.utexas.edu

University of Vermont
Historic Preservation Program
Burlington, VT
www.uvm.edu/histpres

Ursuline College
Historic Preservation Program .
Pepper Pike, OH
www.ursuline.edu/academics/graduate/hp

GRADUATE PROGRAMS WITH CERTIFICATES (OR EMPHASIS)

Colorado State University
Dept. of History
Fort Collins, CO
www.colostate.edu/Depts/Hist/index.html

George Washington University
Graduate Program in Historic Preservation
Washington, DC
www.gwu.edu/~amst/histpres/pres.htm

Oklahoma State University
Applied History Program
Stillwater, OK
http://history.okstate.edu

Pratt Institute
Graduate Center for Planning and the
Environment
Brooklyn, NY
www.pratt.edu/gcpe

Texas A&M University
College of Architecture
College Station, TX
http://archone.tamu.edu/College
/Academics/

Texas Tech University
School of Architecture
Lubbock, TX
www.arch.ttu.edu

University of Arizona
College of Arch & Landscape
Tucson, AZ
http://capla.arizona.edu/preservation/index
.html

University of California
Public History Program
Riverside, CA
www.history.ucsb.edu

University of Cincinnati
School of Architecture and Interior Design
Cincinnati, OH
http://daap.uc.edu/said

University of Colorado, Denver
Historic Preservation Certificate Program
Denver, Colorado
http://thunder1.cudenver.edu/preservation
/certificate.html

University of Delaware
Center for Historic Architecture & Design
Newark, DE
www.udel.edu/CHAD/hpspec.html

University of Florida
Graduate Program in Architectural
Preservation
Gainesville, FL
www.dcp.ufl.edu/hp/hp_icchp.aspx

University of Hawai'i, Manoa
Historic Preservation Program
Honolulu, HI
www.hawaii.edu/amst/historic.htm

University of Nevada
Historic Preservation Program
Reno, NV
www.unr.edu/cla/anthro/Hispres.htm

University of New Mexico
Graduate Certificate in Historic
Preservation and Regionalism,
Albuquerque, NM
http://saap.unm.edu

University of New Orleans
Department of Planning and Urban Studies
New Orleans, LA
http://planning.uno.edu/index.cfm

**University of North Carolina at
Greensboro**
Preservation Concentration
Greensboro, NC
www.uncg.edu/hpms

University of South Carolina
Public History Program
Columbia, SC
www.cas.sc.edu/hist/pubhist
University of Utah
College of Architecture + Planning
Salt Lake City, UT
www.arch.utah.edu/?school_of_architecture

University of Virginia
Historic Preservation Program
Charlottesville, VA
www.arch.virginia.edu/preservation

University of Washington
Historic Preservation Program
Seattle, WA
www.caup.washington.edu/certificates/hp
.html

ASSOCIATED PROGRAMS

Boston Architectural College
Continuing Education Department.
Boston, MA
www.the-bac.edu/x348.xml

ARCHITECTURAL TERMS

balustrade

bargeboard (vergeboard)

bay

To understand architectural styles, one must understand the architectural vocabulary. The terms listed below are commonly used to describe architectural components and elements.

Architrave: The main beam that sets on column capitals and forms the lowest part of an entablature.

Balustrade: A railing composed of a series of upright members, often in a vase shape, with a top rail and often a bottom rail.

Bargeboard: A decorative board running along the edge of a gable (often called *vergeboard*).

Battlement: A parapet wall at the edge of a roof with alternating slots and raised portions.

Bay: A unit of a building façade, defined by a regular spacing of windows, columns, or piers.

Bay window: An exterior wall projection filled with windows; if curved, called a *bow window*; if on an upper floor, called an *oriel window*.

Bond: The pattern of overlapping brick joints that binds them together to form a wall (e.g., common bond, Flemish bond, English bond).

Bracket: A decorative element supporting a wall projection, cornice, or other exterior feature.

Buttress: A mass of masonry or brickwork projecting from or built against a wall to strengthen it.

Cantilever: A projecting structural member, the end of which is supported on a fulcrum and held by a downward force behind the fulcrum.

Capital: The top portion of a column or pilaster.

buttress

Carrara glass: Pigmented structural glass (commonly black) with a reflective finish, used commonly in the 1930s and 1940s.

Casement window: Window with hinges at one side.

Cinquefoil: Decorative element representing a five-leafed form.

Clapboard siding: Tapered wood boards lapped one over another to form horizontal siding.

Clerestory: Windows located at the highest point of an exterior wall, usually for sunlighting of the interior.

Column elements:

casement window

    Capital: The top, crowning feature of a column.

Plinth: The lower square form at the base of a column.

Fluting: Concave grooves running vertically up a column.

clapboard siding

Corbel: An incremented wall projection used to support additional weight, most commonly constructed of brick.

Cornice: The decorative projecting element at the top of an exterior wall.

Cresting: An ornamental ridging at the top of a wall or the peak of a roof.

Cupola: A small dome rising above a roof, usually with a band of small windows or openings.

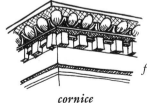

egg and dart pattern
dentils
friezeboard

cornice

Dentils: Rectangular toothlike elements forming a decorative horizontal band in a cornice.

Dormer window: A window and window structure that project from the slope of a roof.

Double-hung window: Window with two sashes, one above the other, each of which slides vertically.

Eave: Lower edge of a roof extending beyond the exterior wall.

Engaged column: A column integral with a wall surface, usually half round in form.

lintel
muntin

double-hung window

Entablature: The larger horizontal form setting on and spanning column capitals; it includes the architrave, the frieze, and the cornice.

Entasis: The subtle bulge in the vertical form of a classical column.

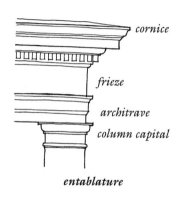

Facade: Usually the front exterior elevation or face of a building.

Fanlight: Fan-shaped window, usually located over an entrance door.

Fascia board: A flat, horizontal board between moldings, typically used with classical styles.

Finial: A decorative ornament placed at the peak of a roof.

Frieze: A decorative horizontal band located just below a cornice or gable.

Gable: The triangular section of exterior wall just under the eaves of a double-sloped roof.

finial

Gambrel roof: A double-sloped barnlike roof, often associated with Dutch colonial architecture.

Hip roof: A roof with slopes in the direction of each elevation, commonly in four directions.

Keystone: Center stone in a masonry arch.

Label: A molding over a door or window.

Lantern: A small turret with openings or windows all around, crowning a roof peak or dome.

Lintel: The horizontal support over a door or window.

Mansard roof: A steeply sloped roof covering the exterior wall of the top floor of a building, named after the French architect Mansart and commonly associated with the Second Empire style.

Modillions: A series of simple brackets usually found in a cornice.

gambrel roof

hip roof

mansard roof

lantern

Mullion: The vertical member separating windows, doors, or other panels set in a series.

Muntin: Wood pieces separating panes of glass in a window sash.

Newel post: Wooden post located at the top or bottom of a stairway balustrade.

Oculus: A round window.

Oriel window: A projection from an upper floor of an exterior wall surface that contains one or more windows.

Palladian window: Large window unit with an arched window in the center and smaller windows on each side.

Parapet: An extension of an exterior wall projecting above the roof plane, commonly used to hide the plane of a low-sloped roof.

Pediment: The gable form at the top of the facade of a classical style structure; also used over windows and doors.

Pilaster: A flat, rectangular partial column attached to a wall surface.

Pitch of roof: The angle of a roof slope, expressed in a ratio of vertical to horizontal (e.g., 6:12).

Porte cochere: A covered entrance for coaches or vehicles, usually attached to the side elevation of a building.

Portico: A covered porch attached to the main facade of a building, supported by classical order columns.

Quatrefoil: A decorative element representing a four-leafed form.

Quoins: Decorative stones at the corner of a building.

Rake: The extension at the end of a gable or sloped roof.

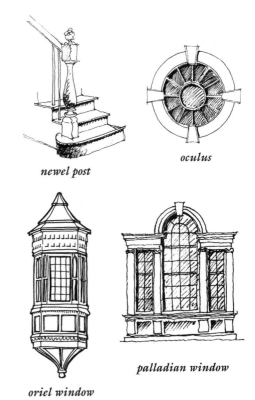

newel post

oculus

oriel window

palladian window

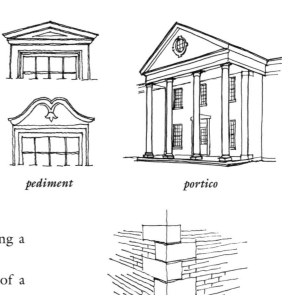

pediment

portico

quoins

segmental arch

turret

Rustication: Large stone blocks or stone forms with deep reveal masonry joints.

Segmental arch: A partial arch form, usually made of brick and located over window or door openings.

Shake: Split wood shingle.

Shed roof: A single-pitched roof, often over a room attached to the main structure.

Sidelight: Narrow window located immediately adjacent to an entrance door.

Single-hung window: Window with two sashes, one above the other, the lower of which slides vertically.

Soffit: The underside of an architectural element.

Terra-cotta: Clay blocks or tiles, usually glazed, used for roof tiles or decorative surfaces.

Tracery: Traditional intersecting ornamental work found in windows.

Transom: A small window located immediately above a door.

Trefoil: Decorative element representing a three-leafed form.

Turret: A small tower located at the corner of a building, often containing a staircase.

Vergeboard: See *bargeboard*.

INDEX

———— ✦ ————

(Page numbers in italic refer to illustrations not otherwise referenced in text. Specific locales or structures are listed under U.S. state name heading.)

accessibility codes, 233–35
Adam style, 67
adaptive use. *see* rehabilitation
additions
    compatible design, 107
    contrasting design, 108
    historic district regulation,
        181–82
    matching design, 106–7
    Secretary of Interior's stan-
        dards, 114–15
Adirondack Forest, 61
Advisory Council on Historic
        Preservation
    membership, 50–51
    origins, 47, 50, 62
    purpose, 49, 50
    resources of, 241–42
    Section 106 reviews, 51–53, 56
aesthetics
    legal basis for historic preserva-
        tion, 122, 123
    regulatory powers of historic
        district commissioners, 132,
        155
agricultural land, 294–95
Alaska, 178

American Heritage Rivers,
        318–19
American Indian Religious Free-
        dom Act (1978), 58
American Institute for Conserva-
        tion of Historic and Artistic
        Works, 199
American Institute of Architects,
        40
American Planning Association,
        271
American Society of Civil Engi-
        neers, 41
Americans with Disabilities Act,
        44, 233–35
America's Industrial Heritage
        Area, 334
Ann Arbor, Michigan
    Carnegie Library, *118*
    Historical Street Exhibit Pro-
        gram, 324–25
    University of Michigan, 106,
        106
    Wilson House, *69, 70*
antiquarianism, 27
Antiquities Act (1906), 31–32,
        61, 315

appreciation, property value,
        264–65
archeological considerations in
        preservation, 114, 137,
        218–20
architectonic technologies, 102
architectural review boards,
        38–39
architecture
    American styles, 63, 102–3
    architects' attitudes toward plan-
        ning and preservation, 292–94
    classical styles, 68–76
    contextual considerations, 103–5
    English influences, 64–68
    historical significance of struc-
        tures, 135, 136–37
    integrity evaluation, 137–38
    post-World War II building
        stock, 302–3
    preservation rationale based on,
        30
    romantic styles, 76–86
    sustainable design, 299–300,
        303–4
    twentieth century design,
        87–103

*The Architecture of Country Hous-
es*, 73, 76
Arizona
    Casa Grande ruin, 30–31, 61
    Mesa Verde, 31, *32*
Arkansas, 178
Art Deco design, 94
Arts and Crafts movement, 91
Association for Preservation Tech-
    nology International, 190
Australia, 220
Beaux-Arts classicism, 74–76
Berman v. Parker, 122, 132
bicentennial, U.S., 12, 62
birds-eye views, 204–5
*Birds-Eye Views: Historic Litho-
    graphs of North American
    Cities*, 205
birthplaces of important persons,
    136, 148
Boston, Massachusetts
    Beacon Hill historic district, 173
    Church Court condominiums,
        109, *109*
    First Church of Christ, Scien-
        tist, *209*, 227–30
    park system, 315, *316*, 326
    Public Library, 71, *71*
    Quincy Market, *277*, 278
    Trinity Church, 78
Brennan, William, 125–26
Breuer, Marcel, 124
Brolin, Brent, 103
building codes
    accessibility requirements,
        233–35
    fire and safety, 232
    rehabilitation challenges, 231
Bullfinch, Charles, 173
bungalow house design, 92–93
Bureau of Land Management,
    266
Burgee, John, 140
business districts, 238
Business Improvement Districts,
    290
CAD, 101–2
California
    Downey, McDonald's restau-
        rant, 142

Mountain View, *256*
Pasadena, Gamble House, 92,
    92
rehabilitation tax credit for
    homeowners, 256–57
Santa Barbara, 20, *21*
see also Los Angeles, California;
    San Francisco, California
Campbell Center for Historic
    Preservation Studies, 190
cash flow analysis, 263
catalog houses, 93–94
Certificate of Appropriateness,
    178, 185
Certified Historic Structures, 250,
    251
Certified Local Government sta-
    tus, 56, 62, 187–88
character of historic structure,
    rehabilitation considerations,
    112
Charleston Principles, 59–60
Chatfield-Taylor, Adele, 14
Chicago, Illinois
    Columbian Exposition, 75–76,
        89, 326
    Grant Park Stadium/Soldier
        Field, 153–54
    Hilliard Homes, 144
    Lake Shore Drive Apartments,
        97, 98
    Marshall Field Wholesale Store,
        78
    Reliance Building, 88
    Robie House, 91, *91*
    Tribune Tower, *86*, 86–87
Chicago School of Architecture,
    87–89
Chinese culture, 24
chronology of development and
    use, 215–16
city council, 289
city lithographs, 204–5
Civilian Conservation Corps, 317,
    332
Civil War sites, 32, 61
Civil Works Administration,
    39–40
Civil Works Administration Act,
    40

Clark, Joseph S., 296
cleaning
    masonry walls, 226–30
    Secretary of Interior's stan-
        dards, 114
Clean Water Act, 53
Clinton administration, 318
Colonial National Historical Park,
    32
colonial period architecture,
    64–65
Colonial Revival, 82–83
Colorado
    Boulder, 116
    Denver historic district, *162*,
        162–63
color and coating analysis,
    199–201
Columbian Exposition (Chicago,
    1893), 75–76, 89, 326
*Commercial Building Energy Con-
    sumption Survey*, 301
Community Development Block
    Grants, 266
community identity
    Charleston Principles, 59–60
    community boundaries,
        172–73
    heritage interpretation, 323
    historic preservation and, 45
    role of downtown areas, 275
    see also local government
*Community Planning: An Intro-
    duction to the Comprehensive
    Plan*, 274
compatible design, 105, 107
completion report, 214
*Complexity and Contradiction in
    Architecture*, 100
computer-aided-design, 101–2
    digital imaging for, 211,
        212–13
concrete construction, 230–31
Conference of Mayors, U.S., 46,
    312–13
Connecticut
    eminent domain case, 133–34
    historic preservation case law,
        122–23
    New Haven, Yale University

Art Gallery, 144
conservation
    activities of, 199
    definition, 199
    masonry analysis and repair,
        201–2
    paint color and coatings analysis,
        199–201
consolidants, 230
Constitutional law
    aesthetic basis for government
        action, 132
    legal exemptions for religious
        buildings, 127–30
    Penn Central case, 123–26
    private property rights, 121
construction debris, 238
construction techniques.
        see methods and materials of
        construction
context, thematic/historic,
    144–48
Contextualism, 103–5
contrasting design, 108
Cottage Residences, 76
Craftsman style, 91–92
cultural landscapes, 326–27
cultural landscapes reports, 218
cultural resource management,
    220
Cultural Resources Geographic
    Information System, 41
Cultural Resources Management
    Guideline, 218
culture
    American architecture and, 63,
        102–3
    cultural heritage tourism, 284,
        321–24
    cultural significance of historic
        structures, 135, 136, 145
    preservation attitudes and
        beliefs, 24–25
    themes and concepts approach
        to evaluating historic struc-
        tures, 145–48
Cunningham, Ann Pamela, 29–30
Daughters of the Republic of
    Texas, 315
The Death and Life of Great

American Cities, 44–45
Department of Commerce, 266
Department of Energy, 301
Department of Housing and
    Urban Development, 266
Department of the Interior
    rehabilitation funding sources,
        265–66
    see also National Park Service
Department of Transportation,
    267, 296
Department of Treasury, 266
depreciation, 304
design review, 115–17
digital images, 211–13
disabilities, people with, 233–35
DOCOMOMO, 143
Douglas, William, 122
Herbert H. Dow Historical
    Museum, 16
Downing, A. J., 73, 76
downtown areas
    importance of, 274–78
    participants in revitalization
        effort, 281
    strategies for revitalization,
        278–79
    trends, 274
    see also Main Street Program
Downtown Development Author-
    ities, 290–91
drawings
    episode, 217–18
    field-measured, 208–11
due diligence, 175
due process law, 121, 129–30, 175
Earley, John J., 230
easements
    on historic properties, 243–45
    on undeveloped land, 247–48
economic development
    community planning and
        preservation, 288–89
    experience economy, 283–87
    historic properties representa-
        tive of, 146–47
    interactions of developers and
        preservationists, 292
    interests of developers, 291
    role of Downtown Develop-

ment Authorities, 290–91
Economic Development Adminis-
    tration, 266
Economic Recovery Tax Act, 250
The Economics of Historic Preser-
    vation, 237
economics of preservation
    benefits of preservation,
        237–39
    building life-cycle analysis,
        304–5
    challenges to calculating,
        239–40
    easements, 243–45, 247–48
    energy budgets, 240
    financial analysis, 257–65
    homeowner tax credits for reha-
        bilitation, 255–57
    Main Street Program strategies
        for downtown revitalization,
        281
    opera house renovation,
        287–88
    purchase of development rights,
        247–48
    rehabilitation costs and bene-
        fits, 240–42
    rehabilitation funding sources,
        265–68
    revitalization of downtown
        areas, 278–79
    tax assessments for historic
        properties, 242–43
    tax incentives for rehabilitation,
        248–50. see also Rehabilita-
        tion Investment
        Tax Credit
    tourism, 278
    transfer of development rights,
        245–47
Edison, Thomas, 37, 38
EDR, Inc., 206
education and training in preser-
    vation, 47, 61
    preservation technology,
        189–91
egress, code requirements for,
    232
Eisenmann, Peter, 103–4
embodied energy, 242

eminent domain, 133–34
employment
    in rehabilitation projects, 241
    role of downtown areas, 276–77
endangered properties, National
    Trust list of, 44
energy efficiency, 299–300, 302,
    305–6
environmental movement
    benefits of rehabilitation vs.
        new construction, 241, 242,
        299–301
    early efforts, 314–16
    historic preservation movement
        and, 46, 55, 313–19
    historic properties associated
        with, 147
    see also sustainable design
episode drawings, 217–18
equal protection law, 121
Euclid v. Ambler Realty Company,
    121
experience economy, 283–87
façadism, 16
    attitudes toward, 117–19
    definition, 117
Faulkner, William, 105
federal government
    early preservation efforts,
        30–32
    National Trust for Historic
        Preservation and, 42
    rehabilitation funding sources,
        265–66
    review of projects affecting his-
        toric properties, 51–53
    role in historic preservation,
        58–59
    State Historic Preservation
        Offices and, 56–57
    transportation spending, 296
    urban renewal movement,
        44–45
    see also National Historic
        Preservation Act (1966);
        National Park Service
Federal style, 67–68
Federal Works Agency, 39–40
Ficke, Charles, 81
A Field Guide to American Houses,

64
field survey, 216–18
Fifth Amendment, 121
Figarsky v. Historic District Com-
    mission, 122–23
fire and safety codes, 232
fire insurance maps, 205–6
First Amendment, 129, 130
Florida
    Fort Myers, 322, 323
    Miami Beach, Berkeley Shore
        Hotel, 94, 94
Ford, Henry, 37–38, 53, 61
foreign affairs, historic properties
    associated with, 147
Fourteenth Amendment, 121
France
    Vezelay, Church of La
        Madeleine, 19, 20
Frommer, Arthur, 292, 321–22
functionalism, 87–88, 89
future of historic preservation
    modern-era building stock,
        302–3
    sustainability goals and,
        300–302
gardens, historic, 325
Gast, John, 13
Gay, Patricia, 312
Gehry, Frank, 101–2, 141
Georgia
    Lower Coastal Plain develop-
        ment review, 53
    Savannah, 157–58
Georgian architecture, 66–67
Gephardt, Richard, 250
Gilmore, James, 283
The Gingerbread Age, 70
glass, window, 224
Glassie, Henry, 64
Goodhue, Bertram, 87, 127
Goodwin, William, 35–36
Gothic Revival architecture,
    76–77, 86–87
gravesites
    of important persons, 136, 148
    Native American, 220
Great Lakes Circle Tour, 318
Greek Revival style, 68–70
greenbelt towns, 316–17

Greene, Charles, 92
Greene, Henry, 92
Gropius, Walter, 97
guidelines and standards
    historic district ordinance,
        173–74
    purpose, 111
    Secretary of Interior's, 112–15,
        132, 174
Gund, Graham, 109, 109
Hamer, David, 164
A Handbook on Historic Preserva-
    tion Law, 187
Hardy, Holzman, Pfeiffer, 110
Heritage Corridors and Heritage
    Areas, 62, 329–35
heritage interpretation, 284,
    321–24
high-definition survey, 212–13
Historic American Buildings Sur-
    vey, 40–41, 61, 208, 209, 211
Historic American Engineering
    Record, 41
Historic American Landscape Sur-
    vey, 41
Historic Context Statements, 148
historic districts
    administrative costs, 179
    alterations and additions to
        structures in, 181–82
    authority of city council, 289
    as barrier to innovative design,
        184–85
    boundaries, 169–73
    commission activities, 187
    commission meetings, 185–87
    commission membership, 173
    conceptual basis of legal provi-
        sions, 175–76
    conceptual evolution, 50
    concerns about, 179–84
    control of new development as
        basis for, 159–60
    criteria and standards for prop-
        erties in, 173–74, 183
    current registration, 50, 269
    design review, 115–17
    developers' attitudes toward,
        292
    early efforts, 38–39, 47, 61,

155
economic effects, 181
enforcement of regulations in, 174–75
establishing, 168–69
justification, 169
legal protections, 50, 123, 155, 183–84
local historic preservation review boards, 58, 59
need for, 176–78
property maintenance regulations, 174
to protect historic properties, 157–59
public relations and promotion as basis for, 163–64
reasons for establishing, 156
redevelopment incentive as basis for, 160–61
regulatory powers, 131–32
review process, 181
scope of ordinance, 178–79
stabilization or increase of property values as basis for, 162–63
takings law considerations, 132–34
tax incentives for establishing, 250
threat of litigation to influence decisions of, 134
time period representation, 164–68
well-written ordinance for, 173–75, 183
Historic Grounds Reports, 218
historic preservation, generally
conceptual evolution in U.S., 12–15
cultural perspectives, 24–25
early efforts, 27–41, 60–61
nouns and verbs conceptualization, 15–18
philosophies of, 18–24
post-World War II evolution, 41–60, 61–62
public interest and support, 9, 11–12, 18
rationale, 11, 12, 14, 297

Historic Preservation Fund, 265
Historic Sites Act (1935), 40, 61
historic structure reports
chronology of development and use, 215–16
completion report, 214
content, 213
physical investigation and field survey, 216–18
process diagram, *214*
purpose, 213
History in Urban Places, 164
Hitchcock, Henry-Russell, 96–97
Holabird and Roche, 153
Housing Act (1949), 44
Howard, Ebenezer, 316
Hunt, Richard Morris, 76
Hurricane Katrina, 9, 310–12
Hurricane Rita, 9
identification and evaluation of historic properties
community role, 139
criteria for exclusion, 148
fifty-year-old rule, 140–42
historic significance evaluation, 135–37
integrity evaluation, 137–38, 139
inventories, 122
legal significance, 122
level of government and, 149
nomination for historic designation, 149–50
overall significance evaluation, 138–39
recent past properties, 142–44
research for, 135
review of federal projects affecting historic properties, 51–53
state role, 55–56
thematic/historic context approach, 144–48
Illinois
Lockport, *332*
Openlands Project, 332–33
see also Chicago, Illinois; Oak Park, Illinois
Illinois and Michigan Canal National Heritage Corridor, 331–34

Indiana
Colombus, 303
Fort Wayne, 29
Indianapolis, 178–79
Madison, *280*
infrared sensing, 212
Institute of Museum Services, 267
integrity of historic property, 137–38, 139
interiors, protection of, 131
field survey, 217
rehabilitation, 195
Intermodal Surface Transportation Efficiency Act (1991), 62, 296
International style, 96–99, 102
Iowa
Davenport, Ficke Mansion, *80, 81*
Italianate design, 70–72
Italian Villa style, 73–74
Jacobs, Jane, 44–45, 46
Japan
Ise City, Ise Shrine, 24–25, *25*
preservation beliefs and practices, 24–25
Jefferson, Thomas, 35, 68–69
Johnson, Philip, 96–97, 101, 125, 140
Kahn, Louis, 144
Keillor, Garrison, 115
Kelo v. City of New London (Connecticut), 133–34
Kentucky, Louisville, Humana Building, *99, 100*
Kniffen, Fred, 64
Knoll Modernism Prize, 144
Labine, Clem, 12
Land and Water Conservation Fund, 266
landmark buildings
criteria for evaluation, 136–37
early preservation movement, 30
legal protections, 125–30
preservation based on historic events, 15, 136
landscapes
cultural, 326–27
historic, 41, 325–26

landscapes (*continued*)
maritime, 327–29
parkways and greenways, 315–17
land values
historic district designation to affect, 162–63
tax increment revenues, 291
teardown trend and, 117
law
aesthetic basis for historic preservation, 122, 132
evolution of preservation case law, 122–30
government right of eminent domain, 133–34
limits of government authority in land use issues, 121–22
property rights protections, 121–22
threat of litigation to influence preservation decisions, 134
see also ordinance(s); takings law
Lawrence, John, 14
Leadership in Energy and Environmental Design (LEED), 306–7, 308
Le Corbusier, 97
Lee, Antoinette, 59
LEED system. *see* Leadership in Energy and Environmental Design
Lééon, Paul, 20
Library of Congress, 40
life-cycle analysis, 304–5
life-cycle cost analysis, 304
living history presentations, 16–18
loan-to-value ratio, 261
local government
Certified Local Government status, 187–88
Charleston Principles, 59–60
city council, 289
different perspectives of participants in planning and development, 288–94
establishment of historic districts, 38–39

historic preservation components of comprehensive plans, 273
property research using records of, 202, 203
right to establish historic districts, 168
role in historic preservation, 58–59
state preservation authority and, 56
threat of litigation to influence preservation decisions, 134
see also community identity
Local Initiatives Support Corporation, 266–67
Longsworth, Nellie, 250
Los Angeles, California
Getty Center and Museum, *141*, 141–42
Walt Disney Concert Hall, *101*, 102
Louisiana, New Orleans, 39, 155, *156*, 311–12
Lowenthal, David, 24
Low-Income Housing Tax Credit, 266
Lynch, Kevin, 104, 172
Maass, John, 70
Maher v. City of New Orleans, 123, 174
Main Street Program, 44, 62
accomplishments, 282–83
activities, 282–83
four-point approach, 280–81
principles of revitalization strategies, 281–82
purpose, 279–80
mansard roof, 81
maps and atlases, 203–6
maritime landscapes, 327–29
Maryland
Baltimore, *45*, 166–68, *177*, 269–70
Carroll County purchase of development rights program, 248
Chevy Chase, 94
Libertytown, Jones House, 68, *68*

Mason, Randall, 239–40
masonry
analysis and repair, 201–2
cleaning, 226–30
exterior walls, 225–27
Massachusetts
Lowell, *163*, 163–64, 330
North Eastern, Ames Memorial Library, 78, *78*
Topsfield, Parson Capen House, 64, *65*
West Boxford, Boxford House, 65, 319–20
see also Boston, Massachusetts
matching design, 106–7
materials of construction. *see* methods and materials of construction
Maybeck, Richard, 76
McAlester, Lee, 64
McAlester, Virginia, 64
McDonald's restaurants, 142, *142*
McMansions, 117
measurement
field survey, 217
measured drawings, 208–11
rectified photography, 212
Meier, Richard, 141–42
Merritt, Schuyler, 316
methods and materials of construction
code requirements, 231–35
colonial period, 64–65
concrete, 230–31
conservation activities, 199–202
costs of new construction vs. rehabilitation, 238
early Chicago high-rise buildings, 88–89
economics of rehabilitation, 237–42
energy efficiency, 305–6
exterior walls, 225–27
facadism, 117–19
Gothic Revival design, 77
Greek Revival architecture, 69–70
interviews with builders to research, 206–7

post-World War II building stock, 301, 302
Richardsonian Romanesque designs, 79
roofs, 221–23
sustainability issues in renovation, 301–3
training for preservation technology, 189–90
windows, 223–25
Michigan
  Alger County, Bay Furnace, 22–23, *23*
  Dearborn, 37–38, 94
  Detroit, 153, 326
  Garden, *327*
  Monroe, *219,* 308–10
  Traverse City Opera House, 287–88
  see also Ann Arbor, Michigan
Mies van der Rohe, Ludwig, 97–98
Minnesota, Minneapolis–St. Paul, *300,* 315
Mission style, 84–85
Missouri
  Kansas City, Country Club Plaza, *84*
  see also St. Louis, Missouri
Modern architecture, 96–99, 102, 103
  recent significant examples, 141–44
Moderne style, 95–96
Moe, Richard, 312, 313
Morris, William, 91
Mount Vernon Ladies' Association of the Union, 29–30, 60, 315
Muer, Chuck, 161
municipal council, 289
National Conference of State Historic Preservation Offices, 56–57
National Council for Preservation Education, 9–10
National Environmental Policy Act (1969), 55, 62
National Heritage Areas, 33
National Heritage Corridor, 62

National Historic Landmarks
  current listings, 33, 151–52
  dedesignation, 152–54
  definition, 150
  nomination and selection, 150–52
National Historic Preservation Act (1966), 9, 27, 155
  archeological protections, 220
  influence of, in preservation movement, 47, 53–55
  major provisions, 46–47, 61–62, 150
  origins, 46
National Park Service
  certification for Rehabilitation Investment Tax Credit, 254–55
  Certified Historic Structure program, 250, 251
  cultural resource programs, 33, 41
  documentation programs, 40, 41–42
  evaluation of historic properties, 145–48
  Heritage Corridors and Heritage Areas, 330–31, 333, 334–35
  historic district listings, 50
  Historic Preservation Training Center, 191
  National Historic Landmark designations, 33, 150–52
  in National Register of Historic Places nominations process, 56
  origins and early development, 32, 61, 315
  preservation activities, 33, 34–35
  "Standards for the Treatment of Historic Properties," 112–15
National Preservation Awards, 144
National Register Information Service, 47
National Register of Historic Places
  current number and scope, 33, 149

dedesignation, 152
evaluation criteria, 136–37
National Historic Landmark designation and, 151–52
nomination and selection process, 48–49, 51, 56, 149–50
origins, 46, 47
owner's objections to listing on, 150
purpose, 47, 49
scope of protections, 49–50, 150
National Trust for Historic Preservation
  With Heritage So Rich publication, 46, 313
  National Preservation Awards, 144
  objectives, 42
  origins, 27, 42, 61, 62
  partnerships, 313
  preservation activities, 11, 42–44
  properties owned by, 43
  resistance to teardown trend, 117
  see also Main Street Program
Native American culture
  archeological research and, 220
  preservation beliefs, 24, 58
  sacred places, 24, 220
  Tribal Historic Preservation Offices, 51, 57–58
Native American Graves Protection and Repatriation Act (1990), 220
Neighborhood Housing Services of America, 267
Neutra, Richard, 143
new construction
  sustainability goals and, 300–301
  trends, 301
  see also additions
New Market Tax Credits, 266
New Techtonic style, 102
New York
  Buffalo, State Hospital, 78
  Rhinebeck, Delamater House, 76

New York (*continued*)
  Tarrytown, Lyndhurst Mansion, 43, *43*
  Water Mill, House at Half Creek, *100,* 101
  see also New York City
New York City
  African Burial Ground, 137
  AT&T (Sony) Building, 101, *140,* 140–41
  Central Park, 326
  Grand Central Terminal, 123–26
  Greenwich Village townhouses, 109–11
  historic preservation case law, 123–30
  JFK International Airport, 136–37, *137*
  Lower East Side Tenement Museum, 43
  Metropolitan Museum of Art, 76
  St. Bartholomew's Church, *127,* 127–30
  urban renewal movement, 45
nomination for historic designation, 48–49, 51, 56, 149–52
North Carolina
  Cape Hatteras Lighthouse, 328–29
  Winston-Salem, 39
Oak Park, Illinois, 184–85
  Cheney House, 184, *184*
  Unity Temple, 130–31, *131*
  Wright home and studio, 43, 194–95
Oglethorpe, James E., 157
Ohio
  Akron, Civic Theater, *285*
  German Village, 159
  Lucas County, 322
  Perrysburg, 29
  Sylvania, 322
Oklahoma
  Norman historic district, *170*
  Oklahoma City, Gold Dome Bank, 144
Olmsted, Frederick Law, 155, 315, 325–26

Onassis, Jacqueline Kennedy, 125
ordinance(s)
  authority of city council, 289
  design review, 115
  developers' attitudes toward, 292
  for establishment of historic districts, 168–69, 173–79
  exemptions for religious buildings, 127–30, 133
  façadism and, 119
  historic district protections, 50, 155
  local–state government relations, 56
  regulatory powers of historic district commissioners, 131–32
  urban growth boundaries, 294
  see also building codes; law
Oregon
  Portland, 116, 307–8
  urban growth boundaries, 294
Otis, Elisha, 88
paint color and coatings, 199–201
Palladian style, 66–67
parkways and greenways, 315–17
partnerships for preservation, 312–19, 329
Pattern in the Material Folk Cultures of the Eastern United States, 64
Penn Central Transportation Company v. City of New York, 62, 123–26
Pennsylvania
  America's Industrial Heritage Area, 334
  Bear Run, Fallingwater, 199–201
  early conservation efforts, 315
  Gettysburg National Military Park Cyclorama, 143, *143*
  Greene County, Reese Grist Mill, *210*
  Planning Code, 272–73
  Uniontown fire insurance map, *205*
  Youghiogheny River, *318*
  see also Philadelphia, Pennsylvania; Pittsburgh, Pennsylvania

Peterson, Charles E., 214
Philadelphia, Pennsylvania
  City Hall, 80
  Cliveden Mansion, 66, *66*
  Independence Hall, 27–28, 60
  transfer of development rights program, 245–46
philosophies of preservation, 18–24
photographic documentation, 211–13, 217
Pine, Joseph, 283
Pittsburgh, Pennsylvania
  Allegheny County Courthouse and Jail, 78
  birds-eye view, *204*
  Station Square, 160–61, *161*
planning, land use
  architectural design process and, 292–94
  components of historic preservation in, 271
  costs, 273–74
  developers' goals, 291–92
  different perspectives of interested parties in, 288–94
  downtown areas, 274–79
  goals, 269
  integrating preservation with master plans, 269–74
  planning commissions/planning departments, 289–90
  residents' interests, 294
  rural preservation, 294–95
  urban growth boundaries, 294
planning commission/planning department, 289–90
political history, 146
population and demographic shifts, 146
Postmodern design, 99–101, 140–41
Prairie style, 89–90
preservation
  case example, 192–93
  definition, 191
  goals, 191–92
Preservation Action, 55
Preservation Briefs, 207–8, 214,

218
Preservation Education Institute, 191
Preservation magazine, 42
preservation technology
    conservation activities, 199–202
    definition and scope, 189
    educational programs and institutions, 190–91
    knowledge and skills for, 189–90
    preservation activities, 191–93
    reconstruction activities, 195–97
    rehabilitation activities, 197–98
    restoration activities, 194–95
    types of interventions, 191, 198–99
Preserve America, 268
Presley, Elvis, 150
private sector
    developers' interests, 29
    early preservation efforts, 29–30
    interaction of developers and preservationists, 292
pro forma analysis, 257–65
property rights
    easements, 243–45
    historic preservation case law, 122–30
    historic preservation components of comprehensive plans and, 273
    historic preservation review boards and, 58
    inclusion in historic district and, 182
    legal framework, 121–22
    National Historic Landmark designation and, 151
    zoning law and, 121
    see also takings law
protection of historic properties, establishment of historic district for, 157–59
public opinion
    community boundaries, 172–73
    concerns about historic districts, 179–84
    evaluation of significance of his-

toric property, 139
    of historic district regulations, 176
    on planning and preservation, 294
    preservation movement, 9, 11–12, 18, 47
Public Works Administration, 39–40
purpose of historic structure, rehabilitation considerations, 112
Queen Anne style, 81–82
radar, 212
Rails-to-Trails projects, 317
reading the building, 207–8
recent past properties, 142–44
reconstruction
    definition, 195
    eligibility for National Register, 148
    indications for, 195
rectified photography, 212
rehabilitation
    alterations and additions in, 198
    case example, 197–98
    economics of, 237–42
    goals, 197
    indications for, 197
    standards for, 33, 112–15, 132
Rehabilitation Investment Tax Credit
    accomplishments of, 250, 251
    conditions of use for, 254–55
    eligibility, 249–50, 251–52
    prior use requirements, 253
    qualified expenditures, 252
    substantial rehabilitation requirement, 252–53
    tax credit, 249, 254
    wall retention requirement, 253–54
religious buildings, 127–31, 133
    National Register eligibility, 148
relocated buildings, 148
Renaissance Revival style, 70–72
replacement of distinctive elements, 114

Reps, John, 205
research and documentation
    cultural landscapes reports, 218
    literature/resource search, 202–3
    maps and city lithographs, 203–5
    measured drawings, 208–11
    oral history, 206–7
    photographic techniques, 211–13
    reading the building, 207–8
    roof construction, 221
    Sanborn Fire Insurance Maps, 205–6
    skills for, 202
    see also historic structure reports
restoration
    case example, 194–95
    definition, 194
    objectives, 194
    Ruskin's conceptualization, 21–22
    standards, 195
    Viollet-le-Duc's conceptualization, 19–21
RESTORE, 190
return on investment calculations, 262–65
Revenue Act (1978), 62
Richardson, H. H., 76, 78
Richardsonian Romanesque, 77–79
Robert's Rules of Order, 186–87
Rockefeller, John D., 36, 37, 61
Romanesque Revival, 77–79
romantic style of architecture, 76–86
roof designs and construction methods, 221–23
Roosevelt, Franklin D., 39–40
Roosevelt, Theodore, 314, 315
rural areas
    preservation concerns, 294–95
    purchase of development rights, 247–48
Ruskin, John, 7, 21–22
Rypkema, Donovan, 237
Saarinen, Eero, 136–37
Sanborn Fire Insurance Maps,

205–6
sandblasting, 114
San Francisco, California
  Alcatraz Island, 151–52, *152*
  Presidio, 34–35
  San Francisco Opera House, 76
  transferable development rights
    program, 246–47
Sauer, Carl, 61, 326
Save America's Treasures, 267
scavenging and looting, 30–31
Schweitzer, Robert, 94
science and technology, historic
  properties associated with,
  147
Second Empire style, 80–81
Section 8 housing, 266
Section of Fine Arts (Federal
  Works Agency), 39–40
Section 106 reviews, 51–53, 56
Sequoia National Park, 61
The Seven Lamps of Architecture,
  22
shingle style construction, 82
shotgun houses, 64
significance of historic property,
  135–37, 138–39
  National Historic Landmark
    designation, 150–52
skyscrapers and high-rise build-
  ings, 86–87, 88–89
social institutions and movements,
  146
South Carolina
  Charleston, 16, 38–39, 61, 155
  Columbia, bus station, *95*
Spain
  Altamira, 17
  Bilbao, Guggenheim Museum,
    101–2
Spanish Colonial style, 84–85
sprawl, 294–95
sprinkler systems, 232
St. Augustine Historical Society,
  315
*St. Bartholomew's v. New York
  City Landmarks Preservation
  Commission,* 127–30
St. Louis, Missouri
  Gateway Arch, 235

Old Courthouse, 221–23, 235
Union Station, 197–98
Wainwright Building, 89, *90*
"Standards for the Treatment of
  Historic Properties," 112–15,
  132, 174, 182
Starbucks coffee, 283
state government
  historic preservation compo-
    nents of comprehensive plans,
    272–73
  historic preservation review
    boards, 58
  homeowner tax credits for reha-
    bilitation, 255–57
  local government authority
    and, 56
  see also State Historic Preserva-
    tion Offices
State Historic Preservation Offices
  in establishment of historic dis-
    tricts, 171–72
  in National Register nomina-
    tion process, 149
  national representation, 56–57
  origins, 47, 55
  responsibilities and authorities,
    55–56, 59
  in Section 106 reviews, 51
Stern, Robert A. M.
Stickley, Gustav, 92
Stipe, Robert E., 274
street exhibits, 324–25
Sullivan, Louis, 76, 89, 102
sustainable design
  building life cycle analysis, 304–5
  case studies, 307–12
  challenges for historic preserva-
    tion, 299, 301–3
  energy performance, 305–6
  importance of preservation,
    299–301
  LEED system, 306–7, 308
  preservation rationale, 304
takings law
  case law, 122–26, 129
  Constitutional provisions, 121
  definition, 132
  eminent domain and, 133–34
  historic district ordinance and,

175–76
  implications for historic district
    commissions, 132–34
tax increment financing, 291
tax policy
  assessments for historic proper-
    ties, 242–43
  building depreciation, 304
  easements on historic proper-
    ties, 243–45
  incentives for preservation,
    248–50
  New Market Tax Credits, 266
  tax credits for rehabilitation and
    preservation, 56, 62, 255–57
  transportation taxes, 296
  see also Rehabilitation Invest-
    ment Tax Credit
Tax Reform Act (1976), 62, 249
teardowns and demolition
  legal basis for denial of right to,
    122–23
  motivation for, 117
  of structures with historical des-
    ignation, 153
  tax incentives for, 248–49
  trends, 117
Tennessee
  Memphis, Graceland Mansion,
    150, *151*
  Nashville, Parthenon, 230–31
Texas, San Antonio, 39
  Alamo Plaza, 158, *158*
theater experience, 285–88
themes and concepts process,
  145–48
3D laser scanning, 212
time, context of, 103–5
title search, 203
Tomlan, Michael, 54, 118–19
tourism, 278, 284
  heritage interpretation, 321–24
  historical preservation linkage,
    321
trails and roads, historic, 317
transfer of development rights,
  245–47
transportation, preservation and,
  296, 315–17
Treatise on the Theory and Practice

of Landscape Gardening, 76
Tribal Historic Preservation
 Offices, 51, 57–58
Trust for Public Land, 319–20
Tudor style, 85–86
Tyler, Norman, 278–79
urban growth boundaries, 294
Urban Renewal Act (1954), 44
urban renewal movement, 44–45,
 249
Venturi, Robert, 100
vernacular architecture, 64
Victorian era, 81
Views and Viewmakers of Urban
 America, 205
Viollet-le-Duc, Eugène
 Emmanuel, 19–21
Virginia
 Alexandria, 39
 Charlottesville, University of
  Virginia, 69
 Loudon County, Belmont
  Manor, *48*
 Mount Vernon, 29–30, 60, 197
 Williamsburg, 21, 35–37, 39,
  195–97

Woodlawn Plantation, 43
walls
 exterior, 225–27
 wall retention requirement of
  Rehabilitation Investment
  Tax Credit, 253–54
Washington, D.C.
 façadism in, 119
 Georgetown historic district,
  39, 165–66
 historic district ordinance,
  178
 historic preservation case law,
  122
 Library of Congress, *74, 76*
 Red Lion Row, *119*
 State, War and Navy Building,
  80
 Union Station, 76
 Wilson House, 43
Washington, George, 197
Washington, Seattle
 Pike Place Market, 192–93
 Pioneer Square, 159–60
 Steinhart Theriault and Ander-
  son Architectural Office, *98*

West Virginia, Huntington,
 275
window designs and construction,
 223–25, 305–6
Wisconsin
 Janesville, Lincoln Tallman
  House, *208*
 Milwaukee City Hall, 215–16
With Heritage So Rich, 46, 313
Works Progress Administration,
 39–40
World Monuments Fund, 144
Wright, Frank Lloyd, 43, 89–91,
 102, 194–95
 Fallingwater restoration,
  199–201
 Unity Temple, 130–31
Yellowstone National Park,
 30–31, 61, 314–15
Yosemite National Park, 61
Zeigler, Arthur, 160
zoning regulation
 agricultural conservation dis-
  tricts, 295
 legal basis, 121
 origins, 39